Secrets of the *Conqueror*

Secrets of the *Conqueror*

The Untold Story of
Britain's Most Famous Submarine

Stuart Prebble

faber and faber

First published in 2012
by Faber and Faber Limited
Bloomsbury House
74–77 Great Russell Street
London WC1B 3DA

Typeset by Donald Sommerville
Printed and bound by CPI Group (UK) Ltd, Croydon CR0 4YY

The right of Stuart Prebble to be identified as author of this work
has been asserted in accordance with Section 77 of the Copyright,
Designs and Patents Act 1988

A CIP record for this book
is available from the British Library

ISBN 978–0–571–29032–1

2 4 6 8 10 9 7 5 3 1

In memory of Arthur Gavshon

Contents

Illustrations

1 Lieutenant Narendra Sethia, August 1980.
(Courtesy N. Sethia)

2 Sethia takes part in an elaborate April Fool prank at the
Royal Naval College, Dartmouth.
Launch of the nuclear-powered submarine HMS *Conqueror*
at Cammell Laird Shipyard, Birkenhead, 28 August
1969. *(PA/EMPICS)*

3 Midshipman Narendra Sethia, aged eighteen, December
1974. *(Courtesy N. Sethia)*
Commander Chris Wreford-Brown, captain of HMS
Conqueror, with Petty Officer Graham Libby, October
1982. *(PA/EMPICS)*
Tim McClement, first lieutenant of HMS *Conqueror* during
Operation Corporate and Operation Barmaid.
(Courtesy T. McClement)
HMS *Conqueror*'s navigator, Jonathan 'Jonty' Powis,
greeting his wife and new-born baby at Faslane after his
return from the Falklands. *(© Herald and Times Group)*

4 Prime Minister Margaret Thatcher and Foreign Secretary
Francis Pym meeting US Secretary of State Alexander
Haig. *(PA/EMPICS)*
Defence Secretary John Nott announces that British troops
are established on the Falkland Islands. *(PA/EMPICS)*

5 The Argentine cruiser *General Belgrano*, after the attack by
HMS *Conqueror*, 2 May 1982. *(AP Photo)*
'Gotcha' – how *The Sun* reported the attack on the Argentine
cruiser *General Belgrano*.

Maps

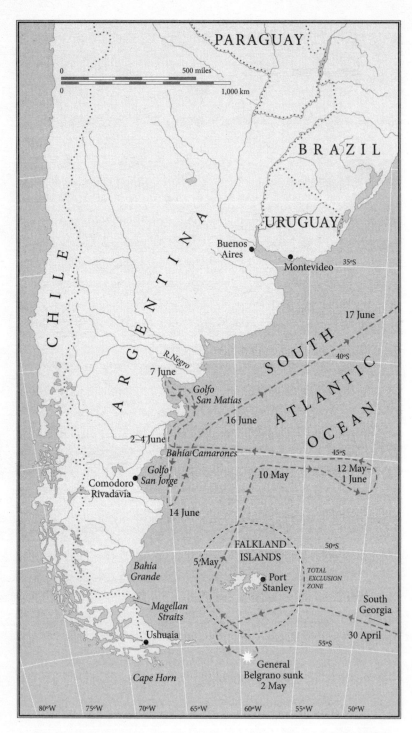

Track of HMS *Conqueror* during Operation Corporate, 1982.

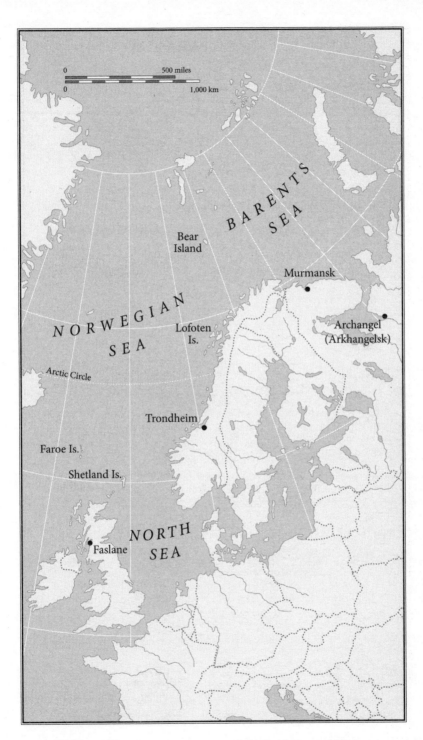

The North Atlantic operational area of the Cold War.

Introduction

This is a story I have waited for thirty years to tell. When I first heard it, I was a producer working on ITV's investigative current affairs series, *World in Action*. Like most people at the time, I was preoccupied with the conflict between Britain and Argentina over the invasion by the military junta of the Falkland Islands. When the Argentines landed, it had seemed like a relic of a bygone age, an echo of our colonial past – more like 1882 than 1982.

It is fair to say that when Britain woke up to the amazing news that we had lost the Falklands, the reaction of most people was to ask 'what are they?' and 'where?' On the day of the invasion, ITV's evening news magazine programme in the north-west of England, *Granada Tonight*, sent out reporters to ask people in the street where they thought the Falklands were. 'Just off the coast of Scotland?' was the most common speculation. 'Yes of course they are off the coast of Scotland,' quipped the presenter back in the studio, 'the trouble is that they are some 8,000 miles off the coast of Scotland, and only about 300 miles off the coast of Argentina.'

Humour quickly turned sour as the television news carried pictures of disarmed Royal Marines lying face down in the street with Argentine soldiers standing over them. Falkland Islanders, we were informed, felt every bit as British as do Cornishmen or the Welsh – probably more so.

Britain and the world watched in amazement as the Royal Navy assembled a Task Force, consisting of ships that most of us had no idea we still possessed, and cheering crowds lined the jetties and coastline as the armada set off to the far end of the world to free our good people from beneath the jackboot of the tyrant. Certainly some jumped-up band of tin-pot generals with too many medals on their chests and too much gold braid on their epaulettes could not be allowed to cock a snook at the British Empire. Just exactly who did they think they were dealing with here?

Three months later, the war was over and our boys were either back or on their way back. Or at least, most of them were. It had been a close-run thing, and far closer than any of us had realised at the time. There was triumph in the popular headlines, there were services of thanksgiving, and Mrs Thatcher (not Her Majesty the Queen) took the salute at the military march-past. But then questions began to be asked. Had the war really been unavoidable? Aside from the fact that it could and should have been anticipated and averted, had it really been necessary to fight at all? Could the matter not have been resolved peacefully through negotiation? Did 649 Argentines and 258 British soldiers, sailors and airmen have to die?

Much of the controversy centred on the sinking of the Argentine cruiser ARA *Belgrano* with the loss of 323 men. It was widely agreed that this action, by the British hunter-killer submarine HMS *Conqueror*, had been the act which had made inevitable an all-out war in the South Atlantic. Not only had it sent the Argentine ship to the bottom of the ocean, but with it had gone any prospects of success for the peace negotiations which were being brokered at the time by Peru with the help of the Americans.

On the face of it, the circumstances of the sinking had been straightforward enough. She was an enemy warship, she was at sea, she was escorted by two destroyers, the British had the chance to sink her, and they did. 'GOTCHA!' yelled the front-page headline of the *Sun*, and by jingo we had taught the 'Argies' a lesson. But, as often happens in political history, it was not so much the original act which was now causing such disquiet, it was the fact that the government had chosen to lie about it. Week by week, revelations began to emerge showing the differing accounts of the military men who had been there, and the politicians back home who had presented the official version of the sinking. There were discrepancies over just about every aspect of the action, including the first time that the Argentine cruiser had been spotted, its actions in the hours before the attack, its position, its orders, and its course and speed at the moment it was hit by two Mark 8 torpedoes, wracked by explosions and consigned to the sea-bed.

Then, when it already seemed inescapable that the government was covering up something very murky, the Defence Secretary told a stunned House of Commons that a log-book from HMS *Conqueror* was missing. The control room log-book contained details of the course, depth and speed of the submarine, and its loss was only discovered more than two years after the war, when a civil servant went in search of it in order to try to answer a question from an MP. Immediately it was widely assumed that the log-book contained information that would contradict some aspect of the government's account of the sinking, and had not been 'lost' at all.

An officer serving in the *Conqueror*, whose personal diary had fuelled much of the controversy about the attack on the *Belgrano*, was accused of stealing the log-book. If indeed he had misappropriated it, then it could not have been a government cover-up. The mystery deepened. The hunt for the author of the diary, and the thief, was on. By this time I was working on the *World in Action* programme and I was one of a number of journalists on the trail of the vanishing log-book and all that it implied.

One evening I found myself in company with a small number of submariners from HMS *Conqueror*, and in the course of several hours a story emerged which, even now as I recall it, I find utterly extraordinary. It is a tale as incredible as the exploits of James Bond, straight out of John le Carré, a story from the wildest part of the front line of the Cold War which was still, at that time, very much liable to go hot at any moment.

My journalistic instincts were aroused and I spent a sleepless night wondering how best I could tell the story I had just heard. In the small hours of the morning, however, I realised that this particular episode could not be made public. I was, and still am, all in favour of freedom of information, and certainly freedom of any information which is kept secret merely because it embarrasses the government. However, this, if anything was, seemed like a genuine military secret: a matter of national security.

At that time I was thirty years old. I thought about the thirty-year rule under which national secrets can be reviewed to see if the passage of time has allowed them to be published. When that came around I would be sixty, and maybe have some time on my hands. In the thirty years since then I have indeed produced three separate *World in Action* programmes dealing with different aspects of the Falklands War, I have been a documentary maker, a commissioning editor, and Chief Executive of ITV. Eventually I left to start my own TV production company where I executive-produced series such as *Grumpy Old Men, Three Men in a Boat, The Alastair Campbell Diaries* and various documentaries featuring Michael Portillo.

Today I am sixty. I still do not have time on my hands, but I do have a hankering to tell the story I first heard thirty years ago. So, in November 2010, I asked Alastair Campbell to put me in touch with the right person in the Cabinet Office, and there followed eight months of negotiation. In that time the Ministry of Defence considered my various requests to interview on the record some of the people involved, to be allowed to put aside the Top Secret classification of these events, and to tell the real story of what happened on board HMS *Conqueror* in 1982.

My arguments were simple and, I believed, compelling. First, the enemy we were confronting at the time – Soviet Communism – no longer exists. It is twenty years since the demise of the USSR and the days of cat and mouse games beneath the oceans of the world are largely over. Secondly, today's students of the Falklands

War and its causes would, without this story, be entirely misled by what is currently the official account of what happened on the submarine *Conqueror*. Third, and most important of all, the true and until now hidden story reflects extremely well on all those on the British side who took part in it, and we owe it to them and what they did that it should be known and even celebrated.

In the end the men from the Ministry refused. Well, they didn't refuse completely. They said that while they would not release any present or former Navy personnel from their obligations under the Official Secrets Act, they also would not actively stand in my way or seek to prevent publication.

It has not been easy. While all who were intimately involved with the following story are free to speak quite openly about most aspects of the Falklands War, they have not been free to speak about the other matters. Those are still classified 'Top Secret'. In many cases talking to them has felt like getting blood out of a stone. In the end, all those who decided to contribute to this narrative took great care not to reveal any information which could genuinely be of use to an enemy. Through a mix of what I learned in that conversation just about thirty years ago, the eyewitness testimony from some of those involved, careful research in the archives, a lot of help from the Naval Historical Branch, patient study of the accounts of the various submariners who have told related stories here and abroad, the Freedom of Information Act and the odd inadvertent slip of the tongue, the real story can at last be told.

Like all good stories, this one begins with a central character of more than average interest.

1

Something about a Sailor

Narendra Sethia was born in Edinburgh on 14 May 1956. His father Babulal had been born in Rajasthan in north-west India into a wealthy Marwari family, a group famous for their entrepreneurial skills and strict adherence to religion. Babulal was a Jain, and believed that every living being has a soul, and that therefore it was imperative to be kind to all creatures.

Babulal, or BL as he was known, came to London from India after World War II and worked in a successful jute business which had been set up by his uncle. KC Sethia (1944) Ltd advertised for a secretary and the successful applicant was Marjorie Joan Vennard. Marjorie, known to all as Joan, had been working as a clerk in the Admiralty. She was already married with two children, Barry and Carole, but her husband had been in a Japanese prisoner of war camp and could not work, making her the sole breadwinner for the family. History does not recall the precise sequence of events, but when BL moved to Scotland to start his own company, Sethia Wools, Joan went with him. The relationship and the business both prospered and in 1951 their first son was born. He was named Babulal after his father, then came Krishna and finally Narendra.

When the youngest was six months old, the Sethia family moved to a huge rambling house in Haslemere called Grayswood Place. The business was booming and they were living in handsome style. There was the big house in Surrey, a uniformed nanny to take care of the children and, later, a flat in Mayfair.

BL had strong views about the importance of education and was determined to do what was best for his three sons. However, he did not think it wise to encourage them to compete, and so decided to send the three boys to different schools. All were sent away at an early age to board, and from the start Babulal and Krishna proved to be conscientious and diligent. Narendra on the other hand was proving himself to be something of a handful. Having attended and been asked to leave a series of prep schools, he surprised and delighted everyone by managing to gain a place at one of the top three public schools in the country. Their pleasure was to be short-lived.

'My time at Harrow was not happy,' says Narendra. 'Although my older brothers had passed through Rugby and Eton with distinguished records, I was quite unable – or unwilling – to match their performance.'

Narendra bridled at the strict discipline at the school, as well as the enforced religious instruction, casual racism and snobbery. The ethos of the school was neatly summed up in the admonition of the Assistant Headmaster to a group of Harrovians found lounging about at the roadside. 'For goodness sake – stop behaving like grammar school children!' The remark made a big impression on Narendra and reinforced his natural inclination to rebel.

When his inability to conform led to his expulsion from Harrow at age fourteen, it looked as though the family was running out of options for his continued education. However, BL was patient and prosperous and eventually managed to have him accepted at a small boarding school called Langley, in Loddon near Norwich. This was a chance to settle down, but still Narendra smoked and drank and continued to frustrate his parents and teachers alike by consistently performing well below his abilities.

His two older brothers were continuing their education, and both were eventually to become distinguished surgeons. Narendra showed no such inclination, and everyone around him began to wonder what would become of the youngest son of the family. Narendra was good-looking, highly articulate, and sociable in the extreme – but showed absolutely no sign whatsoever of being willing to knuckle down and do very much actual work.

Considering his rejection of authority and discipline, it is surprising that one of the few things which did attract Narendra was the school's Army Cadet Force. Everyone was amazed when he announced that he thought the next step after leaving school might be a career in the military. If he had been so lamentably unable to observe the rules imposed by a series of schools, how on earth would he cope with the far greater discipline required by the armed forces? Nonetheless, there was relief all round that the boy seemed at last to want to apply himself to something – anything – and so the next question was which service he wished to try for. Narendra was in no doubt.

'The Navy,' he announced. When asked why, he replied that he had a great uncle who had been on a ship, he was fond of swimming, and he thought the dark blue uniform looked so much smarter than khaki. What better reasons could there be?

In the summer of 1972, Narendra Sethia found himself on his way to an Admiralty Interview Board at Gosport. He took the precaution of having a sensible haircut and was careful to choose the school uniform featuring the fewest cigarette burns. The board process lasted for three days and consisted of a battery of intelligence tests, a lot of swinging from ropes in the gymnasium, and what seemed to him to be an endless series of interviews.

'We note from your records,' he was asked at one of them, 'that you attended Highfield Boarding School at the age of eight, but appear to have left rather abruptly at the age of nine. Would you care to tell the board why that was?'

Narendra was very clear that he did not care to tell the board the reason – but realised that he had little choice. He gilded the lily only slightly: 'I was asked to leave sir.'

There was a lengthy silence and rustling of papers.

'And we note from your records, Sethia, that at the age of thirteen you won a scholarship to Harrow but that at the age of fourteen you . . . er . . . left. Would you care to tell the board why that was?'

Once again, Narendra felt quite certain that he did not care to give the reason to the board. 'I was asked to leave sir.'

By now the questioner was running out of patience. 'But why were you asked to leave?'

'Well sir, I ran away sir.'

'But why did you run away, Sethia?'

'I didn't like it sir.'

'And what shall you do if you enter the Navy and then decide that you don't like it?'

Narendra knew that a truthful answer would end the interview far more quickly than it had begun, but he had also learned enough about negotiating with authority to know when it was a good idea to play the game.

'Well sir, I believe that I have now matured sufficiently to appreciate what my responsibilities are and so a similar occasion would never occur.' He lived to fight another day.

When asked later to write an essay entitled 'The Generation Gap', Narendra wrote four pages in which he despised the rebellious trends of modern youth and praised the virtues and wisdom of all grown-ups. We will never know whether or not they believed a word, but a week later Narendra learned that he had won a scholarship to Dartmouth. All he had to do was to pass his A levels . . .

The Navy was now paying his school tuition fees and so the pressure to pass was redoubled, but still Narendra's indolence out-weighed his motivation and he failed all but one of the exams. He left the school in the summer of 1973 and crammed with a private tutor for four months, only then finally achieving enough passes to get him into the Navy.

There remained six months before he could join up, and so the family thought it might be a good idea for him to use the time to gain some relevant experience. After all, he had just joined the Navy, and no one really knew for sure whether he liked the sea. So BL arranged for his youngest son to be seconded to a cargo ship bound for West Africa, and in March 1974 the seventeen-year-old set off on the MV *Egori* of the Elder Dempster Lines. The ship left Liverpool, bound for the west coast of Africa, with stops at Sierra Leone, Gabon, the Congo and Angola. She carried chemicals, whiskey, cars and machinery on her way out, and copper and wood on the way back. This was the first time Narendra had been away from the disciplines of school or home and his natural hedonistic instincts ran wild.

I smoked and drank myself into oblivion with monotonous regularity. In Angola I met my first prostitute and in the Congo I had my first puff of marijuana. I did everything I could possibly think of, and of which my parents would undoubtedly disapprove.

For the best part of six months he immensely enjoyed this first taste of more or less complete freedom, and felt that he had learned a few of life's lessons along the way.

On the very first evening at Britannia Royal Naval College, Dartmouth, along with 123 other recruits, Narendra was sent to see the barber. The shortness of the back and sides was matched by the close cropping on the top, and all the cadets emerged looking like freshly shorn sheep. They were given a haphazard range of shoes, socks, trousers, pullovers, caps and battle-dress, and after lots of mixing and matching and swapping items with one another, they each had a complete uniform which more or less fitted. Then the real business of the college took over their lives. The Dartmouth training was demanding and exhausting, both physically and mentally.

The day started at 0600 with parade training or an early morning run, and ended at 2300 with kit-marking, boot-bulling, uniform cleaning and inspections. We quickly learned that a speck of dust on a jacket, an unshaved hair on a chin or a stain on one's stiff collar were all unacceptable – and resulted in extra inspections and parades.

The formal lessons were in discipline and seamanship, navigation, engineering, communications, supplies, logistics and history.

In addition the young recruits were also being taught about the conduct which was expected of an officer in Her Majesty's Royal Navy. There were lessons and demonstrations, for example, on how to behave and how not to behave at a cocktail party – including what not to do if a gherkin accidentally fell down the front of the dress worn by the admiral's wife.

The work was hard and the play was hard, and forty of the original cohort left after the first term. Among those who remained there was plenty of humour and camaraderie. Narendra had always enjoyed a practical joke, and there was lots of scope for these. One of them was scaling the clock tower which overlooked the parade ground and bending the hands outwards so that they continued to turn but became invisible when viewed from below. Another was stealing a senior officer's car and driving it at break-neck speed around the grounds. Narendra and friends once stole a steam-roller and drove it across the parade ground during the morning drills.

One morning, Sethia was summoned to meet his divisional officer and wondered what he had done wrong this time. All the divisional officers were present. The master-at-arms marched him in, he saluted and then went through the formal routine of removing his cap and standing to attention. The divisional officer, Lieutenant Commander Nicholas Cocks, looked at Sethia and said: 'Your father's dead, Sethia. I gather you had been expecting it.'

Actually, Sethia had not been expecting it, and the announcement in a public place came as more of a shock to him than the sensitive lieutenant commander had anticipated. The unwelcome news was swiftly followed by the revelation that BL had been a lot less wealthy than he appeared, and that the large house and apparently substantial bank balance were scarcely enough to pay off a long queue of creditors who had successfully been held at bay but now wanted their money.

Faced with a lot of debts and complications, Joan Sethia left the country for Barbados where some family assets remained. Suddenly his father had died, his mother had gone abroad, his brothers were away at university and, for the first time in his life, Narendra felt alone. On the other hand, he was no longer expected to spend his time off at his parents' home, and so another restraint on his pursuit of hedonism was taken away.

On 5 January 1975 Narendra Sethia was assigned to continue his training on board the assault landing ship HMS *Fearless*. The ship headed for South America and the Caribbean, and suddenly life in the Navy began to feel a lot more as he and his new friends had hoped it might be. In between exploring and getting to know every inch of the vessel, and then painting and polishing them, there were trips ashore to some of the most exotic locations in the world. In Colombia, a group of young officers was detained for being drunk in charge of a tricycle. In Bermuda the mopeds they had hired were stolen and so they stole some others to replace them. In St Vincent, a midshipman ferrying guests to and from a cocktail party on board ship managed to pull away just as the island's governor was straddling the gap between the ship and his boat. The result was a very wet and angry governor and a very embarrassed midshipman. A fellow crew member, who was laughing so hard that he fell over the stern of the boat, was punished with two days' extra work for leaving his place of duty without permission.

It hardly needs saying that most of the recruits failed their examinations, and Narendra was among those who had to do an extra term, and then stayed on in Dartmouth to do a further year of academic study – physics, engineering, computing and meteorology. He finally passed out and was assigned as a junior officer on a mine-hunter, HMS *Bossington*. The entire ship's company consisted of only five officers and twenty-eight crew, and so everyone put their hand to everything. Sethia's unofficial rank among the younger officers was SLJO – which stood for 'Shitty Little Jobs Officer'.

After a spell on the frigate HMS *Brighton*, in October 1977 Narendra was assigned to the majestic aircraft carrier *Ark Royal* for her final deployment to the United States and the Mediterranean. The carrier and her crew received a warm welcome in many places, including Fort Lauderdale where a banner hoisted on the quayside read 'Welcome British Ship Royal Ark'. It was a sad and moving occasion for the ship's company when, on 4 December 1978, *Ark Royal* steamed up the Hamoaze estuary for the last time, to the accompanying cheers of many thousands of well-wishers, and berthed alongside in Devonport.

Three months later, in March 1979, Sethia was sitting in his office as the carrier was being dismantled around him when the telephone rang. He picked up the receiver and a voice said: 'This is Nick Hunt, Captain of Britannia Royal Naval College, Dartmouth.' Well used to the practical jokes which were part of everyday life in the Navy, Sethia made a rude remark and was about to hang up when the caller said: 'Go and find a copy of the Ministry of Defence phone directory, find my number and call me back.' Sethia still presumed that he was being set up and that when he called the number, the real Captain Hunt would not know who on earth he was and the young officer would have made a fool of himself. Not wishing to take the chance, however, Sethia did just that, and his call was answered by Captain (later Admiral Sir Nick) Hunt.

Hunt told Sethia that he had a proposition to put to him and asked if the two men could meet the following Saturday in the Royal Oak pub in Meavy on Dartmoor. Sethia duly arrived at the pub, and over lunch and a few beers, Hunt outlined his plan.

There are three rules for spoofs in the Royal Navy – they must be original, they must be funny, and they must not cost the Ministry of Defence a single penny. Hunt's idea fulfilled all three. It was an elaborate plan to play an April Fool prank on his senior colleagues at Dartmouth, especially his second-in-command, the Commander at the College, Neil Blair.

Visits to Dartmouth by very senior military officers and dignitaries were frequent occurrences and Hunt had decided that he was going to arrange a visit – of a Saudi Arabian prince. The plan was that on 31 March 1979, his Excellency Prince Muhammad Saud al-Musad, the Amir of Al-Bahah, Prince of Al-Mamlakah al-Arabiya as-Saudiya, would visit the College, inspect a parade and hold discussions with senior officers about the possible purchase of Lynx helicopters for the Saudi Navy.

The only thing was that Sethia was to be the prince. He immediately said he was game and started thinking of ways to make the plot even more elaborate.

An order was sent to the College that an extremely important visit was going to take place. Key officers were briefed about the need to show every aspect of the College in its best light. Even the Flag Officer Plymouth, Vice Admiral Sir Peter Berger, took Commander Blair aside one day and said, 'I see you've got that Saudi chappie coming soon, Blair. Look here, this is a jolly important visit and I can't over-emphasise the importance of it in the light of current UK–Saudi relations.'

Sethia's older brother Krishna was up at Oxford at the time, and so he was invited to join the visit, playing the part of Mr Kassim Hajar, 3rd Secretary at the Saudi Embassy in London. If anyone had checked with the Saudi Embassy, they would have found that Mr Hajar was indeed the 3rd Secretary there.

Sethia needed to look the part so he visited the London theatrical costumiers Berman & Nathan and rented the most splendid Arab robes available. Black staff cars were hired, a special programme was printed, including the Prince's biography which stated that his hobbies were falconry, alpine skiing and fast cars – adding that he was the proud owner of two Maseratis. Hunt paid for everything from his own pocket.

As 31 March neared, Admiral Berger sent a signal to Dartmouth, simply reading 'His Excellency delayed one day. Will now arrive Sunday.' The message thus avoided using the words 'April 1st'.

We met up at an officer's house close to the College [recalls Sethia]. Our group consisted of myself, the prince; my brother Krishna; Captain Hunt; Lieutenant Commander 'Louis' Armstrong; a gentleman who was a friend of Louis's, recently retired from the Foreign & Commonwealth Office, but who still had his FCO card; another friend of Louis's who was large and wore an ill-fitting suit with bulges, and one of the officers from the College who was in on it and had organised the visit from within.

The convoy of three black staff cars drove up to the College at 11.00 a.m. sharp and was met at the front door by Captain Hunt, Commander Blair and several other officers. They had all been briefed on how to bow and on the correct way to shake the Prince's hand. Captain Hunt welcomed the Prince.

'Your Excellency – what would you like to do? We can either go for a tour of the College, or we can go to my house for informal discussions, or . . . aha! the Sunday church service is about to begin.'

'I will go to the church!' said Sethia in broken English, and to the consternation of the others he strode off in the direction of church, entourage in tow, and with the large fellow with the ill-fitting suit scanning the roof-tops for potential snipers.

The group arrived at the church entrance and was greeted by an oleaginous priest who opened the service with the words 'Ladies and gentlemen, today we are blessed with an event of great ecumenical importance and are honoured by the attendance of His Excellency Prince Muhammad Saud al-Musad.' For most of the service, Sethia held his hymn book upside down and smiled benignly at everyone around him.

The collection bag arrived and of course I had no money, but the captain's wife, immediately sensing my predicament, grabbed the bag from me and passed it to Krishna, saying at the same time 'Funny English custom, isn't it?!' I snapped my fingers and told Hajar to deal with it – and later a furious Krishna told me that all he'd had on him was a ten-pound note and rather than face embarrassment, he'd put that in the bag.

The church service came to an end and the Prince and his entourage were escorted by Commander Blair down a long corridor lined with midshipmen standing to attention on both sides. The entourage ended up on the quarterdeck, a large area which can accommodate dozens of people and has a statue of King George V at one end. Coffee and snacks were served, but the Prince's bodyguard had to taste everything before it was handed to him. Eventually it was time for speeches and a formal end of the visit. As 'the Prince's English is not too good', Mr Hajar (Eton and Oxford in real life) was to make the speech on his behalf.

'His Excellency would like to thank you for his all too brief visit to your College,' said Krishna. He glanced around him at what must be one of the most beautifully maintained buildings in Britain and continued: 'He is sorry that you have to work in such poor surroundings, and imagines that your refurbishment programme must be well under way by now. He would therefore like to make a donation to help with your restoration and repairs.'

At this, the Prince reached into his robes and produced a cheque drawn on the Imperial Bank of Saudi Arabia. It was made payable 'to the esteemed bearer' and was to the value of one penny. Blair, speechless, blinked at the cheque, scratched his head, looked around him at the smiling faces, got the joke and everyone collapsed in hysterical laughter. The story of this spoof was repeated for many years, and Hunt reckoned that it was one of the best pranks carried out at the College in the twentieth century.

Despite the great times he had enjoyed touring the high seas, and the frequent practical jokes, the experience of dismantling *Ark Royal* at the end of her distinguished life made Narendra feel restless. Suddenly it felt as though his career was at a turning point. He had been impressed by the loyalty and unique brand of camaraderie he had witnessed among members of the submarine service, and so he applied for submarine training.

The training course at HMS *Dolphin* in Gosport and the Royal Naval College in Greenwich lasted for four months, after which

Narendra was appointed to the nuclear-powered fleet submarine HMS *Courageous*. Once again he spent three months crawling on hands and knees in every deep corner of the bowels of the vessel, learning the position and function of every valve and pipe and switch and piece of electronics. At the end of the training he passed his submariner's qualification, entitling him to wear the badge of the two dolphins – the equivalent of the pilot's 'wings'.

Narendra Sethia left HMS *Courageous* and in May 1980 he was appointed as supply officer on board another nuclear-powered submarine, sister-boat to *Courageous*.

This was Her Majesty's Submarine *Conqueror*.

2

The Silent Service

HMS *Conqueror* is the most famous British submarine ever launched. Two hundred and eighty-five feet long, with a beam of thirty-two feet, she is an Improved Valiant Class submarine with a complement of 120 officers and men. Today, HMS *Conqueror* is still the only British nuclear submarine to have fired her torpedoes in anger, and the only one ever to have sunk an enemy ship. She is also responsible for a number of other remarkable 'firsts' which have hitherto remained shrouded in official secrecy.

Unlike her two sister boats, *Churchill* and *Courageous*, which were built at Vickers in Barrow, *Conqueror* had been built at Cammell Laird in Birkenhead. There had been suspicions of sabotage during her build, and her sea trials were dogged by a number of teething problems. She eventually took five months longer to be accepted into service than did *Courageous*, and cost £5 million more. Once she joined the Royal Navy submarine fleet in November 1971, however, she proved to be a state-of-the-art fighting machine. She was at the time the last word in a long tradition of underwater warfare.

Submarines have a history going back to the sixteenth century, but ther true significance and military potential had only begun to be understood with the success of German U-boats in World War I, when they sank nearly a million tons of Allied shipping in just three months between November 1916 and February 1917. This led to their further development through the 1930s and their pivotal role in World War II.

The statistics of the destruction of Allied shipping in the WWII Battle of the Atlantic take the breath away. Between 1939 and 1945, 3,500 Allied merchant ships along with 175 Allied warships, were sunk. Some 72,200 Allied sailors and merchant seamen lost their lives: 72,200 seamen – the equivalent of the total population of modern-day Carlisle – blown up or drowned in the icy waters of the Atlantic. The Germans lost 783 U-boats and 30,000 submariners – three out of every four members of the entire U-boat fleet.

The Allies eventually won the Battle of the Atlantic, but it had been a close-run thing. On the very day that Adolf Hitler took his own life in a bunker in Berlin, the Germans sent the first of a brand-new type of submarine into action, of a design which could, had more of them been completed and delivered sooner, have made a significant impact on the last months of the war. The Type XXIs (and the smaller Type XXIIIs) were the first submarines designed primarily to operate submerged, as opposed to boats which spent much of their time on the surface and only dived for short periods when either under attack or carrying out an attack. The Type XXI boasted three times the battery capacity of its predecessors and could run at 17 knots beneath the waves, which was faster than some of the Allied warships sent out to hunt them. It also brought enhanced underwater range of up to 72 hours at 5 knots. It was far quieter than its predecessors, making it harder to detect when submerged.

The effectiveness of the German undersea campaign in the North Atlantic was lost on neither the Allies nor the Soviets, and no sooner had hostilities come to an end than there was an unseemly scramble to divide up the most advanced boats among the victorious powers, and to locate and recruit German expertise. Past sins were quickly forgiven as former Nazi U-boat designers and engineers settled into their new homes – the lucky ones finding themselves living in a comfortable house in a prosperous suburb in Connecticut, while the less fortunate found themselves sent to downtown Murmansk, on what would prove to be the wrong side of the Iron Curtain rapidly descending across Europe.

Political tension turned into military rivalry, and just three years after the end of World War II, in 1948, the primary operational function of the US and UK submarine fleet was announced as the monitoring and interception of Soviet submarines slipping out of their bases in northern Russia, potentially to attack British and Allied merchant vessels. This unseen and largely unheralded cold war under the sea lasted for four decades and its code-name was Operation Holystone.

The mainstay of Britain's front-line submarine fleet in the post-war period were A Class diesel-powered boats, which were now given a range of enhancements that would allow them to cope with the more challenging task at hand. These included fitting improved radar warning equipment so that they could detect aircraft while remaining at periscope depth; a so-called 'snorkel', which allowed them to run engines, re-charge batteries and change the air in the boat without having to surface; and much better optics in the periscope for improved night vision. They carried a crew of sixty-five men, who lived closely together for up to ten weeks at a time, in conditions which were desperately cramped and every bit as noisy as the engine room of hell.

When these submarines left port, the crew would have no idea where they were headed. When they returned, most often they had only an approximate idea of where they had been. In the early days they would be completely out of touch with their loved ones for the duration of their mission. In later years members of the crew might receive a weekly 'familygram' – a message limited to forty words which, by tradition, was never allowed to include bad news. Many submariners preferred not to receive any messages at all while on operations; there was nothing they could do about any domestic problems, so they thought it better not to know about them.

One of the main difficulties in the long operational patrols was the limited supply of fresh water. This meant that many crew members would wash neither themselves nor their clothes for the entire period of their mission. Taken together with the diesel fumes which permeated clothes and skin and everything else, the smell must have been eye-watering. However, since everyone on board smelled equally bad, there were few complaints other than those from wives and girlfriends when the submariners got home. A stoker on board the diesel-powered A Class submarine HMS *Alliance* recalled how his wife would put his clothes through three cycles of the washing machine, and then hang them for several days on the line to try to remove the smell of the submarine. It did not work.

Personal comfort and hygiene apart, the most significant shortcoming of traditional submarines by the end of World War II was the danger of detection. Radar could find any surfaced submarine and even detect a periscope or snorkel head, and improvements in sonar and anti-submarine weapons meant that even a deeply submerged submarine was far from safe. Limited range, caused by the obvious need to refuel, was perhaps the greatest restriction. What the Navy needed was a vessel which could remain underwater more or less indefinitely, go where it liked, and sustain itself with fuel, air and water for extended periods. They urgently needed a truly stealthy submarine.

US scientists and engineers set to work straight after the war to try to realise the vision of Hungarian physicist Leó Szilárd, who had been the first to suggest that it might be possible to induce a nuclear chain reaction and then harness the resulting energy to power a submarine. The keel of what was to be USS *Nautilus* was laid at General Dynamics' Electric Boat Division in Groton, Connecticut, by President Harry Truman on 14 June 1952, and the world's first nuclear-powered submarine was launched two years later. She was named after the submarine in Jules Verne's *Twenty Thousand Leagues Under the Sea*, and over the following three years was to clock up a remarkable 60,000 miles in exercises and sea-trials. The size of the reactor meant that she was forty feet longer than the A Class but her performance was staggering: she could dive to 600 feet, with a surface speed of 22 knots and a submerged speed of 25; what is more she could circumnavigate the globe at that speed without a pause. In one trial she did the 1,300-mile trip from her home base to Puerto Rico in 90 hours. *Nautilus* was also the first submarine successfully to navigate a passage under the North Polar ice, thereby adding a further dimension and a new front line to the Cold War against the USSR.

The nuclear-powered submarine fleet instantly became the decisive element in the balance of power between the East and West, and the Soviets were quick to respond. Nikita Khrushchev had succeeded Josef Stalin as leader of the USSR in 1953, and immediately set about modernising and expanding the Soviet submarine fleet. The first Soviet nuclear-powered submarine, *K-3 Leninskiy Komsomol*, was launched in 1957 and just five years later it challenged the supremacy of the USS *Nautilus* by reaching the North Pole under water.

Britain was not far behind. In 1955, the Royal Navy took part in a series of exercises with the US Navy, and the improved speed, stealth and ability of *Nautilus* to remain submerged more or less indefinitely meant that she ran rings around the British vessels. It was quite a shock, and it was Lord Mountbatten who persuaded the Americans to share their technology with the UK. Britain's first nuclear-powered submarine, HMS *Dreadnought*, was laid down in 1959 with an American reactor and propulsion system, and finally commissioned in 1963.

The arrival of nuclear-powered submarines was to change the rules of the game for ever.

It is not easy, in the second decade of the twenty-first century, to summon up the real experience of the Cold War for those who did not live through it. Those who did will never forget the ever-present background fear shared by old and young, and by rich and poor, that their world seemed to be a push of a button away from coming to an end.

It was only a decade and a half since the end of all the devastation of World War II but now, for the first time in human history, military enemies had the capability to annihilate each other. At times of stress between East and West, the prospect of instant death flashing across the sky seemed to be a very real and imminent possibility. For many weeks during the summer of 1962 for example – when Narendra Sethia was just six years old – the people of the United States and of the United Kingdom (as well as, presumably, many of those in the USSR), almost literally held their collective breath as President John F. Kennedy and Premier Nikita Khrushchev confronted each other over the attempted siting of Russian nuclear missiles on the Caribbean island of Cuba. Parents exchanged anxious glances but tried to mask their concern from their children; children nevertheless picked up the tension in their households and heard the almost funereal gravity in the voices of TV and radio newsreaders. In churches and Sunday schools and school assemblies up and down the country, prayers for peace were spoken. Little ones were given an extra hug as they were tucked into their beds at night.

The two leaders drew back from the brink and what had threatened to become a very brief and very final hot war was averted. However, the frosty relations which had existed between the two new super-powers since their forces squared off in Berlin in 1945 continued to escalate into a full-blown Cold War.

Both sides in the arms race were now frantically developing and building ever more numerous and ever more deadly land-based nuclear missiles – more deadly because of their increasing destructive power, but equally because of the improved accuracy of their targeting. However, this very accuracy also made the missiles vulnerable to those of the other side. No matter where one power decided to site its nuclear arsenal, in its own country or in the territory of a 'satellite' state, and no matter how well camouflaged and protected the site might be, it was always going to be vulnerable to a direct hit by enemy missiles. If only it were possible to launch a nuclear missile from a site that was mobile, far away from landmarks or centres of population, from a place which was difficult to detect or target.

If the development from diesel-powered to nuclear-powered submarines had changed the rules because of the time they could spend under water, it was the arrival of submarines capable of launching ballistic missiles and threatening the enemy's cities which changed the game entirely. Since it was never going to be possible to monitor every inch of every ocean, suddenly there was the prospect of being on the receiving end of a nuclear attack quite literally 'out of the blue'.

Nuclear submarines came to be divided into two categories – the hunters and the hunted. The hunters could be nuclear-powered, but carried only conventional weapons because their main purpose was to locate, track and destroy the submarines carrying nuclear weapons. The hunted were usually nuclear-powered, and also carried inter-continental ballistic missiles which could destroy the major cities of the enemy without warning or even after their home country had been hit by a surprise attack.

The ability to locate, track and potentially to destroy enemy submarines, which had always been important, was now even more crucial. Somewhere out there, roaming any and every corner of the oceans, at depths which hid them from satellites and put them out of reach of current weapons systems, were silent killers which could at the press of a button destroy your cities and annihilate millions of your people. It is impossible to overstate how this priority eclipsed all others; the high command of every nuclear power recognised that nothing was more important to their respective defences than to be able to keep track of enemy submarines.

Since a submarine, submerged beneath periscope depth, is essentially almost totally 'blind' and unable to see the enemy, it follows that it is vital to be able to hear ships of the opposing side. Anyone who has seen movies involving submarines is familiar with the intermittent 'ping' which increases in frequency as the target gets nearer, and most of us who paid attention at school know that what we are hearing is the noise made by a pulse of sound sent out from a submarine or surface ship, and bouncing back to be picked up by listening devices on board. The sooner the pulse returns, the less distance it has travelled, and therefore the nearer the object it has detected. This is what is known as active 'sonar' – sonar being short for 'sound navigation and ranging'.

The ocean is also naturally a noisy place. Sensitive passive sonar listening devices pick up hiss and whistle from the surface waves, song from dolphins, that peculiarly haunting croon made by whales, clicks and ticks from fish, and then have to disentangle from all that the rumble of sometimes scores of diesel engines within a range of hundreds of miles.

An individual sound signature of a surface ship or submarine consists essentially of three elements: there is the continuous noise coming from her internal machinery, there are the specific sound frequencies coming from her propulsion systems, and then the low-frequency sound caused by the vibration from her propeller. Taken together they can locate a ship or submarine accurately and may even enable a skilled sonar operator to identify an individual vessel.

During the Cold War what all that meant was that when an unidentified vessel came within range, the first things the operator needed to analyse would be number of propellers and propeller blades, and the revolutions per minute at which they were turning. There were certain combinations that could quickly identify the class of vessel – for instance a 'one-by-four' (a single fast-revving crude and noisy prop with four blades) at 300–400 rpm would very likely be a fishing trawler. A vessel with a five-bladed propeller and slower revs was very likely to be a smaller warship, while something much larger, like a carrier, would have up to four propellers.

Conqueror's single propeller had seven blades and at 4 knots the rpm would be only 30 – the approximate rule was that 7 rpm would produce 1 knot of speed. In the 1980s some submarines were fitted with what was known as a 'whizzer' – this was a new design of propeller that had dozens and dozens of blades, very close together. The advantage of the whizzer was that it cut down on noise by eliminating some of the things that would be detectable with a regular propeller.

The primary source of propeller noise was 'cavitation' which was caused by air bubbles forming and collapsing near the propeller blades, this often being the result of a blade that had damage or excessive wear. The degree of cavitation could also indicate other things – cavitation from the blades of a dived submarine would tend to be higher-pitched than the cavitation from a submarine on the surface; even the cavitation from an oil tanker that was fully laden and thus had a deeper draft, would be different to the sound of the cavitation when the vessel was unladen.

Additionally, it was often possible to pick up the frequencies of individual pieces of equipment being run aboard a target – 'Aha, yes, that would be a 440AC air conditioning unit' or 'They've just fired up a turbo-generator' or whatever.

While East and West were in neck and neck competition in many areas of submarine warfare from the start of the Cold War, for a long time noise-reduction and sonar technology were critical areas in which the British and Americans were miles ahead. More sophisticated technology and techniques on the Western side, coupled with the fact that Soviet submarines were generally larger and far noisier, meant that the operational balance beneath the waves was hugely in favour of the West.

Until one day the balance began to tilt the other way.

Officers and crew in British and American submarines going about their business and believing themselves to be undetected could suddenly receive an unexpected 'wake-up call' in a highly dramatic and unnerving fashion. Sonar screens lit up with a vivid brightness, and there would be an instant high-pitched screech from transmissions which started loud and got louder. This was a sign that a Soviet submarine had located and was tracking them, and had suddenly turned on active sonar at close quarters. What it meant in effect was, 'I have you in my sights and I could have destroyed you if I wanted to.' Submariners referred to this as being 'bounced'. It was an unnerving experience for anyone on board, as well as for intelligence analysts back at naval headquarters in Britain and the USA. Suddenly, on more occasions than were comfortable, Soviet submarines had proven themselves able to find, track and 'bounce' their Western counterparts. If that were not alarming enough, now the Soviets seemed to be able to locate underwater sensors which had been placed in strategic positions by the NATO side to assist in the pinpointing of enemy craft. Whether it was to mislead or deliberately cook a snook at Western commanders, some of these devices had even been repositioned so that they gave an inaccurate reading to anyone monitoring their output.

These sudden improvements in technology on the Soviet side naturally led the British and American security services to wonder whether the advances had been home-grown within the USSR, which would be worrying enough, or whether they had been given some help by spies based in the UK or the USA. It was a fair question to ask, not least because there had in recent memory been an unfortunate series of catastrophic security breaches. To the chagrin of the British, all of them involved British subjects.

For example there was dismay among the defence intelligence community when, in 1960, the CIA received an anonymous letter informing them that information was reaching the Soviets from the Admiralty Underwater Weapons Establishment at Portland in Dorset. This was where the Royal Navy developed and tested equipment for undersea warfare – including sonar technology.

It is not hard to imagine how the suggestion of a leak to the Soviets of information about sonar would have been received by the Americans. Many on the American side were already deeply suspicious of the 'old boy network' based on Oxford and

Cambridge Universities that seemed to run the British Intelligence agencies, and harboured serious reservations about sharing technology with the Brits at all. Now here was the possibility that these most critical of all military secrets – underwater weapons and detection systems – might have been compromised.

It turned out that the letter had been sent to the CIA by an officer in Poland's Ministry of Public Security named Michael Goleniewski. Goleniewski was deputy head of military counter-intelligence and later head of the technical and scientific section. He had worked for the Soviets as a spy all through the 1950s, and at the end of it he decided to extend his activities across the Atlantic, being given the code-name Sniper and eventually defecting to the West in 1961. It is perhaps just as well that Goleniewski's information was taken seriously at the time because at a later date, after his defection, he claimed actually to be Tsarevich Alexei Nikolaevich of Russia – that is, the little boy with haemophilia shot with the rest of his family by Bolsheviks in a cellar in Yekaterinburg in 1918. Needless to say, Goleniewski wasn't Alexei. (Aside from anything else, Goleniewski was eighteen years younger than the murdered tsarevich would have been – and he wasn't a haemophiliac.)

For the moment, however, Goleniewski's information had credibility and caused instant alarm. The CIA informed Britain's MI5 and a mole-hunt was instituted. Goleniewski claimed not to know the name of the spy but said it sounded something like 'Huiton'. He was also able to obtain some of the documents that had been received from the spy, which helped to narrow down the list of suspects still further.

In the light of what happened next, it is perhaps surprising that suspicion had not already fallen on Harry Houghton. Houghton was a former Navy rating who had become a civil service clerk at the research base at Portland, and was living a lifestyle which should have been instantly recognisable as unaffordable on his modest salary. He drank heavily and was very generous when buying rounds in the pub. At a time when car ownership was relatively rare, Houghton had just bought his fourth.

MI5 put Houghton under surveillance and soon realised that he had a mistress. Her name was Ethel Gee, and she was a filing clerk who handled a whole range of highly sensitive documents to which Houghton himself did not have access. MI5 began to follow the couple and soon learned that they made regular trips to London, where they would meet a man later identified as Gordon Lonsdale. Lonsdale and Houghton were seen to exchange packages. MI5 now began to watch Lonsdale as well, and followed him to Ruislip in north-west London where he visited an antiquarian bookseller, Peter Kroger, and his wife Helen. The Krogers were also put under surveillance.

On 6 January 1961, Ethel Gee left the naval base with pamphlets containing details of a sonar device. On the following day all five spies, Houghton, Gee, Lonsdale and the Krogers were arrested in London by detectives from Scotland Yard's Special Branch.

Houghton's story amply illustrates the adage that in espionage matters truth is stranger than fiction. He claimed at his trial that he had been blackmailed by the Russians into spying for them. While he had been working in Poland in the 1950s, he had had an affair with a female black-marketeer and was told that she would be arrested if he did not start spying. In March 1961 Houghton and Gee were both sentenced to fifteen years in prison. They were released surprisingly early and married in 1971.

Meanwhile, hard on the heels of the humiliation caused by the Portland spy ring, came another spy story which must have challenged the credulity even of the Americans.

In World War II, William John Christopher Vassall had been a photographer with the Royal Air Force, after which he got a job as a clerk at the Admiralty. In 1952, he had been posted to the British Embassy in Moscow where he worked for the naval attaché. Moscow in Stalin's declining years was a harsh and unhappy environment for everyone, and perhaps especially for the very few Westerners who found themselves living there. Vassall's loneliness was compounded by the fact that he was homosexual – homosexual acts were illegal then in both Britain and the Soviet Union. However, he was eventually introduced to the homosexual underworld of Moscow by a man named Mikhailsky who worked in the embassy. Vassall was invited to a party where he was encouraged to drink heavily and was then photographed in a compromising situation with various men. The party had of course been set up by the KGB, who used the photographs to blackmail Vassall into spying for them. Over the next few years, Vassall gave the Soviets many hundreds of classified documents, including information on British anti-submarine equipment.

Vassall was betrayed when Anatoly Golitsyn, a senior KGB operative, defected to the United States. The KGB immediately ordered Vassall to suspend his activities while he might be under suspicion. Some within the Western Intelligence community already harboured doubts about the information coming from Golitsyn, so the tip-off about Vassall was taken less seriously than it might have been. Even so, it might be thought surprising that he was next given a job as private secretary to a junior minister in the Admiralty, Tam Galbraith, at which point Vassall resumed his espionage.

Vassall eventually made the same mistake that others in his position often seem to make, and began to enjoy a lifestyle which obviously could not be funded by his salary. He moved to a flat in prestigious Dolphin Square in London and threw expensive parties, explaining that he had been left money after the death of a relative. He was finally arrested in September 1962. In the closets of this clerical grade civil servant earning £750 a year, investigators found thirty-six suits, most of them hand-made in Savile Row, thirty pairs of hand-made shoes, and a vast supply of silk shirts, underwear and pyjamas. In a secret drawer in his desk they also found three expensive cameras, one of which was especially designed for photographing documents.

Vassall made what he claimed was a full confession, but once again, the secrets he said he had betrayed did not cover all the information thought to have reached the Soviets. This led the security services to wonder whether there was another spy still operating somewhere in Naval Intelligence. Vassall served ten years of an eighteen-year prison sentence and was released in 1972. He changed his name to Phillips, was employed for a time by the British Records Association and later worked for a firm of solicitors in Gray's Inn.

No sooner was the dust beginning to settle on the sorry story of John Vassall than there was a third breach of military security in a closely related area. This incident was to cause still more severe embarrassment for the hapless British security services.

Sub-Lieutenant David Bingham served as a weapons electronics officer aboard a Type 12 anti-submarine frigate called HMS *Rothesay* but had previously served as the torpedo anti-submarine officer (TASO) on a nuclear submarine. Bingham had what seemed to be the excellent good fortune of being married to a mesmerising and charismatic wife, with whom he had four children. However, it was perhaps especially unlucky for someone in his position to find that the delicious Maureen was not only devoted to him, but was also addicted to shopping and to gambling. Maureen's appetite for spending eventually led her to the realisation that Sub-Lieutenant Bingham's pay was not sufficient to finance her needs, so one fine day in 1970 she travelled to London, knocked on the door of the Russian Embassy, and offered the services of her husband to the KGB.

Maureen was welcomed inside by consular officials, who invited her to return some time later. They recommended that if anyone asked what she was doing at the embassy, she should say that she was carrying out research for a book on 'housewives of the world'.

In order to demonstrate the truth of her claims about her husband's position, Maureen Bingham had photographed pages from an exercise book which he had been using for notes. However, she had deliberately induced some 'camera shake', the effect of which was to blur the images so that the information on the prints was tantalising but unreadable in its detail. Later she would claim that she never intended to give any useful information to the Russians and that she was effectively 'taking them for a ride'.

Bingham discovered what his wife was up to and was thrown into a panic. However, Maureen appears to have persuaded her husband to go along with her plan because, on 11 March 1970, Sub-Lieutenant and Mrs Bingham met the Russian assistant naval attaché, who gave them £600 (around £7,000 at today's values) and told them to use some of it to buy a camera and a light meter at a shop in Portsmouth, and to meet their controller eleven days later outside Guildford Cathedral. At that meeting, Bingham was given more money and told to photograph whatever secret documents came his way. All went according to plan and by August the couple had received a sum said in different reports to be £2,800 or £3,200, which was close to twice his annual salary. In exchange he handed over a range of confidential and secret documents giving details of operational procedures, forthcoming naval exercises, and some details on the use and operation of sonar.

Maureen Bingham's excessive spending continued over the following months, and things got so bad that she had to sell the family car, which would have been reasonable but for the fact that it was the subject of a hire-purchase agreement and so technically was not hers to sell. It is perhaps disappointing that when a solicitor wrote to Bingham's senior officer on behalf of his clients asking for the sub-lieutenant's address because of an urgent need to contact him about an accumulation of unpaid bills, no concern was expressed or alarm raised.

Eventually the Russians became irritated that the 'camera shake' which had afflicted Maureen's first pictures also marred a good many of the documents they had received in subsequent months and began to suspect that they were indeed being taken for a ride. Now in total despair and at a loss about what to do next, Bingham approached a senior officer and confessed to his spying activities. Next day he was visited by an officer from Special Branch, to whom he confided that he had just taken nineteen pain-killers, and was confined to hospital.

Bingham came to trial in 1972. Newspaper reports described his activities as 'beyond belief' and Bingham himself was called 'the most despicable traitor in the history of post-war espionage' which, in the light of other recent cases of treachery, should have been a difficult title to win. The defence counsel described the case as 'a story of almost incredible folly' whilst the judge observed that David Bingham's confession read like 'a badly written spy-novel – a lurid melodrama of secret assignations, signals that involved leaving empty packets of cigarettes in rural telephone boxes and posting church notices to addresses in Kensington'.

At Winchester Crown Court, David Bingham confessed to photographing naval documents and as a result was sentenced to a total of 126 years on twelve counts, to run concurrently. Via some convoluted judicial arithmetic, that converted to an actual sentence of twenty-one years.

Maureen was also arrested and charged with offences under the Official Secrets Act. She was examined by a psychologist and the report stated that she was a pathological liar. Maureen was eventually sentenced to two and a half years in prison. She served her sentence and almost thirty years later, in 2002, was convicted of making false claims for social security benefits amounting to £14,000. She claimed that her time in jail – especially having to associate with Moors murderer Myra Hindley – had caused her to suffer from depression.

David Bingham was released from prison after serving only seven years of his sentence. He changed his name to Brough, remarried, and became the manager of a small hotel in Bourne-mouth. He also became the vice-president of the local Conservative

Club. In February 1997, during severe gales, he crashed his car into a tree and died from his injuries. He was fifty-six.

All three breaches of security – Houghton, Vassall and Bingham – had involved leaks of material related to anti-submarine warfare and a wide range of other secrets, and so Intelligence services on both sides of the Atlantic now concerned themselves with the consequences of the three bizarre lapses. What secrets had been compromised? Which operations were now vulnerable? How would what the enemy had learned be put to advantage in the perpetual game of catch-up which was being played across the globe?

Though much of what had been passed over to the Soviets in the three cases of espionage was tangentially relevant to anti-submarine warfare, none of it seemed to be directly responsible for the sudden improvement in submarine noise-reduction and sonar technology on the Russian side which was otherwise so difficult to explain. How could British and American Intelligence find out what the Soviets now knew, and how they had come to know it?

3

Silent Messengers of Death

The sudden and dramatic improvement in the Soviet anti-submarine capability, and its possible relationship to recent breaches of military security, were very much in the collective consciousness of the Intelligence community in general and the submarine service in particular when HMS *Conqueror* was commissioned into service on 9 November 1971. The primary purpose of the submarine would be to become part of the unending exercise in underwater sparring which was now the active front line of the Cold War.

However, *Conqueror's* first operation on active duty involved a different adversary. On New Year's Eve 1971 intelligence was received that the Irish Republican Army was planning to ship a cargo of weapons across the North Sea for use in their newly relaunched armed campaign for a united Ireland. Until now, the IRA had been getting most of its new and replacement weapons from Republican sympathisers in America – often smuggled to Britain on the liner *Queen Elizabeth II*, via Southampton and later in smaller cargo vessels across the Irish Sea. More recently, though, word had been received that the IRA had agreed a deal with Colonel Gaddafi in Libya, and that a wider range of perhaps more lethal munitions might be on their way. There was no such thing as a bank holiday for the submariners and despite the unsocial timing, the company of the *Conqueror* was quickly scrambled. But no sooner was the submarine at sea and the search begun, than new orders were received.

NATO has long operated a series of fixed sonar devices known as SOSUS (Sound Surveillance System), which permanently monitor ship and submarine movements on the most sensitive sea routes. On this occasion, the SOSUS which listened out for intrusions into the Clyde had detected the presence of a Soviet submarine in the area used by the British nuclear submarine fleet to approach and depart their base. The sound signature of the target suggested that she was a Victor Class nuclear-powered hunter-killer or SSN. This was taken as a sign of the increasing boldness of the Soviet submarine fleet. Some fast re-prioritising took place and *Conqueror* was ordered to break off from hunting the Irish and instead to go in search of the Russians.

The fixed SOSUS system operates at very low frequency and thus has long range. This means that precise accuracy is poor, but the advanced sonar on *Conqueror* enabled her to track down her target quickly. She was able to confirm that her quarry was indeed a Soviet Victor boat.

This was the first time that a Soviet submarine had been detected this close to the naval base at Faslane, and so there was no protocol describing how the situation should be handled. The last thing that either side wanted was a collision between the boats, but on the other hand neither wanted to be the one to back down. There followed what was essentially an underwater game of blind man's buff, with neither vessel able to locate or predict the position of the other with precision. At one time the two boats passed within 500 feet of each other which, in these circumstances, counts as a very near miss. On this occasion, after a nerve-wracking few hours, the Soviet vessel was the first to blink and she turned and left the area.

Life on board the *Conqueror* quickly fell into a pattern of patrols that lasted for between eight and eleven weeks, and then spells in base of perhaps six weeks for repairs, training and recuperation. Frequently intelligence would have been received about the movement of a Soviet submarine or a spy-ship disguised as a trawler and flying the flag of an Eastern Bloc country, and *Conqueror* would be instructed to track down and follow the suspect. Sometimes there would be rumours of developments in the other side's military capability – a new ship or submarine – and the task would be to search the oceans to try to find and photograph the target vessel. On one occasion there was panic in the Ministry of Defence about the launch of a new Alfa Class Russian submarine and *Conqueror* was tasked to find and snap a picture or record the acoustics of one. The operation was officially known as Operation Swain, which bored submariners speculated must have been an acronym for 'search whole Atlantic if necessary'.

Like their predecessors in the A Class diesel boats, the men on *Conqueror* and the other SSNs in the fleet had no idea where they were going, and often had little idea where they had been. The difference between life on board the earlier A Class diesels and the nuclear boats was the difference between taking the old night-mail train from London to Glasgow and the new high-speed inter-city sleeper. Neither was especially comfortable, but in the second there was at least the feeling that someone had made an effort. Being in the diesel boats felt like being a spare part thrown about inside a giant engine; the crew were a kind of after-thought once the engines and weaponry had been taken care of. It was equally impossible to be on board a nuclear submarine for long without being aware that it was 100 per cent about business, but at least someone seemed to have noticed that men had to live on board too.

At 285 feet long and 33 feet wide, *Conqueror* was almost four times the length and breadth of an inter-city railway carriage. It was the sort of vessel that looks very big when you are outside it, and feels small when you are inside. The hull was in the shape of a cigar, tapering from front to back, and with a large fin (frequently, mistakenly, known as a 'conning tower') just forward of the centre. For the most part, the vessel was divided into three decks, upper, middle and lower. Passageways between compartments were narrow and two crew members passing each other had to turn sideways. There were no exercise facilities and no way, of course, of playing any sports. For that reason, submariners had something of a reputation for becoming a little podgy and unfit. Commanding officers and first lieutenants were supposed to keep an eye on individuals who started to become ungainly or unhealthy and to send them on fitness courses – but in practice this happened only very rarely.

At the very front of the submarine – the bows – was the housing for the fixed sonar – as close as it could be to the enemy and as far away as possible from the interference caused by the boat's own engines and propeller. This is properly the 'business end' of the vessel because underneath the sonar, in the nose of the submarine, were six torpedo tubes racked in two columns of three.

Immediately behind the torpedo tubes were the torpedo compartments. Huge, heavy and unwieldy steel tubes tipped with high explosive warheads would be winched by cranes through hatches into the boat, rested upon harnesses and stowed on racks, one above the other. When preparing to fire, the tubes were opened, the torpedoes lined up carefully, and then slid inside ready for firing. Immediately another torpedo would be lined up behind for instant reloading should that prove necessary. The submarine could carry a total of thirty-five torpedoes.

Also in this compartment was an escape tower – for use either by divers who were needed to undertake operations outside the boat or, in emergency, as a means of evacuating the submarine. Every submariner has participated in an exercise simulating such an escape, and everyone who has done so remembers vividly the day the exercise took place. Professional divers are present in the training tank to ensure that the trainee breathes out as he ascends from deep water to the surface. If the divers do not see air-bubbles indicating that the candidate is exhaling, they swim forward and land a hard punch in the trainee's stomach. This is tough love, because air expands as the depth decreases, and failure to breathe out while floating to the surface has resulted in burst lungs, embolism and death.

Still moving from bow to stern, on the upper deck was the space where the officers spent most of their time on board. On the port side were two two-berth cabins which felt much like the sleeper compartments on that overnight train, and then the only single cabin on board the submarine, which was reserved for the captain. On the starboard side was an eight-berth cabin for the other officers. Sleeping spaces were usually in bunks stacked three-high, and were tiny, with only a curtain providing a modicum of privacy. The standard bunk was six feet two inches in length, and if a man of average build lay flat, he had around eighteen inches of headroom. Lack of space forced some on board to store clothes under their mattresses, thereby reducing the headroom still further. There were no bed-sheets – each man had a sleeping-bag made from nylon – which quickly began to smell from the sweat and dirt. A submariner's entire kit and personal property had to fit into a cupboard the size of an average left-luggage locker on a railway station platform. As well as the smell, the other ever-present thing was noise. Every second of every day – machines, pumps, generators, turbines, periscopes, bulkhead doors, whatever – there were thousands of systems that created a continuous background hum.

Next door to the bunk-space was the officers' wardroom, maybe twenty feet by fifteen, and looking like the sixth-form common room in a minor public school. Wood-panelled, it contained a table with a few chairs, a TV and some book-shelves, with cupboards concealing the bar.

Still going sternwards on the upper deck, and now immediately below the fin, was the sound room and then the control room. Senior officers could literally fall out of their bunks and within a few yards be inside the brains of the submarine. The environment looked like a mix between Jules Verne and Willy Wonka's (original) Chocolate Factory – a mass of dials and tubes and cables and controls and screens and wires and printed read-outs. There were spaces for the navigator and for the sonar operators, and for the operators of the diving planes which control the depth and orientation of the boat. In the centre of the control room were two periscopes – one for general use by the captain or officer of the watch called the search periscope, and another, known as the attack periscope, monocular to make it smaller on the surface, but with enhanced optics for photographs and targeting.

The feelings of isolation and claustrophobia that some people may have experienced were exacerbated by the fact that there were inevitably no portholes. The use of 'white lighting' was the only visible indication that helped the crew to know that it was daytime. In night periods, lighting was usually switched to dim red, and when the submarine was at periscope depth on dark nights, the control room would be in 'black lighting'; any interior lights would make it impossible for anyone on the periscope to see clearly outside.

If going on watch when the control room was operating in black lighting, officers and men would have to stand still for five minutes in the doorway to give time for their eyes to adjust to the dark. Sometimes the instrument panels were so dim that it was all but impossible to make out the readings, even from just a few feet away.

Directly below the control room, on the next level down and accessible via steel ladders, were the sleeping areas for senior and then junior ratings – much like those above them, but slightly more spartan and much more overcrowded. There was constant 'hot-bunking' – the bunks were often shared by two men according to their watches.

Down one further deck to the bowels of the boat and there were bathrooms and laundry facilities and storage areas but also, nearest the bow, a sonar console space where the electronics of the boat's listening gear were housed.

Heading now from midships towards the stern the cigar began to taper. The next compartment occupied the full beam of the boat and housed the nuclear reactor. Everything back from here towards the stern was related to powering the submarine: diesel generators in the motor room, turbo-generator space and storage.

Aside from family and friends, what many on board missed more than all else was the sense of anything in their surroundings originating in nature. There were no windows, and no sight or smell of anything from the natural world. Even the watch pattern defied the ordinary rhythms of the body clock. Six hours on and six hours off made it more or less irrelevant whether it was day or night.

The experience of living at such close quarters, united by the common bond of the earnestness of their task, produced among the submariners a very particular kind of esprit de corps. Much like the few astronauts who have ever visited the moon, submariners have an air about them which seems to hint that they know things the rest of us can never know. There is a cohesion and sense of solidarity which perhaps comes from their awareness that, albeit for a short time, they have taken part in something of historic and biblical profundity. Get close up to the 'silent messengers of death' which are their machines, and you can begin to get an idea why this might be so. These submarines are nothing less than the chariots of modern war, embodying the most advanced marine technology humankind is capable of producing at any particular moment. Stand on the top of the fin and imagine nearly 5,000 tons of menace a few feet beneath the surf around you and carrying you towards the enemy at 28 knots, and perhaps you can get an inkling of why these men take a special pride in their calling.

At sea, and among friends and comrades, submariners communicate with each other in a language they have made their own. They are constantly exchanging 'dits' about their various adventures. They know each other's strengths and weaknesses as they might if members of a large family. Nothing that happens on board can be concealed for long. Mistakes are usually owned up to immediately because to fail to do so can be a matter of life or death. Sometimes errors are lampooned, as might be traits of personality that annoy or entertain. They do not stand on ceremony, but they have a respect for officers and a discipline which is certainly rare in the armed services, and may indeed be unique.

Bring them ashore, however, put them among civilians, and they become very different animals. Partly this is because the requirement for security has been drummed into them from the very first minute of their service. More than that, it is a state of mind which does not require recognition from mere mortals. It is enough that they themselves know what they do, and they seem to have little need for the rest of us to know, or even to be suitably grateful.

4

Project 2000

Such had been the advances in Soviet capability in terms both of noise-reduction of their own submarines, and their ability to detect enemy vessels, that the Western powers began to feel something close to panic. Whereas in the mid-sixties it is fair to say that UK and US listening technology was ten years ahead of the Russians, by the mid-seventies the gap had become smaller and smaller, and was now too tight for comfort. The latest Soviet submarines were far quieter than their huge and noisy predecessors, and their sonar capability seemed to have been massively enhanced in a very short period.

The security breaches by Houghton, Vassall and Bingham were the cause of enormous concern, but did not in themselves seem to account for the Soviets' technical advances. Intelligence services on both sides of the Atlantic wondered whether there was another security breach somewhere else. If only it were possible to obtain an example of some key equipment being used by the Eastern Bloc – an analysis would then show whether it was home-grown, or a copy of similar kit being used in the West.

It was the Americans who first came up with the idea of trying to capture an example of the top secret equipment known as the towed-array sonar system. The towed-array was an ingenious listening device which enabled the user to get a two-dimensional fix on a target, and also to avoid a good deal of the noise from the engines of the ship deploying it. The system involved towing a cable up to two miles long, along the length of which were fixed a series of hydrophones. This 'array' of listening devices was then trailed behind the submarine or another suitable vessel. Whereas a single ship-board sonar could detect the direction from which a sound was coming, but not necessarily the distance away or the depth of the vessel emitting the noise, the ability of the towed-array to listen at various points along a line meant that these sonars could form a triangle with the object they were tracking. Thus it was possible to get a two-dimensional fix on the target. And because the listening took place at a series of points at some distance from the vessel using it, the towed-array also gave the opportunity to eliminate the noise caused by the mother-ship.

Deploying the towed-array from a ship or a submarine was a tricky business. Firstly, in the early days at least, such was the unwieldy nature of the apparatus that it had to be fitted by means of a barge coming alongside and connecting the kit to a short stub-cable emanating from the towing vessel. The array was also not accurate while the ship was altering course and could take as much as half an hour to settle once a new direction was established. Perhaps worst of all, once fitted, it effectively made the towing vessel up to two miles long – with all the attendant risks from ships or submarines passing in its wake.

Notwithstanding all these problems, once it was operating, this new technology was highly effective, and had played a major part in the advantage enjoyed by British and American submarines. However, within a short period following its introduction, Soviet sonar capability seemed to be equally as effective, if not more so, than that operated by the NATO side. Intelligence sources determined that the Soviets were using a towed-array system of their own. It was essential, said intelligence analysts, to obtain a sample of the Soviet version so that it could be taken apart and examined.

So it was that a highly secret project was set up within the Special Navy Control Programme (SNCP) to plan a dangerous mission. The code-name given to the daring project to obtain a Soviet towed-array, preferably without the enemy knowing that it had been taken, was Project 2000.

The top secret SNCP had been active since the 1950s and was designed to monitor movements by the Soviet fleet. Nuclear-powered submarines from the British and American fleets had been specially fitted with the most sophisticated state-of-the-art listening and tracking equipment, and would sit quietly off Arch-angel or Murmansk keeping a vigilant eye or, more accurately, ear, on the movements of Soviet submarines and surface vessels. The operations were usually initiated by the Navy, but some had also to be coordinated with the RAF, which would be asked to put up a Nimrod maritime patrol aircraft to activate Soviet defence systems to which the submarines could then tune in.

Twice a week, at the Ministry of Defence in London, the Director of Naval Intelligence would give a full briefing about the deployment of Soviet vessels to the head of DS5. DS5 was the liaison point between the military and senior ministers. If politicians were to retain ultimate control and responsibility for this critical element of the defence of the realm, they needed to understand and to approve details of SNCP operations which could become diplomatically sensitive.

Since many of the operations took place inside Soviet territorial waters, they were technically illegal under international law and were likely to lead to a serious international incident if anything went wrong. Hence each operation had to be cleared individually – with the Ministry of Defence, the Foreign Office, and the PM's office. One mission request was turned down because the Foreign Secretary at the time, Geoffrey Howe, was on a visit to Moscow and the Foreign Office delayed the operation until he was clear of Soviet airspace.

Only half a dozen civil servants and the Secretary of State were to know about Project 2000, and only those few on board British and American submarines who needed to know were indoctrinated into the operation. So sensitive were the political dimensions of the task, that only the Prime Minister would be able to give the go-ahead for British participation in any significant steps.

Already there was a dispute with the Soviet Union about maritime borders, the Soviets claiming a twelve-mile limit around their vast coastline, while the UK would concede only three. An adventure within twelve miles of the Soviet coastline could be perceived, technically, as an act of war; the added factor of a blatant act of piracy might lead to a full-scale diplomatic row. Or worse.

How was such an undertaking ever going to be possible, and who would carry it out?

Needless to say, the British and American submarine services work closely together, and frequently participate in joint exercises and equipment testing. Few things in this world are absolute, but as a general rule, when the two sides are pitted against each other in this area, and despite technology on the American side which is frequently superior, the British usually win.

This is not a factor of their overall experience and expertise. It is a function of the nature of their training. American submariners are trained to do everything – really everything – by the book. If the vessel they are tracking does this, they do that. If it does that, they do this. If it changes course twenty degrees west, you are supposed to do the following. If it dives, you do the following. Tell an American submarine commander a situation, and he will tell you the responsive action in his sleep. Their discipline is unimpeachable.

The training and culture of the British submarine officer is different. Of course they will learn and know and be able to repeat and respond to every eventuality as second nature; however, by tradition they are given a level of discretion and judgement which may seem surprising in so critical a role. A British submariner will explain that it is in the nature of the service that officers are out of touch with base for long periods of time. In so hostile an environment as the deep waters of the ocean close to or inside enemy territory, and sitting on board thousands of tons of state-of-the-art technology, there is a lot which can go wrong – and does.

No doubt any American submariner reading this will find it too harsh and too general and, like many generalisations, it may be unfair. By definition it can only be subjective and anecdotal. British submariners cite as evidence the relatively large number of US Navy submariners who have been cashiered from the service for what could be regarded as very minor breaches of the rules. More tangible evidence is provided by the fact that while the minimum depth of water in which a British submarine is allowed to operate when fully submerged is 44 metres (and as little as 30 with special permission), the equivalent minimum for the Americans is 100 metres. Trusting the judgement of the captain seems to have different boundaries on opposite sides of the Atlantic.

Whatever were the reasons, it was agreed between the Americans and the British that the Royal Navy would be in the front line of the attempt to acquire a towed-array from the Soviets. It was also noted at the time that the diplomatic fall-out from discovery might be less severe if it was a British rather than an American boat which was involved.

Every aspect of the various attempts to obtain and bring back a towed-array used by the Soviets is still classified top secret, and such information as can be gleaned is fragmentary at best. We know, for example, that in the middle of the 1970s, *Conqueror's* sister boat HMS *Churchill* made two attempts to steal a Soviet array. Essentially these efforts were not very much more sophisticated than a deliberate manoeuvre designed to get the submarine caught up in a cable which was being towed by a spy-ship flying a flag of the Eastern Bloc, so that it might be wrenched away with brute force. These spy vessels, known as AGIs – short for Auxiliary General Intelligence, were usually disguised as trawlers and were operated by both sides in the Cold War.

Given that the towing cables were some three inches thick, and the sensitivity of the equipment on board a submarine, it is surprising that there was not a serious accident. On the second occasion, however, there was a brief and dramatic tug of war at sea, which led to explosives being dropped over the side of the trawler. *Churchill* had become ensnared in the array and enough damage was done to the submarine's planes to oblige her to return urgently to Faslane for repairs. The official story was that the vessel had been snarled up in fishing nets.

Plainly, if Project 2000 was going to be successful, a new and more radical approach was going to be needed. Desperate needs required desperate measures.

For those who first heard about it, the idea behind Operation Barmaid certainly smacked of desperation. Secret operations which most people would have regarded as dangerously reckless were the everyday currency of life in the submarine service, but this proposal was as outlandish as anyone had ever heard.

Operation Barmaid was a sub-set of Project 2000, and the basic idea behind it sounded simple, even if slightly insane. Two huge pairs of mechanical pincers would be constructed which would be capable of cutting through a three-inch steel cable. They would measure approximately twenty feet long, and the cutting jaws of the pincers would be operated remotely via electronic connections. These pincers would be attached to the bows of the submarine, one on each side, with the wiring being fed into the boat and operated from a special control area. The pincers would not be a permanent fixture on the boat; only if intelligence indicated that a towed-array was in use, would the equipment be made available. Divers would attach the kit to wooden brackets which were to be fixed permanently to the hull.

Rather than cutting the cable of the towed-array neatly, which would immediately give the game away to anyone examining it after it had been severed, the jaws of the pincers would 'chew' their way through it, leaving open the possibility that the cable had frayed or snapped rather than been cut. At the same time, another giant pair of pliers would grip the severed end of the cable to prevent it from sinking irretrievably to the bottom of the ocean.

In order that the submarine would not be blundering about completely in the dark, cameras would be installed on the front of the vessel, and a series of monitors inside the boat would enable the officers in the control room of the submarine to peer through the gloom and get an idea of what they were doing. All the submarine had to do, it seemed, was to locate and approach a vessel – submarine or AGI – which was dragging a towed-array sonar system. Then they would need to sneak up underneath and behind it at the series of critical speeds and angles that would allow their approach to be unheard and undetected, get close enough in the murky waters to locate the cable behind the towing vessel, and then manoeuvre with sufficient precision to place the jaws of the pincers around the cable.

Considering that the vessels concerned were equipped with the very latest listening technology, merely the task of approaching one of them and remaining undetected was a challenge. Once it had been located and approached, following a Soviet submarine truly was a game of blind man's buff. Hearing the submarine at a distance was not necessarily a huge problem, but then coming close to it and staying with it as it slid through the water, required nerves of steel. The faster both boats travelled, the less effective was the ability to listen and pinpoint the enemy craft. Ploughing along at 20 knots, into the dark water, knowing that somewhere up ahead of you is 5,000 tons of menacing steel, sounds like madness. Add to all this the fact that, in order to check whether they were being followed, Soviet submarines were quite likely to do a sudden halt, effect a 180-degree turn, and come back along the previous direction of travel, and you have a recipe for terror. This move was known as a 'crazy Ivan', for the good reason that it was a manoeuvre frequently favoured by the Soviets, and it was extremely dangerous.

Having located, sneaked up on, and followed the vessel towing the array, the British submarine would need to exercise precision manouevring to line up the pincers with the towing cable, gnaw through it, and then secure it so that it did not immediately plummet into the impenetrable depths. The sudden reduction of weight and drag caused by the loss of the cable would inevitably be felt by the towing vessel, which would be bound to go straight onto the alert. Simultaneously, the considerable weight which had now been shed by the towing vessel would instantly be added to that of the British submarine, giving her the task of coping with being thrown out of equilibrium while at the same time remaining undetected. Next, the submarine would need to remain undiscovered while she withdrew from the area, and then send out divers to secure the towed-array properly to the hull, and return with it to base where it could be examined by experts.

What could be simpler?

5

Operation Barmaid – The First Round

It is May 1980, and in Britain the public is gripped by the real-life drama being played out live on television from the Iranian Embassy in Kensington. Six armed men have stormed the building and have taken twenty-six people hostage. These include the uniformed bobby who had been standing guard outside the embassy, Police Constable Trevor Lock.

It is one year since Britain's first woman Prime Minister was elected on a platform of getting tough on trade unions and getting tough on foreigners – immigrants, refugees, and the European Economic Community. So far, though, Margaret Thatcher has not had her real mettle tested or proven, and a very public siege in the heart of London provides just such an opportunity. The Prime Minister's prestige as a no-nonsense and decisive leader is undoubtedly enhanced when spell-bound TV viewers watch Britain's Special Forces – the SAS – retake the building, rescuing most of the hostages and meting out instant and merciless justice to the terrorists.

On the other side of the Atlantic that same month, the mood is just the opposite. The most powerful nation in the history of the planet is still coming to terms with the failed attempt by US Special Forces to bring home the fifty-two American diplomats being held hostage in Iran. As if the humiliation of the original hostage-taking has not been enough, an untimely sandstorm cripples the helicopters attempting to land the Delta Force unit and the rescue mission is aborted. As the US force prepares to leave Iran, one of the helicopters crashes into a C-130 Hercules transport aircraft carrying fuel and a group of servicemen. The resulting fire destroys the two aircraft, killing eight Americans. The remaining helicopters are left behind and the rescue force has to make a run for it. The debacle effectively sounds the death-knell for President Jimmy Carter's hopes of being re-elected the following November. He will be defeated by former Hollywood actor Ronald Reagan, setting the scene for an unusually strong transatlantic special relationship between President and Prime Minister.

Away from the headlines that May, Lieutenant Narendra Sethia joins Her Majesty's Submarine *Conqueror*. The submarine is in the Royal Navy dockyard in Chatham, undergoing repair and refit. Unlike a normal ship, where officers and crew mostly know their own job and not those of others, an officer on a submarine is required to know every valve and circuit – simply because he might be the person nearest to it when something goes wrong. Sethia spends much of the next weeks crawling on his hands and knees through every compartment of his new home.

That part of the time when he was not exploring the intimate entrails of *Conqueror*, Sethia spent exploring the night spots of Chatham. Preferring the company of members of the crew to that of most senior officers, Sethia would consume copious amounts of alcohol in the local bars with his friends before repairing to one of the town's Indian restaurants and consuming even more. Of the several characters who were his regular accomplices, most prominent was Leading Writer Colin Way. His job was to ensure that all ship's records were up to date and could be located when needed. At 6 ft 2 in and 19 stone, bearded and bespectacled, he was universally known as 'The Bear'. Way was as large in character as he was in stature, and the two men were to become inseparable. However, Sethia soon began to get a reputation among the boat's senior officers for being just a little too close to, and familiar with, members of the crew, and some of them frowned upon it. Sethia reasoned that if he did his job in a totally professional manner when on duty, what he did off duty was his own affair.

Though generally preferring the company of junior members of the crew to that of fellow officers, Sethia did make an exception for the TASO, Charles Hattersley. In the boot of his sports car, Hattersley routinely carried a white dinner jacket, a shooting stick, a hamper, ski boots and a set of golf clubs: everything a gentleman needed for a leisurely weekend. Charlie was every bit as partial to a drink as Sethia, and in a local restaurant one evening he took exception to the way he was being treated and threw a table through a plate-glass window. He and Sethia made a run for it and took refuge in a frigate which was in the dry dock. The two drunken officers walked up the gangplank, said good evening to the officer of the day, and went down to the wardroom where they opened a bottle and waited for a more senior officer to tell them to leave.

By the beginning of June *Conqueror* was close to being ready for action and Commander Morley Stephens, the captain, carried out some manoeuvres in local waters to test the systems, and some man-overboard drills to get the crew back into operational mode. On 17 June *Conqueror* said goodbye to Chatham and proceeded at a leisurely pace up the east coast of Britain and around the north of Scotland, at periscope depth the whole way, and arrived back in Faslane four days later, fresh from its refit and now thoroughly tested. The officer of the day wrote in the control room log, 'The submarine is in very good shape. Let's keep it that way.'

Soon after *Conqueror* was back alongside in Faslane, three Americans arrived without fuss or fanfare at the Royal Navy submarine base. They were dressed in civilian clothes and if they distributed business cards, these would have described them as working for General Dynamics – a company known then and now as, in effect, the engineering and technology arm of the Central Intelligence Agency. The three men checked into an unremarkable guest house in Rhu, just a little way down the coast on the way to Helensburgh. For several days the three Americans were involved in secretive talks with the captain, Morley Stephens. Also involved in the discussions from time to time were the executive officer, Tony Poulter, the submarine's weapons engineering officer, Mike Garland, the navigator, David Southcott, and the marine engineering officer, David Hall.

The cloak-and-dagger behaviour of the group invited interest from other officers left out of the discussions, but enquiries were discouraged. Over the course of the following weeks the three Americans made a series of low-profile visits to Faslane. Eventually, one at a time, some twenty of the boat's most senior and key crew members were called into a private office. They included the *Conqueror*'s sonar officer, Robin L'Oste-Brown, Leading Stoker Simon O'Keeffe, and ship's control officer, Narendra Sethia. Eventually the list would also include the navigator, Jonathan 'Jonty' Powis, and the new executive officer, Tim McClement.

The Official Secrets Act was and is the law of the land and, like all laws, applies to everyone. However, as serving members of Her Majesty's armed forces, each of the men now signed a new declaration to say that they were aware of, and would abide by, its restrictions. What is more, as officers aboard one of Britain's nuclear-powered submarines, they knew that the special sensitivity of their work meant that they were never allowed to speak about what they did. Submarines regularly go on patrol for several months at a time, leaving family and friends in complete ignorance of their location, duration of absence, or mission. Never is a word said to anyone about where they are going, where they have been, or what they have done while they have been away. That is the reality of their calling.

Even against that background it was clear that there was something unusual about the operation on which they were now to be briefed. One by one, each was reminded yet again that they were subject to the OSA, but there was more. The secrecy and sensitivity of what they were about to be told could not be over-emphasised. Many of their own superior officers were to be left in ignorance of the operation. Not only were they not allowed to speak about it with others on the submarine, but they were never to speak of it to anyone for the remainder of their lives. None of them was left in any doubt that the severest consequences would follow the slightest breach of security.

At the end of the meetings, each was required to sign a piece of paper. It was headed 'Actin Wintel – Top Secret Umbra'. There would eventually be some twenty-five names on the paper. These would include the First Sea Lord; Commander-in-Chief, Fleet; Flag Officer Submarines, and Captain of the 3rd Submarine Squadron. At the top of the list was the Prime Minister, Mrs Thatcher.

The same three Americans made several visits to Faslane over the following months and then, in the first week of August, the submarine was sent for an unscheduled period in dry dock. Curiosity among the crew was heightened still further as a large framework built from scaffolding was erected around the front of the boat, and great sheets of canvas were placed across the entire underwater section of the bow. Crew members and dock-workers watched in amazement as armed Royal Marines were stationed in the bottom of the dry dock, and access to the submarine's bow was restricted to no more than a dozen of the signatories to the top secret undertaking.

At the same time, on board the submarine, a large black curtain was erected in the control room around the navigation table, and custom-built operational and monitoring equipment was installed behind the screens. Two white lines were drawn on the floor, and a sign posted noting that only specifically authorised personnel were allowed to cross the lines. More specialist equipment was installed in the sonar console space, which is forward of the control room and two decks below, and this compartment was then declared out of bounds to all except the select few.

'None of us was told where the Barmaid equipment itself had come from,' said one young officer from the submarine, 'but it was generally assumed that these men from General Dynamics had been responsible for putting it together.' When not in use on the submarine, the kit would be kept in high-security storage in the Faslane base.

On 19 August the work was complete, and the dry dock was flooded, concealing the results of all that mysterious work.

'This is the first night out of dry dock so be vigilant', wrote the officer of the day in the log. 'We are afloat.'

The *Conqueror* spent the whole of September and October 1980 carrying out exercises in local waters in order to become acquainted with the Barmaid equipment. The idea for the operation was entirely novel, and every aspect of the kit and the way it worked would need to be tried and tested and tested again. There was no instruction manual for this kind of project – for the officers and crew of the *Conqueror* it was a matter of trial and error. In the forward sonar compartment, Ron Brooks, 'Bungy' Williams, David ('Reggie') Perrin, Graham ('Horse') Libby, Kevin Nicholls, Nick Webster and Mike Lewis were among those trained in operating the pincers which were designed to grab and saw through the steel cable, and then the powerful jaws which would clamp around the apparatus to prevent it from sinking to the sea-bed. There were complex hydraulics to get right, ultra-sensitive manoeuvring to seek to perfect, a whole new system of communications within the submarine to work out and then to practise. For several weeks, the submarine would head out of its base in Faslane and choose an unsuspecting fishing boat or cargo vessel as a guinea-pig for its 'underwater looks', practising following and approaching undetected, and coming up as close as possible for the proposed underwater snip.

The manoeuvre which would be necessary if the submarine was to execute the Barmaid operation successfully is one of the most dangerous in the underwater repertoire. In the short period going from deep to shallow or to periscope depth, the vessel is effectively 'blind'. Speed and turbulence make the periscope itself useless. Equally the sonar is virtually ineffective because sound waves bend and behave unpredictably at different depths, temperatures and concentrations of salinity; and of course the submarine is at power and therefore generating noise of its own.

Finally it is very difficult to use a sonar to 'look' upwards. There have been a number of reported incidents of submarines coming up to periscope depth and holing a vessel on the surface, and many more unreported incidents of one submarine colliding with another – hazards known in the trade as 'black icebergs'.

Faslane has the advantage of being tucked away in the deep waters of the Firth of Clyde and of being located in a relatively remote part of western Scotland. The disadvantage, so far as the submarine's company was concerned, was that there was very little to do in the area during time off. Sethia, the Bear and the TASO Charlie Hattersley were among those who made regular trips just down the coast to Helensburgh where favourite bars included the Imperial Hotel, better known as 'The Imps' and the Bar-L. Both were also favourite haunts of some of the local women, who could feel confident of being outnumbered and in demand, and who frequently expressed surprise to find officers such as Sethia and Hattersley mixing among the crewmen.

With his father having died and his mother now living in Barbados, Sethia would spend his periods of leave in Surrey with his friend Tony Blake – universally known by his nickname 'Bones'. Sethia had met and befriended Bones when the former had been a civilian guest at a mess dinner. Bones had literally thrown all 6 ft 5 in of himself into the boisterous games which followed the meal, and was last seen that evening leaving the mess covered with bruises and with his shirt and trousers torn. Nonetheless he had a big smile on his face and at that moment, Sethia recognised him as someone who shared his own *joie de vivre*, and determined to get to know him better. Bones was studying Town Planning at Cheltenham Art College, but his mother had recently died and had left him a large rambling country house to which Sethia was drawn at every opportunity.

'He was a rogue and a drunkard,' said Sethia later, 'and yet he was intelligent and well-read. More than that, he was a rebel and a wanderer at heart.'

Indeed, it emerged that, after he had finished his studies, Bones was planning to set off round the world in a small yacht. He had intended to go with a friend, David Phillips, who had chosen to get married instead, and so now he was looking for someone else to accompany him.

I was out sailing with Bones in the Solent [said Sethia]. It was a lovely August day with beautiful weather and a comfortable sea. He asked me if I wanted to take Dave's place and sail around the world, and with barely a moment to consider, I said 'Yes!' He actually seemed quite shocked by my immediate response.

Sethia returned to Faslane and submitted his resignation letter, informing his superiors that he planned to set off around the world in a small yacht. Despite his unconventional behaviour, he was considered to be a promising young officer, and one in whom the Navy had invested a lot of training and resources. Immediately he was summoned to the offices of the Captain of the 3rd Submarine Squadron, Captain (later Rear Admiral) Jeremy Larken. Larken was a keen sailor himself and asked Sethia all about the yacht he intended to use for the trip.

All I could tell him is that it was small and fat and had a mast. He looked a trifle surprised that I planned to sail around the world on a vessel thus described. He then asked me if I 'aspired to command' and I said that, yes, if I had planned to stay in the RN, I may well have switched back to the Executive Branch – the branch in which I had originally joined the RN – so that I could one day have a command.

At that, Larken sent a signal to the captain of a diesel-electric submarine that was operating the submarine officer's command qualifying course (known as the 'Perisher'). He told the submarine's skipper that there was an officer who 'wants to leave the service for admirably adventurous reasons but who aspires to command'. He asked if there was room for Sethia to accompany the submarine to observe part of its Perisher course.

Sethia spent a week on board the submarine, accommodated at

a hotel on the island of Arran, and being shuttled with the other officers at the crack of dawn every day out to the waiting training vessel. They would go out until well after dark, conducting one practice attack after the other. Sethia found it both exhilarating and exhausting. When he left the Perisher submarine, Captain Larken again summoned him to a meeting.

'Well? So what do you think?'

'It was amazing,' said Sethia, 'but I'm still leaving.' His resignation stood, and the process to find his replacement as supply officer on board *Conqueror* began.

The nuclear submarine continued to carry out short missions and exercises to test the Barmaid equipment, taking only a four-day break at the end of September in Hull. A friendly hockey match arranged with the local women's police team ended with fifty drunken submariners invading the pitch and kidnapping the opposition goalkeeper, who was also attacked – in the friendliest of ways – while on traffic duty the following day in the city centre. The officers and crew of the *Conqueror* worked hard and played hard, and it would not be long before an opportunity arose to test their skills and the equipment which had been so carefully installed in the submarine.

In November 1980 a report was received from Intelligence that a spy-ship disguised as a trawler had been seen operating a towed-array in an area off the Kola peninsula, north-west of Murmansk. Lacking the network of fixed and mobile listening devices which were routinely employed by the UK and USA, the Soviet Northern Fleet tended to concentrate their anti-submarine warfare efforts in this region, patrolling a fan-shaped area spreading out from their submarine base at Murmansk. *Conqueror* had received some damage to a periscope and was alongside for repairs in Faslane when the word came. The repairs were given more urgency and last-minute checks were made on the Barmaid installation. In the control room, the curtain concealing the specialised kit was still in place, and the sonar compartment which housed the controls for the pincers was out of bounds to anyone not on the exclusive list.

'Do not forget security now we are alongside,' wrote the officer of the day in the control room log, 'e.g. classified compartments are safely locked and checked regularly. Remember SECURITY.'

On 14 November *Conqueror* was ready to go. It was not thought likely that the mission could be completed successfully at this early stage, but the sighting did seem to present an opportunity for a dummy run at the very least. Just hours before departure another name was added to the short list of people who 'needed to know' about Operation Barmaid. Grant Louch had just joined the boat as a weapons engineering rating and immediately was summoned and put through the same rigorous interview to which other signatories had been subjected. Suitably impressed, he was required to sign the top secret confidentiality form. The list included the same pantheon of the highest-ranking officers of the Navy.

'I was well-used to the idea of chasing around after Soviet submarines,' said Louch, 'but none of the other submarines were doing anything like this operation. It was a complete revelation.'

Just four hours later the mechanical pincers were fitted to the *Conqueror* and she was off in a great hurry. Her destination was unknown to anyone except the captain and a handful of the most senior officers. *Conqueror* remained on the surface as she edged her way down the Firth of Clyde and into the North Channel. Once in open water she submerged and turned north, running up the narrow channel between Harris and Skye.

For the next five days, *Conqueror* sailed north and north-east, on a heading which took her parallel to the Norwegian coast but staying well clear of it. On 18 and 19 November the submarine turned east, leaving Norway's Lofoten Islands to starboard. Now she was approaching the area where intelligence had spotted the AGI. Some of those who participated in the exercise believe that the target ship was flying a Polish flag and was called *Ribachiy*.

Vessels of this type were bristling with radar and antennae of every description, and were on the look-out for aircraft, ships, submarines or electronic transmissions of any kind. It was hoped that when eventually located, the AGI would be at anchor, giving *Conqueror* a fighting chance to approach her from the deep and to locate the towed-array in stable conditions. However, when eventually the AGI was detected, she was on the move. An attempt was nonetheless made to approach the ship from below and to put the submarine into a position where she would be able to retrieve the towed-array if the opportunity presented itself. Very quickly it was realised that there was little or no chance of performing the operation on a fast-moving target, and after some careful approaches, the attempt was abandoned.

Despite this setback *Conqueror* spent two weeks – much of it in silent mode – stalking its target. Eventually the attempt was given up altogether and *Conqueror* headed home in time for Christmas. Though there was disappointment, no harm had been done, the enemy had not been aware of the operation, and the exercise had been a good rehearsal for another attempt whenever the opportunity should arise.

6

Crazy Ivan

American anxiety that the Soviets had made a significant advance in sonar technology was raised still further with the launch of the Victor III Class of submarine. US Intelligence had obtained a photograph of the new vessel under construction, revealing the presence of a large tear-shaped pod some thirty feet long and ten feet across near the stern of the boat. All the great minds huddled to discuss what this mystery bump might conceal. Some thought it might be a new and perhaps quieter method of propelling the boat. Others that it might be a new on-board sonar. One popular opinion, however, was that it might house a new kind of towed-array sonar system – exactly the apparatus which had so significantly enhanced the Soviets' listening capability in the world's oceans. Plans were swiftly made to try to get as close as possible to the new Victor III, in order to photograph and examine the strange bulge.

In April 1981, the American nuclear-powered submarine USS *Drum* was ordered to the waters around Vladivostok where it was thought most likely that the Victor III might be operating. The submarine waited around for several weeks before eventually her radar picked up what seemed as though it might be the submarine's silhouette. The good news was that it was resting on the surface, which might mean that it was preparing to go on exercises the following day. The bad news was that it was inside Peter the Great Bay, which was an area usually congested with Soviet warships. USS *Drum* approached stealthily at periscope depth and gradually eliminated all the other clutter from her sonar, until eventually she neared her target just off Popov Island, outside Vladivostok. The Navy photographer was preparing to snap his pictures through the periscope, when a warning indicator in the control room signalled that the submarine had been detected by enemy radar. A glance through the periscope was enough to reassure Captain Michael Oliver that the Victor III was taking no aggressive action, and so in the control room of the *Drum* they assumed that no alarm had been raised. The Soviet submarine was now just 900 yards off the port side, and the photographer, William Craig Reed, kept snapping away.

They might now have regarded their mission as having been accomplished, but between them Reed and Oliver decided that since the sun had been behind the enemy submarine, they would be able to take better pictures by sneaking around the other side, so that the light would be behind them. Oliver also suggested that Reed might put on a wet-suit and go for a swim in the bay to see if he could take even better pictures. These were cold and crowded enemy waters, but nonetheless Reed began to get kitted up. Minutes later he had entered the escape hatch and was waiting for the order to exit the submarine.

The USS *Drum* began to dive in order to commence its manoeuvre across to the other side of the Soviet submarine when the officer of the watch, Nick Flacco, realised that the VHF aerial wire had been left trailing outside the vessel and needed to be retrieved. There was what seems to have been a brief moment of confusion while the *Drum* was returning to periscope depth. As the vessel neared the surface the captain once again took the periscope and just had time to glance through it and shout 'Emergency dive!' – but it was too late. Instantly a thunderous boom shook the boat and the radioman who had been reeling in the aerial tumbled down the ladder and hit the deck hard.

'Why aren't we diving?' yelled the captain. The order was given to flood the forward trim tanks but the submarine still failed to dive. The two boats had collided and become entangled.

The US submarine lurched backwards and forwards, the sound of metal on metal deafening as water began to pour in through hatches above the crewmen's heads. The boat was flooding.

Meanwhile the diver, Reed, was still in the escape hatch where the collision had knocked out the lights and his oxygen supply, and was desperately trying to work out what to do.

Eventually the *Drum* yanked itself free but it was not yet safe. Soviet helicopters had been scrambled and were dropping sonobouys in the waters all round them to try to pinpoint their position. As she fled south, it became clear that a number of anti-submarine destroyers and gunboats were heading towards a narrow gap ahead, attempting to cut off the only route to safety. This was a life or death moment for the *Drum*; everyone in the boat's company knew that the captain would take the vessel to a depth where the pressure of water would implode it, rather than to allow it to be captured by the Soviets. Then, suddenly, the *Drum*'s sonar picked up the sound of a metallic crunch some way in the distance, and gradually the number of enemy vessels in pursuit began to diminish and dissolve. It later turned out that another American nuclear submarine, USS *George Washington*, had collided with a Japanese freighter not far away, effectively providing a decoy for the *Drum*'s escape. The submarine managed to make it into open water, but spent the next two days sneaking around the bottom, the crew listening to the sound of patrolling vessels above them and the occasional explosion from a depth-charge – some close enough to rattle the crockery.

When the *Drum* eventually made it to the safety of Apra harbour in Guam, she was immediately covered in tarpaulins so that Soviet satellites would not be able to photograph the damage. As was often the case with Cold War special ops, the boat's logs were altered so that there was no official record that USS *Drum* had ever been in Peter the Great Bay. Two years later, thanks in part to the photographs taken in this incident, US Intelligence confirmed that the pod on the Victor III was indeed the housing for a new kind of towed-array sonar.

Also in 1981, *Conqueror* herself had what felt like a near-death experience involving a Victor III. The British submarine was on a normal patrol and was trailing the Soviet vessel in what should have been a relatively routine operation. Narendra Sethia was the ship control officer on watch when, in the early hours of the morning, there came a sudden and very loud, sharp and high-pitched sound from the sonar screen on the port side of the control room. The whole screen lit up brightly, instantly dazzling the sonar operator. This was an example of a so-called 'bounce' by which an aggressive Soviet submarine would send a signal that a hunter had been spotted and was now itself a potential target. Everything seemed to happen at once – the captain and first lieutenant came rushing to the control room and within seconds of the flash on the sonar screen, the submarine's sensors could see that the Victor III had made a 180-degree turn and was now coming straight back towards the British submarine. A 'crazy Ivan'. At the same time she was transmitting actively – another blatantly aggressive gesture. If the manoeuvre was anything more sinister than a scare-tactic, the next thing they would hear would be the sound of torpedo bow caps being opened – which would have raised the stakes still further. Rather than risking an escalation of the confrontation, *Conqueror* took evasive action and rapidly retreated from the area. When later all the information was sent to Northwood for analysis, it was calculated that the Victor III had been driving directly towards *Conqueror* and had passed within a few hundred feet.

There was to be yet a third close encounter in that same summer, in the Barents Sea, when Her Majesty's Submarine *Sceptre* was following an unidentified Soviet submarine, but lost the trail for about half an hour. *Sceptre*'s weapons officer, David Forghan, said later that 'there was a huge noise. It started very far forward, sort of at the tip of the submarine, and it trailed back. It sounded like a scrawling. We were hitting something. That noise lasted for what seemed a lifetime, but it was probably only a couple of seconds or so. Everybody went white.' Later inspection of the damage indicated that the *Sceptre* had been hit by a much larger submarine. She hurried back to the floating dock at Faslane for repairs before returning to Plymouth; the crew were told to say, if asked, that they had encountered an iceberg.

Then, just six months after the first exercise exploring the possibility of grabbing a Soviet towed-array in the North Atlantic, *Conqueror* was at it again. It was the end of June 1981 and this time the submarine was on a routine patrol when Intelligence reported that a spy-trawler from the Eastern Bloc was deploying a towed-array sonar somewhere in the Mediterranean, just off the coast of north Africa.

Conqueror was ordered to load torpedoes, food and equipment and be ready to set sail within thirty-six hours. However, there was a civil servants' strike at Ministry of Defence shore establishments, and all the land-based storerooms were shut and locked. The supply officer of another submarine, Peter Godwin, conferred with Sethia and they set up what they dubbed an 'Emergency Control Centre' on the lawns outside the shore wardroom – taking good care to ensure that they were equipped with a striped umbrella to keep off the sun and with a case of beer to hand. The two men decided that, if they were to carry out their primary duty to defend the nation, it would be necessary for them to break into the storerooms in order to put to sea. The chief civilian officer was the only person in authority still at work, so Godwin and Sethia marched down to the Ministry of Defence Police booth at the entrance to the submarine base and told the duty sergeant that they were about to break into the storerooms and that he had better accompany them as a witness. The officer was speechless and had no text-book response – but he accompanied the naval officers as they tore off the padlocks, opened the stores, and then sent their own men to bring fork-lift trucks in order to load the stores. *Conqueror* ended up sailing on time, and when the striking civilian employees found out what had happened, there was an enormous row.

On 20 June *Conqueror* set off due south in haste. By this time Morley Stephens had been replaced as captain by Richard Wraith.

Despite Sethia's initiative in ensuring adequate supplies for the operation, not all of the kit required for an interception was on board, and so on 1 July *Conqueror* made an unscheduled stop in Gibraltar where the Barmaid equipment would be delivered and loaded. It was made clear to all on board that the submarine would be leaving again on the following morning.

Among those on the trip who wanted to go ashore were Narendra Sethia, Colin ('The Bear') Way, Robin L'Oste-Brown, Jonty Powis, John 'Soapy' Coulthard, Phil Buckley, Paul Taylor, Mike Lewis and Simon O'Keeffe. Grant Louch would have liked to have been on the trip, but missed it because he had swapped tours with another submariner who was getting married. The only trouble was that they were not allowed to go ashore in their submariners' overalls, and none of them had any civilian clothes. An unsuspecting civilian who was delivering kit to the vessel found himself physically overwhelmed by a group of submariners, who removed the shirt and trousers that he was wearing as well as the spares of both in his luggage. The Gibraltar representative of Bernard's Naval Tailors was then summoned to the submarine and asked to bring a pile of civilian clothes. While the majority of officers and men went ashore to the local bars, a smaller group went off to spend the evening at one of their favourite haunts.

There was no sign outside 'Strings', or any other external evidence that it was a restaurant; it was very small, with not more than half a dozen tables. The owner was Peter Wheatley, whose cousin was Dennis, the famous author of satanic thrillers. Peter was said to have been cashiered from the Army when ADC to the governor of either Australia or New Zealand (no one seems sure which) for 'an indiscretion with a fellow officer'. There were only a couple of staff – very friendly Moroccans – and although the menu was small, the food was fabulous and the attention to detail impressive.

The opportunity for a break and some booze in the middle of a tour of duty was rare and unexpected, so full advantage was taken. The group was described by one member as being in a state of 'advanced relaxation' and were not amused when they realised that it was nearly dawn and they were overdue back on board.

Only a few hours later, at 09.00 on 2 July, *Conqueror* slipped quietly out of Gibraltar and headed east into the Med. The AGI had been sighted off the coast of Algeria, but these were crowded waters and the submarine had to steer a course between large numbers of pleasure boats and cruise liners, while of course always keeping alert to the possibility of coming across a Soviet submarine.

This is the kind of operation for which the *Conqueror* had trained and trained. New officers on board were frequently put through a baptism of fire in the waters of the Firth of Clyde where they would need to steer a course in between cargo vessels, fishing boats, pleasure boats and ferries – all of which can be difficult enough for the pilot of an ordinary ship when other vessels can see you and take evasive action of their own. Locating a crowd of other ships, predicting their course and speed, and nudging your course between them when your own vessel cannot be seen and avoided, can test the seamanship of even the most highly trained submariner. That said, the sonar signatures of the Soviet AGIs were well-known to the sonar operators on board *Conqueror*, and they knew what they were looking for.

Departing Gibraltar, *Conqueror* travelled east and east-north-east, running fast at an average depth of around 500 feet. She covered 234 miles in the fifteen hours until 24.00, by which time she was in the vicinity where the AGI was last reported to have been operating. At midnight *Conqueror* slowed and came up to periscope depth, retracing her steps in search of her target. At around 10.00 on 3 July *Conqueror* finally located the AGI, and followed her at a leisurely pace heading more or less due west. An hour later *Conqueror* began to close in.

Now came the real challenge. How could *Conqueror* remain undetected while approaching an Eastern Bloc ship, part of the purpose of which was to listen out for and analyse the sound signatures of NATO submarines? Not only was the vessel stuffed with all the most state-of-the-art electronic and signals intelligence kit available, but she was of course also deploying a towed-array sonar, which would be likely to stretch out for a distance of perhaps 3,000 yards behind.

Fortunately the average depth in the Mediterranean is around 5,000 feet, with extremes closer to 17,000, so once *Conqueror* had located her target she had plenty of room to go deep and come up behind and beneath her, making use of a 'blind spot' in the AGI's sonar caused by its own propulsion system.

As in the previous exercise in the Barents, once again the AGI was on the move, and the task of trailing her with enough precision to be able to line up the pincers with the towing cable and sever it was going to be hugely challenging. The captain, now Richard Wraith, ordered the crew to stop any activities which might make a noise, and every member of the submarine's company was focussed on the task ahead. The approximate course and speed of the AGI had been calculated from the initial visual contact, and now the *Conqueror* dived to 120 feet to update all sonar checks before making her final approach. At around 2,000 yards, the submarine returned to periscope depth. Through the magnifying lens the captain could now see the snaking cable of the towed-array dipping into the water behind the trawler. Like a swimmer taking a last deep breath of air before diving, *Conqueror* once again submerged to 120 feet. Soon the turbulence caused by the AGI's propellers was visible through the scope and Wraith issued a series of speed adjustments to the helmsman. A little faster, a little slower.

Once the progress through the water of the two vessels matched, Wraith gradually increased the speed of the submarine in order to close the gap. Gradually, gradually, and then finally, the AGI's propellers came into view through the periscope, sharp steel blades spinning in a blur through the water. Any collision would be disastrous – on board the submarine the notion of those steel blades ripping through their vessel's casing was terrifying; yet the operation demanded that the submarine and the trawler come close enough to kiss beneath the water. Now the turbulence caused by the propeller and the wake from the trawler began buffeting the submarine dangerously, and suddenly inside the sub they heard the sound of contact. Wraith knew that he had not hit the trawler, and quickly realised that they had come into contact with the cable towing the array. He gave the order to steer to port and gradually to reduce speed, and the *Conqueror* pulled out of the gap between the boat and the trailing cable, allowing the AGI to open up the distance between them.

Now the sonar operators were listening hard to reassure themselves that their presence had not been detected by the spy-ship. The AGI was continuing her course and speed, and there seemed to be nothing to indicate that she had noticed the bump. After an hour *Conqueror* surfaced to check for any consequences of the collision. The damage was confined to some superficial scraping to the submarine's fin.

Once the captain was sure that the alarm had not been raised, he decided not to press his luck any further, and the submarine disengaged and slowly continued her journey west and out once again into the Atlantic.

Four days later, at 09.00 on 7 July, HMS *Conqueror* engaged in two hours of 'angles and dangles' – the name given to a set of exercises in which the submarine is cranked up to full power and, when it reaches very high speed, the planesmen are given orders such as 'starboard 30'. The submarine then heels, and the planes act like aircraft ailerons, so that, when doing almost 30 knots, the submarine can plunge 500 feet within seconds. 'Angles and dangles' are good training for the fore- and after-planesmen in controlling the boat at high speeds. Doing them was also a perfect cover story, if needed, for the otherwise inexplicable manoeuvres which the submarine might have been seen carrying out when it was actually involved in trailing the AGI. After lunch that day the *Conqueror* turned north, making a fast passage back to Faslane for repairs to her fin. She arrived at 14.00 on 10 July.

Conqueror spent the remainder of 1981 on routine patrols and exercises, waiting for another opportunity to try to complete Operation Barmaid. None came, and in the first three months of 1982, she was due to take part in exercises with the US Navy at the Atlantic Undersea Test and Evaluation Center in the Bahamas. So, the following January, HMS *Conqueror* set off across the Atlantic.

7

'Their Way of Life is British'

One of the features of life in the world of *1984* as portrayed by George Orwell, is that yesterday's enemy is suddenly your friend, and yesterday's friend is suddenly your enemy. It rather felt that way in the first few days of April 1982 when Britain woke up to the news that the Falkland Islands had been invaded by Argentina.

If the British thought about Argentina at all, they thought about her in terms of football or corned beef – but they did not think of her as an enemy. There were close historic ties between the two nations; Britain was among the first countries to recognise Argentina's independence from Spain in 1825, and at one point in the nineteenth century Argentina accounted for fully ten per cent of the UK's entire overseas investment. There was vigorous and friendly sporting competition, especially through a shared interest in horses in general and polo in particular. In 1912 the Harrods department store opened its first and only international branch in Buenos Aires.

Just 300 miles off their coast, the 200 islands of the Falklands collectively add up to an area about half the size of Wales, with a population at the time of about 1,800. Most are descendants of Scottish, Welsh and English sheep-farmers and are of course outnumbered by the sheep, by a factor of about 200 to 1.

If knowledge of the location of the Falklands was limited to diligent students of geography, only those with an even more specialist interest in history knew much about the background to this unexpected conflict. Look at a map of the world produced in Britain, and the tiny group of islands way down in the South Atlantic are labelled 'Falkland Islands', coloured pink, and followed by the letters 'Br' in brackets. Buy a map of the same area anywhere in South America and the islands are labelled 'Islas Malvinas' and are followed by an 'Ar' for Argentina.

The dispute over sovereignty began not long after the islands were originally discovered – most probably by an Englishman called John Davis in 1592. Helpfully, the first person known to have made landfall was also an Englishman, John Strong, who went ashore nearly a hundred years later in 1690 to take a closer look at the penguins. The next eighty years or so were characterised by intermittent bouts of figurative and literal sabre-rattling as the French, Spanish and British squabbled over parts or all of the islands. Only in 1833 did Britain's appointment of a governor mark the start of 150 years of continuous British administration.

The Argentines, however, had been making noises about their claim to the Falklands at varying levels of intensity since the 1820s. By the 1980s catastrophic economic problems and the unpopularity of the military government in Argentina contributed to the usefulness of the islands as a nationalist diversion, and the noises from Buenos Aires began to reach a roar in the early part of 1982. The most recent rumblings about a possible invasion had been seen off five years earlier by the then Foreign Secretary David Owen, by the simple expedient of dispatching a nuclear submarine and two frigates to the region and letting Argentina know through the good offices of the Americans that he had done so. However, far more overt indications, over many months, that the Argentine junta under General Leopoldo Galtieri was considering a similar move were taken less seriously by Mrs Thatcher's government, and by the time Britain realised that the threat was real, it was too late for deft gunboat diplomacy.

Even taking into account the domestic pressures that the military government in Argentina was facing, the timing of the invasion at first seems odd. In Britain, severe cuts in the defence budget, already announced by John Nott, would have meant the withdrawal of the Royal Navy patrol ship HMS *Endurance*, which provided the only meaningful British military presence in the South Atlantic. They also included the sale of the Navy's two aircraft carriers, *Hermes* and *Invincible*, to India and Australia respectively – without which it would have been impossible for Britain to contemplate a military response (short of a nuclear attack) to an invasion. All of these measures were in the public domain, so why did the Argentines not wait just a few months for them to be implemented? The answer to the puzzle turns out to be one of those accidents of history which has unforeseen consequences.

In the second half of March 1982, Britain's fleet of nuclear submarines was on the annual training exercise based in Gibraltar – Operation Springtrain – when word began to circulate that the Argentine sabre-rattling might be getting more serious and become something more than theatrical. A group of scrap-metal dealers had landed on South Georgia and raised the Argentine flag, a provocative and irritating act, but not much more. Politicians and admirals were contemplating sending one or two submarines in the direction of the South Atlantic, much as David Owen had done five years before. While they were pondering their next move, two Soviet Victor Class submarines were spotted operating in the Western Approaches, and the submarine which was at that moment designated as the 'sneaky' boat – HMS *Superb* under Commander James Perowne – was dispatched to pursue them. Word of *Superb*'s departure from Gibraltar reached Buenos Aires, and in London the Ministry of Defence did nothing to contradict the rumour that she might well be on her way to the South Atlantic. From the Argentine point of view, if *Superb* was indeed heading for the South Atlantic, and arrived before an invasion, she would be a mortal danger to the ships on which any Argentine invasion would necessarily rely. It was later reported that this was the precipitating factor which led General Galtieri to push ahead with the full-scale invasion more quickly than otherwise he might have done – a mistake which would prove to be the defining one of the conflict. Had he been able to wait another six months, history might have been very different.

There followed a few days of frantic diplomatic activity as realisation finally dawned that the threat of invasion was real, and by the time Mrs Thatcher persuaded President Reagan to phone the Argentine President to urge him to think again, the invasion force was on its way.

The Falklands garrison usually consisted of some forty Royal Marines, but because it was a period of hand-over and there had been rumblings of possible action by the Argentines, there were at the time some eighty-four Marines on the islands. This also might have been mistaken for good planning, had it not been for the fact that, due to a logistical snafu, most of their weapons were on board a ship bound for South Georgia. So, with twenty of them out of action for one reason or another when the Argentines came into view, many of the sixty-four who were effectively operational had to hurriedly arm themselves with what they could find or gather up from the local equivalent of the Home Guard.

Perhaps it was just as well that the British armed forces and island irregulars were so outnumbered, because had they been fully armed and prepared, the British Marines might have put up a fight and suffered heavy casualties. As it was, the arrival of more than 10,000 troops made the odds untenable, and when the press printed the photographs of British servicemen lying face down on the ground as Argentine soldiers stood above them, the shockwaves caused the pillars holding up the Thatcher government to tremble.

Defence Secretary John Nott had a talent for always looking irritated even when he was relaxed, and so it was an unusually vexed Secretary of State who gave a press conference to announce formally that the islands had been overrun. 'Had the Marines been given orders to surrender if faced with overwhelming odds?' asked a reporter. Nott looked as though someone had fed him a bad oyster.

'The British never give orders to anyone to surrender,' he said, and he assumed 'that any member of the British armed forces does not surrender.'

Nott's discomfort about having effectively been caught out by the invasion was no doubt exacerbated by his serious reservations on the subject of what could be done about it. Already relations between the armed forces and politicians were at a very low ebb – Nott's announcement of defence cuts had hit the Navy hard, and when First Sea Lord Sir Henry Leach assured Mrs Thatcher that he could assemble a task force capable of sailing to the Falklands and liberating them, there were some who suspected that he was taking the opportunity to make a political point – that you never know when you will need the Navy until you need it. Leach's assurances were greeted by Nott with scepticism at best.

Nevertheless, now in possession of such an assurance, John Nott went on to confirm to the press that a substantial Navy task force sufficient to meet the Argentine invasion had been put on standby, though 'it has not yet been given orders to sail'.

Those orders to sail were going to be subject to whatever happened in a hastily called session of Parliament, which would be the first time the Commons had met on a Saturday since another British military blunder in Suez in 1956. On the eve of the debate, the Chairman of the Conservative Party and Paymaster General Cecil Parkinson had dinner at his club with the Secretary of State for the Environment Michael Heseltine.

'He and I sat,' said Parkinson later, 'as a couple of politicians over dinner, speculating about what it would do to the government if this was a failure. And it would be a disaster.' Whatever the likely fate of these and other secretaries of state, there could be little doubt that the career of the Prime Minister herself was at stake.

Already Britain's first woman Prime Minister was deeply unpopular. The country was in the grip of an appalling recession, and many blamed her uncompromising monetarist policies for unemployment at a record level of over three million. It was less than a year since there had been rioting in Brixton, and Toxteth in Liverpool, and her recent approval rating of 23 per cent was an all-time low for a sitting PM. When she and her front-bench ministers went into the debate in Parliament on that Saturday morning, it is fair to say that anything was possible – including the fall of her government.

At first the House was in sombre mood as Mrs Thatcher described recent events, and informed MPs that even as she spoke, a Royal Navy task force was assembling with a view to setting off to the South Atlantic. Even at this early stage, she was at great pains to assert that nothing in the Argentines' recent behaviour could reasonably have alerted her government to the imminence of an invasion, and she took the opportunity to underline the remoteness of the islands and the difficulties and expense which would have been involved in defending them effectively in the face of long-term grumbling from the Argentines. Her sense of righteous indignation shortly began to give way to a more aggressive tone, and as the debate went on, she seemed to grow in confidence and determination. At last there were the first signs of those far distant echoes of Churchill which were increasingly to characterise her utterances on the subject of the war.

'The people of the Falkland Islands,' she intoned, 'like the people of the United Kingdom, are an island race. They are few in number, but they have a right to live in peace, to choose their own way of life and to determine their own allegiance. Their way of life is British; their allegiance is to the Crown.'

When the Leader of the Opposition Michael Foot stood up to reply, there were shouts of 'speak for England' from the Tory benches. This was an echo of a famous interjection by Tory MP Leo Amery in 1939, encouraging Labour's Deputy Leader Arthur Greenwood in his opposition to Neville Chamberlain's continuing under-estimation of Hitler. (It was Amery who, in a later debate, repeated the even more famous remark originated by Cromwell

– 'In the name of God, go!' – which finally ended Chamberlain's leadership.)

Foot did indeed 'speak for England' in the sense that Amery must have meant it – taking the government to task for its failure to anticipate and head off the invasion, but joining unreservedly with the conviction that 'something must be done'.

Criticism of the government's negligence did not come solely from the official Opposition. In a speech which would have jangled a few nerves on the front benches, the Chairman of the influential 1922 Committee, representing Tory back-benchers, launched a scathing attack. Edward Du Cann lamented that it was astounding that the government was so woefully ill-prepared and apparently also hesitant about its response.

'Let us hear no more about logistics,' he declared, '. . . or about how difficult it is to travel long distances. I do not remember the Duke of Wellington whining about Torres Vedras. We have nothing to lose now except our honour.' In those days Mr Du Cann plainly felt able to take as read that his Honourable Friends would know that Torres Vedras was in what was then relatively distant Portugal and that Wellington had ordered fortifications there some 170 years earlier.

It was left to the Ulster Unionist MP and Old Testament prophet Enoch Powell to utter the words which, perhaps more than any, would stiffen the resolve of the Prime Minister. The Right Honourable Lady had often, he recalled, been referred to as 'The Iron Lady'. In the next weeks and months, he predicted, the House and the country would learn of what metal she was made.

Shortly before the end of the debate, the Argentines got a little bit of unsolicited help from the Member for Merthyr Tydfil, Ted Rowlands. Rowlands had been a minister of state in the Foreign Office in the previous Labour government, and in his attempt to criticise the government and the Intelligence services for their failure to warn of the invasion he told astonished MPs that our intelligence in Argentina had always been extremely good, and that he could not believe that this had changed. You could almost see the jaws dropping as he continued, 'I shall make a disclosure. As well as trying to read the mind of the enemy, we have been reading its telegrams for many years. I am sure that many sources are available to the government, and I do not understand how they failed to anticipate some of the dangers that suddenly loomed onto the horizon.'

According to Hugh Bicheno in his book *Razor's Edge: The Unofficial History of the Falklands War*, 'Argentine embassies used the same, top of the line, Swiss Crypto AG machine systems as their armed forces, so this was the precise equivalent of publicly announcing, during World War II, that the Allies had broken the Enigma system used by the Nazis.'

The debate was adjourned at 2 p.m. and the Prime Minister had survived – for the moment. She left the chamber with determination in her step and looking ready for the fight. While there had been plenty of criticism of the government for failing to predict and prevent this outrage, there was unanimity that the take-over could not be left unanswered. It was not only the prestige of the Prime Minister that was at stake – it was the position of Great Britain on the world stage, and MPs of all parties were determined that so important a concession would never be made without a fight.

Over the following days, general amusement among the public turned to amazement and thence to general bemusement as politicians and the press worked themselves into a positive frenzy of indignation. There was surprisingly little debate in the press and media about the rights and wrongs of the original claims for ownership of the islands; to the headline writers, it seemed clear that British sovereign territory had been invaded by forces from a military junta, and this could not be tolerated. The Falkland Islanders, the public was assured, regarded themselves as every bit as British as did the residents of the Isle of Wight, and were now suffering under the tyranny of an undemocratic regime. The tabloids had a field day.

British chests swelled with pride as an armada of Navy ships, the like of which had not been seen since World War II, was quickly assembled and set a course for the South Atlantic. Cheering crowds lined the jetties and Union flags and banners conveyed messages of encouragement. Very few imagined that the Task Force would reach its destination before a diplomatic solution was found, allowing our boys to return to the serious business of keeping the Russians at bay and preventing the Cold War from ever turning hot.

8

'Two Bald Men Fighting Over a Comb'

At the beginning of 1982, HMS *Conqueror* had been on a three-month overseas deployment, carrying out simulations and exercises with the US Navy at the Atlantic Undersea Test and Evaluation Center (AUTEC), which is based on Andros Island in the Bahamas. Much of the time had been spent testing the Mark 24 torpedo, known as the Tigerfish. The weapon was far more complex in its targeting and electronics than the more familiar and tried and tested Mark 8, and there were serious reservations on board about its reliability.

These exercises can be demanding and exhausting, as the capabilities of boat and men are pushed and tested to the limits. When the project was completed there had been an opportunity to take a couple of weeks of rest and recreation – at Cocoa Beach on the American mainland.

It was there that two of the submarine's officers, Jonty Powis and Narendra Sethia, found themselves delayed in a refreshment establishment, and remembered with only half an hour to go that they were required back at the boat for the wardroom cocktail party. They befriended the American driver of a 24-wheel truck who was memorable for the tight white T-shirt which he wore stretched over his three stomachs. Rather the worse for wear himself, he agreed to sandwich the two officers into the front seat of his cab for the journey back through the town to the submarine. Recognising a genuine military emergency when he saw one, he switched on a siren and began sounding his horn. Now making enough noise to wake the dead, he roared off at sixty miles an hour through the streets until they got to the dockyard. The huge rig screeched to a halt just as the smartly uniformed skipper and first lieutenant – Richard Wraith and Tim McClement – had clicked their heels to attention on the upper casing of the submarine to greet the mayor of Cocoa Beach. The senior officers were not amused.

By the end of March 1982 *Conqueror* was back at her home base at Faslane, and in need of some repairs, so the crew were given leave while the work got under way. Officers and men dispersed to their homes and their loved ones, but with the diplomatic alarm bells now reaching a crescendo just two days before the invasion, the call went out to the crew to return to the boat and prepare for war.

The duty officer when the call came was the navigator, Jonty Powis. Jonty's family has a distinguished naval history; he has seen a letter written by one Sarah Powis in 1680 complaining about her husband's Navy pension. Jonty was always going to go into the Navy, and always going to become a submariner – 'for exactly the same reason that if you joined the Air Force in 1939 you would want to be a fighter-pilot'. Submarines were 'where it was at'.

Powis was enjoying his career in the Navy, but had been thrust into the job of navigator of a nuclear submarine quickly – too quickly in his own view. He had skipped a stage in his career path when he received a call at his office in the MoD one day telling him that there had been an unexpected vacancy because someone had broken a leg, and asking him if he wanted to become the navigation officer on board *Conqueror*. Powis replied that he did not think he was ready, and put down the telephone. Only then did he begin to wonder whether he had just made the biggest mistake of his life. Quickly he sought advice from a senior colleague who told him to wait for twenty minutes and then return the call to say he had reflected on the offer and changed his mind. Jonty managed to wait for twelve minutes before returning the call, and in May 1981 he had taken up his post on *Conqueror*.

All the same, at only twenty-six years old, and just eleven months into his new post, Jonty Powis had not properly found his feet. Yet here he was, duty officer when the emergency came, and charged with the instant responsibility of recalling the crew and starting the preparations to store for war.

The immediate problem was that everything about the submarine revolved around the enemy being the Soviet Union and the battleground being the hostile waters around north Norway and the Barents Sea, and occasionally the Mediterranean. No one knew the first thing about the military capability of the Argentines or indeed very much about the South Atlantic. Powis went in search of the most up-to-date copy of *Jane's Fighting Ships* he could find, to try to learn about this new enemy navy. Meanwhile he asked his wife – who was seven months pregnant at the time – to go out to buy him a Spanish phrase book, two magnetic compasses, and spare torches – the kind of stuff you might pack in case an emergency arose on a camping trip.

Meanwhile he started rummaging around trying to find charts of the South Atlantic, and the best he could locate were 200 years old, drawn in black and white, and clearly marked 'not for navigation'. Powis was to pass many a happy hour on his way to the South Atlantic colouring in the charts to make them slightly more suitable for the critical requirements of navigating hostile seas in the heat of battle.

On that same day, Narendra Sethia was in Edinburgh – giving evidence in a court case about a traffic accident in which he had been involved the previous year. A contingent of officers and men from *Conqueror* had been undertaking a sponsored walk from Helensburgh to the submarine's affiliated town of Fleetwood in Lancashire. At around dawn, when the group was somewhere up in the hills close to the English border, they were resting in a school bus just outside a farmhouse on the verge of a narrow country road. The driver, one of *Conqueror*'s stewards called Donald MacLeod, had gone into the farmhouse to buy milk. It was a foggy dawn and all of a sudden there was a tremendous screaming of brakes from behind, and an eighteen-wheel truck smashed into the back of the bus. The lorry-driver was left unconscious and slumped over the wheel. The bus folded up like a concertina, and Sethia and the others were thrown about, but amazingly sustained no lasting injuries. The group continued to Fleetwood in a private vehicle while picking glass out of their hair. MacLeod had been charged in connection with the accident and Sethia had been in court as a character witness.

He wrote in his diary:

Got the train at 1540 and ended up with a couple from Edinburgh who, amazingly, had also spent their morning as witnesses in the county court. Eventually got back to Faslane at 1830, had a drink and went home. Staggered to the Navigator's house clutching a bottle of wine and drank there until latish. Then to bed!

The next day's entry had a rather different tone.

Shit! . . . arrived on board at 0815 to find that Argentina has invaded the Falklands and we are in the throes of storing for war. Everything seems to be happening.

Sethia had become very good at his job on board *Conqueror*, but off duty his unconventional behaviour in the company of ratings was seen as unbecoming of a Navy officer. And while he enjoyed and found exciting many aspects of the long patrols into the North Atlantic and Barents Sea, he also found much of it desperately boring. It was now nineteen months since he had resigned from the Navy, but his replacement as supply officer had been delayed, and Sethia was becoming impatient. His friend Bones was already on the south coast and was busy preparing their boat for its trip around the world, and so Sethia at first regarded the invasion as an irritation which was likely to come to nothing, but would certainly delay his departure. The only comfort was that it might provide an opportunity to save some money ahead of the trip.

Leading Stoker Simon O'Keeffe was at his home in London when the telephone rang and he was told to report back to the submarine base immediately. Simon comes from an unusual family background for a submariner – his father was the well-known and hugely respected publisher Timothy O'Keeffe, described in the *Review of Contemporary Fiction* as 'among the most important publishing editors of the century'. Simon had grown up in a home where poets, artists and novelists were likely to be among the regular dinner guests. Usually when an unexpected phone call came from the Navy, it meant that intelligence had reported that an AGI or Soviet submarine had been spotted and they were off on a 'sneaky' to try to intercept it. This time a glance at the TV news was enough to alert Simon to the idea that he might be going to a very different kind of operation.

Colin Way, better known as 'the Bear', had gone from Scotland to his home in the Isle of Wight, only to be greeted by a telegram ordering him to return to base immediately. As it was around 1 April, he thought someone was playing a practical joke, and had to be assured in no uncertain terms that the order was in deadly earnest.

The TASO, Robin L'Oste-Brown, was at his home in Twickenham when the call came to return urgently to the submarine. Robin had joined the Navy in the first place largely because the service would pay to put him through university. He had been on full Navy pay all through the three-year course studying physics at Oxford, and had been shunted into submarines after he had achieved his degree. In common with a great many others who joined the armed services in the days long before Iraq and Afghanistan, the idea of actually having to fight a war had never really occurred to him. He had not been following the news and had no idea of the reason for the emergency until he arrived in the *Conqueror*'s wardroom and found everyone watching the television.

Leading Seaman Derek Higgins was a big Manchester United fan and had tickets for the Saturday afternoon match against Leeds at Elland Road. He had heard a rumour of an urgent recall to the submarine but was keen not to miss the game. Midway through the match his name was announced over the tannoy and he was ordered to report immediately to Faslane. He just had time to return to his home in Doncaster to collect his kit and, assuming that the operation was another mission to see off an intrusive Soviet submarine, the last thing he said to his mother before closing the door was 'I'll see you in three weeks.' He saw her again three months later.

Weapons engineering rating Grant Louch was already in Faslane, part of the team sorting out repairs and maintenance following the exercises in the Bahamas. He had been following the news carefully and knew exactly why there was such urgency to recall the crew.

The boat's executive officer, Tim McClement, had just arrived with his wife and eight-month-old baby at his in-laws' home in Bath when he got the call. He had to abandon the family and set off instantly for Faslane.

Conqueror had a new captain. Commander Christopher Wreford-Brown had begun his submarine training at HMS *Dolphin* on the same day in 1968 that the Warsaw Pact tanks had rolled into Czechoslovakia. He had been appointed to *Conqueror* some months earlier, but had taken up the post only forty-eight hours before the emergency call. From the start Wreford-Brown exuded professionalism and natural authority, but was perhaps a more unusual and introspective personality than his predecessors, Morley Stephens and Richard Wraith. His rather quiet speaking voice irritated some of the men – at times of tension on board it was not unknown to hear someone grumble, 'Will you fucking speak up?' – however, the irritation was toned down when it was discovered that Wreford-Brown's wife suffered from hearing-loss and that he himself was a proficient lip-reader.

The order had gone out to store for war, and for the crew of the *Conqueror*, the process of loading was made much more enjoyable than usual because, for once, the SSNs, the hunters, were given a higher priority than the missile-laden SSBNs. Later there was to be much controversy about whether Britain had sent nuclear weapons to the South Atlantic, but for the moment anyway, it was clear that the nuclear-powered *Conqueror* was more suitable for the job in hand than a submarine designed to carry nuclear missiles.

Self-sufficient in fuel, air and water, the only factor limiting *Conqueror*'s ability to stay at sea was the possibility of running out of food, so storing for war meant that they needed to load as much of it as they could. Normally an SSN storing for patrol would prepare for ninety days, but on this occasion *Conqueror* needed to be ready to be away for as long as possible. Every spare nook and cranny in the boat was filled to capacity, and then they began to line the floors of corridors and some of the compartments with tins of food eight inches high, which then became the floor. For taller members of the crew like 'the Bear', it meant weeks and weeks of stooping as they made their way around the decks.

A couple of showers and lavatories were taken out of action and used as larders. Store-rooms and fridges were filled to the doors – which led to the added complication of having to stow the food in the reverse order in which it would be consumed. Sethia and the chef had to write a three-month menu plan, and then fill the fridges, freezers and dry stores from back to front so that the food could be taken out in the right order to fit the menus. If the tin of sardines you wanted was at the back of the store-room, you were going to have to wait for the best part of three months before you could get near it.

With every available spare space full, *Conqueror* was informed that she would be carrying an important and bulky extra cargo down to the South Atlantic. In the middle of the night, on the eve of departure, nine members of the Special Boat Squadron (SBS) arrived in Faslane with a pile of their equipment weighing nine tons. Somehow everything was squeezed in, and final preparations were being made before sailing. Next morning Commander Wreford-Brown was told to embark another five SBS men. These had driven the 500-mile length of the country in a bus and arrived in broad daylight. To the horror of Sethia and the others responsible for packing the submarine, the special forces soldiers proceeded to unload canoes, skis, guns and bombs. In what was perhaps an effort to confuse any Argentine spies, the bus parked next to the submarine was marked 'Royal Marines Sky Diving Team'.

The SBS team were housed in their own area in the torpedo compartment in the bows of the submarine. The space is wet and noisy, with none of the relative comforts available for officers and crew in the rest of the boat. Not at all inconvenienced, the SBS men lived up to their reputations by spending their time doing press ups and pull ups and sharpening their knives. One day Sethia was working at the typewriter in the ship's office when one of the SBS men, a monster of a man with very few teeth, came to the office door, smiled a gummy smile and said, 'Here, catch!' He then threw a grenade directly at Sethia. Fortunately he had not removed the pin, but even so, the supply officer found himself struggling to see the joke. Playing with hand grenades on a nuclear submarine did not seem like a terrific idea – but Sethia did not necessarily want to be the one to point that out. Only the SBS commander, David Heaver, mixed freely in the officers' wardroom, and was always keen to run a movie at any hour. Heaver was unusually baby-faced for someone in his line of work, but his appearance belied reality. His reputation among his men was that he was 'good with a knife'.

Shortly before the submarine slipped its moorings from her Faslane berth to head off to war, the men of HMS *Conqueror* were advised to ensure that their wills were in good order and up to date.

There were no crowds out on the jetties when *Conqueror* set her course for the South Atlantic. Though there was no particular need for secrecy at this early stage of the mission, the submarine could make faster progress when submerged, and she proceeded at a depth of 500 feet and her maximum speed of close to 28 knots.

Sethia's replacement as supply officer arrived in Faslane very shortly after the *Conqueror* had set sail. Plans were made to fly Lieutenant Commander Mike Screech out to meet the submarine at Ascension Island, and there to relieve Sethia so that he could fly home. In the event, pressure for space on board transports to Ascension, coupled with the uncertainty that *Conqueror* would put in there at all, meant that the plan had to be abandoned and Screech would need to wait for the submarine's return. It was one of those 'sliding doors' moments in which, if Screech had arrived a few days sooner, Sethia would have played no part in the war and so much of what followed would have been different.

The passage south of over 8,000 miles was conducted flat out [recalls Jonty Powis], 21 days in the full power state reading one routine [transmission of radio traffic] every 24hrs and devouring the news. The submarine must have woken every Atlantic sonar operator; she had two uninsulated turbo-driven feed pumps for the full power state, which screamed.

Anticipating a long period at sea, some of the officers and crew decided to try to break the boredom by embarking on a beard-growing competition. Narendra Sethia and Colin Way were among those who shaved off their existing beards to ensure a fair start. Competitors included Commander Wreford-Brown, and his second in command, Tim McClement. There was much entertainment as several members of the crew embarked on what would be a 'corporate beard' between them – one growing the left-hand side of a moustache, another growing the hair on the right-hand side of the chin, and so on.

The captain was determined that there would be no opportunity for boredom or complacency, and instituted a constant round of activities designed to adjust very quickly everyone's skill-set and mind-set from the Cold War to a potentially very hot and old-fashioned conventional conflict.

'The new captain and the XO kept us busy with drills and practice attacks,' said Powis. The officers and crew of the *Conqueror* were completely familiar with all the operational practices used by the ships and subs of the Warsaw Pact countries. This, however, was something very different. 'We had a whole new threat to learn as the Argie forces were a mix of US, UK, French and local platforms.'

'We had been at war all our lives,' said one of the weapons ratings, William Budding, 'but all we had ever done was the Cold War, and then we went down to the Falklands. We had been chasing Russians all our lives.'

'You've got to understand that we were very much Cold War warriors,' said Powis. 'We follow people around and photograph them and do sneaky things like that. The idea of firing torpedoes at somebody? We had all practised it, but it wasn't part of our repertoire of tricks.'

The submarines and the surface ships of the Task Force were now steaming headlong towards a likely conflict situation, but no one had the first idea of what would happen when they got there. Was their job simply to provide a demonstration of determination, forcing the hands of the Argentines while the diplomacy did its work? Would there be a fight, and if there was one, what sort of fight would it be?

The *Conqueror*'s executive officer was clear that nothing would be left to chance. McClement insisted that the men keep up the drills and practices for up to sixteen hours a day so that the actions required became second nature. He felt a strong conviction that the lives of all on board might depend on it, and was determined that they would be in the best possible state of readiness. It was a difficult and exhausting time.

The Americans seemed to regard the entire conflict between Argentina and the UK as irritating and anachronistic but, more importantly, it was a worrying diversion from the really important business of squaring up to the Soviets. It was only two years since the Soviet invasion of Afghanistan had ended a period of relative detente between the super-powers, and the subsequent American boycott of the summer Olympics in Moscow had added to the tension. There was talk from both sides about the deployment of cruise and SS20 nuclear missiles in Europe, and overall, relations between the super-powers were at their lowest ebb since the Cuban missile crisis.

In the midst of all this, there was concern that the oldest ally of the US was in danger of neglecting its Cold War responsibilities. The British deployment to the South Atlantic of six hunter-killer submarines – five nuclear-powered and one diesel-electric – from their routine patrols in the North Atlantic was a worry. More than that, the Americans were concerned that, if the conflict became prolonged, the Soviets might be tempted to come in on the side of the Argentines. Shortly after his unsuccessful attempt to intervene with Galtieri to prevent the invasion, President Reagan wrote a personal note to Mrs Thatcher: 'I want you to know that we have valued your cooperation on the challenges we face in many different parts of the world. We will do what we can to assist you here.'

Privately Reagan was reported to have echoed the sentiment originally penned by the Argentine poet Jorge Luis Borges – that the Falklands conflict felt like 'two bald men fighting over a comb'.

On 7 April the US State Department produced a paper assessing the prospects for the outcome of a military engagement. It made a particular point of the vulnerability of the British Task Force in trying to operate so far from its home waters:

The effectiveness of the fleet, far from its maintenance bases, will rapidly deteriorate after its arrival on station ... If Thatcher fails to redeem her reputation and the nation's honor, she could be finished as Tory leader and Prime Minister. Yet military action is full of risks and a British re-conquest, if feasible at all, is likely to be expensive.

The last thing that the Americans wanted was for Mrs Thatcher to lose her job and, worse still, for there to be a General Election resulting in her replacement by the Labour leader and former CND activist Michael Foot.

On the same day – 7 April – the British government announced that from the following Monday, it would impose what was to become known as the Maritime Exclusion Zone around the Falklands.

From the time indicated, any Argentine warship and Argentine naval auxiliaries found within this Zone will be treated as hostile and are liable to be attacked by British forces. This measure is without prejudice to the right of the United Kingdom to take whatever additional measures may be needed in exercise of its right of self-defence under Article 51 of the United Nations Charter.

This was important, because up until this point the British had been acting solely under the authority of Article 51 – the right to self-defence. Even the Task Force Commander, Sandy Woodward, had opined that this meant that he could not fire unless he was fired upon – a statement which infuriated most of the British press and politicians back at home. Now, with this announcement, it was clear that Britain regarded this circle around the Falklands as the area of hostilities, and that any ship or submarine found within it would be liable to attack. It seemed to follow from this that if you were outside it, you were safe – unless you were presenting an immediate threat to the Task Force which would justify a response under Article 51. This distinction was to become important.

Two days later, on 9 April, President Reagan sent Secretary of State Alexander Haig on what was to be a brief attempt at shuttle diplomacy before things really got out of hand. Mrs Thatcher's Foreign Secretary, Lord Carrington, had now resigned and been replaced by Francis Pym. After a five-hour meeting in Downing Street, Haig wrote a memo to Reagan outlining the situation as he saw it: 'The Prime Minister has the bit between her teeth. She is clearly prepared to use force.' Mrs Thatcher was insisting on a return to the status quo ante, though Haig noted that Foreign Secretary Francis Pym:

. . . does not share her view and went surprisingly far in showing this in her presence. All in all, we got no give in the basic British position and only the glimmering of some possibilities, and that only after much effort by me, with considerable help not appreciated by Mrs Thatcher from Pym. It is clear they had not thought much about the diplomatic possibilities.

On board the submarine *Conqueror*, any idea that the Falklands dispute might be settled by diplomacy rather than by bullets was greeted with dismay. Sethia recorded in his diary: 'We're all a bit pissed off because we know what that means – 12 weeks away while the politicians fart and blush "negotiating". What a total waste!'

He need not have worried. After two crossings of the Atlantic, Haig declared himself unable to find a solution acceptable to both sides, and returned to Washington.

Sethia had not kept a regular diary since childhood, when his mother had warned him about the dangers of entrusting his innermost thoughts to paper which anyone could read. However, he had always enjoyed writing and, in view of the possibility that he could be going to war, he had begun to keep a regular daily narrative. Technically it was a breach of the Official Secrets Act to record operational material, but no one thought anything about it or commented as Sethia sat at the table in the officers' wardroom and wrote down his thoughts on the progress of the submarine.

Another of the ways that Sethia broke the boredom while on watch was to draw elaborate cartoons in the margins of the control room log. The log was one of the records of passage which was routinely kept on board the submarine. It was classified as a confidential document, but kept on an open shelf by the chart table in the control room. Each log had sixty-two pages, one double spread for each day of the month. The left-hand page was divided into twenty-four hours, and each hour the officer of the watch was required to record the course, engine speed and depth. The right-hand page was divided into sections, enabling the OOW to record significant events, routine maintenance, as well as notes about special security measures. When the submarine was alongside in port, the left-hand pages were left blank; when she was at sea, anyone with a routine knowledge of navigation could use the log to work out the vessel's position, and perhaps the kind of exercise the submarine was carrying out.

Keeping up maximum speed and maintaining maximum efficiency in a nuclear submarine is not an easy matter at the best of times. The skill is in keeping what is known as the 'trim' – which means maintaining neutral buoyancy in the varying conditions. Neutral buoyancy means that, sitting in the water without power or momentum, the boat will neither rise to the surface nor sink. On this mission, *Conqueror* was carrying significantly more weight than usual in the form of all that extra food, as well as the SBS and their equipment. Her displacement was changing constantly – the submarine produced up to fifty tons of fresh water every day, as well as discharging hundreds of gallons of sewage and other waste into the ocean. In all those circumstances, it can be a tricky task to 'catch a trim' at high speed because it is difficult to tell whether the boat is maintaining her buoyancy and remaining level because of the balance of weight within her, or because of her momentum through the water.

On day five out of Faslane, in the middle of the night, there was a sudden and unanticipated shut-down of the nuclear reactor, and the submarine began to lose speed and very rapidly started going down. Narendra Sethia was on watch as the trimming officer: 'As we slowed down, it became apparent to me that we were so heavy that I was having a problem pumping out enough water fast enough to maintain her buoyancy and so she started sinking for a while.' The submarine was going down so fast that some

2,500 gallons of the water used to stabilise her had to be pumped out as quickly as possible. 'Eventually, I think at about 700 feet, I'd pumped out enough water to be able to get the boat to rise and had her back in neutral buoyancy.' What had seemed like a potentially very critical situation had been narrowly averted.

By the middle of April, the growth of stubble on Sethia's face had started to itch, the photocopier had developed a fault, and he was having nightmares about the submarine running out of food.

'Have seen most of the good films,' he wrote in his diary. 'Little news from the outside world except that "negotiations continue".'

Much of Sethia's time was spent reflecting on the preparations for the trip round the world which he was planning as soon as this mission was over and he could return to base. He and the navigator discussed whether Sethia might be able to make use of some of the submarine's out-of-date Admiralty charts which would otherwise be incinerated.

After nearly three weeks at sea the *Conqueror* was approaching South Georgia, some 900 miles east-south-east of the Falklands. The British high command had decided to attempt to retake these islands first – perhaps to concentrate the minds of the Argentines while the main Task Force was still on its way. The British government realised that they would need new rules of engagement to cover any operation to retake the islands, and so on 23 April a statement was issued reiterating the Maritime Exclusion Zone and adding that the British government:

wishes to make clear that any approach on the part of Argentine warships, including submarines, naval auxiliaries or military aircraft which could amount to a threat to interfere with the mission of British Forces in the South Atlantic will encounter the appropriate response.

This statement was of critical importance, because it was this warning against which the action against the *Belgrano* would be measured.

The following morning *Conqueror*'s sonar detected what sounded like the classic signature of a submarine running diesel engines, and it seemed to be close by. Jonty Powis thought that this was likely to be one of only four submarines in the Argentine Navy, the *Santa Fe*. She was a former US Navy vessel, launched in 1944, and bought from the Americans in 1971. The *Santa Fe* had played a small part in the invasion of the islands when it landed tactical divers at Yorke Bay on the Falklands, who then marked out the beach for the main amphibious landing.

Commander Wreford-Brown was summoned and *Conqueror* went to action stations, rising to periscope depth with torpedo tubes loaded and ready. No vessels were in sight, so it was assumed that the target submarine was below the surface and just beyond visual range. The captain ordered *Conqueror* to go deep again and resume the search, but by this time contact had been lost. They did everything they knew to relocate the target.

'We tried all sorts,' said Powis, 'going shallow again then deeper, active sonar, sprinting beyond supposed maximum range and looking back at the target actively and passively; all fruitless. We came shallow again to make a contact report having given up hope of regaining contact.'

The *Sante Fe*'s reprieve was short-lived. Next day she was caught on the surface by helicopters from the *Plymouth*, *Brilliant*, *Endurance* and *Antrim*, which disabled her while she was entering Cumberland Sound en route to reinforce the Argentine garrison at Grytvyken. She ended up sinking alongside the jetty there, while her crew and cargo of Argentine marines ran ashore for cover.

'This brought us to the realisation that we were actually at war and could have fired real torpedoes at a real target full of real people,' said Powis. 'Furthermore they would probably have a go at us too if we were careless. We became sharp.'

On board *Conqueror*, the fourteen SBS men were anxious to join in the operation to re-occupy South Georgia but, to their evident dismay, the assault plan had no role for them. Later when *Conqueror* surfaced to off-load them into a helicopter for transfer to the destroyer HMS *Antrim*, a huge wave suddenly swept over the deck and carried one of them into the icy waters, along with *Conqueror*'s own Petty Officer Graham Libby. The ship's helicopter quickly moved into place and lowered its single rescue hoist above their heads. Libby was wearing only his waterproofs and immediately felt the warmth from his body draining away into the frozen sea. The SBS man had on his dry suit, but neither was keen to remain in the water for long. There was a brief exchange of glances between the two men: who would avail himself of the rescue hoist and who would remain in the ice-cold mountainous waves? The question answered itself; both men managed to secure themselves into the harness and were brought back on board at the same time. Libby was put into a bath to try to get his circulation going again, and spent six hours recovering on board HMS *Antrim*. When rescuers removed the trousers of the SBS man they were amazed to see that his legs were pink and the blood was circulating normally. These men had been trained in the Arctic, and a dip in the South Atlantic seemed to be a matter of very little concern. Eventually the men from the SBS troop were air-lifted successfully by helicopter to the destroyer.

Meanwhile the SAS had been in action to retake the islands of South Georgia. There had been little resistance, but two British helicopters were destroyed in the appalling wind and rain. There was palpable relief when Defence Secretary John Nott emerged into Downing Street with the Prime Minister to announce the results of the action.

Nott had a curious way of pronouncing the 'Georgia' in 'South Georgia' as though it had three syllables, but otherwise managed to remain calm while announcing the liberation. One look at the Prime Minister beside him was enough to see that she was clearly in her element – no doubt relieved, and also justifiably proud of the prowess of her servicemen.

Having informed waiting journalists that South George-ee-a
had been liberated with few casualties on the Argentine side
and none on the British, Nott failed to mention that two British
helicopters had crashed and been wrecked in the course of the
action. He did say, however, that British helicopters had engaged
the Argentine submarine *Santa Fe*. As he did so, he was careful
to add the words 'because it posed a threat to our men and to
the British warships launching the landings' – words which had
been chosen very carefully so that they chimed with the precise
wording of the warning given to the Argentines on 23 April. It
remained the case that no state of war had been declared, and the
British government had plainly been made aware that any action
had to be justifiable under international law.

Nothing of a showman himself, Nott could not resist the
temptation of ending with something of a flourish, when he
announced that the commander of the operation to liberate
South Georgia had sent the following message (which might just
as easily have been sent by Nelson): 'Be pleased to inform Her
Majesty that the White Ensign flies alongside the Union Jack in
South Georgia. God save the Queen.' By this time, Mrs Thatcher's
facial expression was the very picture of satisfaction, and when
an unfortunate reporter had the temerity to follow up with
the perfectly legitimate question, 'What happens next?' he was
rebuked by Mrs Thatcher's famous command not to ask questions
but merely to 'rejoice' and congratulate our troops. The unhappy
journalist might have been forgiven for thinking that his job was
to ask questions and report the news, rather than to rejoice, but
by the time the follow-up question, 'Are we going to declare war?'
was asked, Mrs T was on her way back inside Number 10.

Now attention returned to the main task in hand on the Falklands
Islands proper. The operation being undertaken by the Royal Navy
was among the most ambitious naval missions of its kind ever
mounted. Its Task Force included the two aircraft carriers, *Hermes*
and *Invincible*, seven destroyers, five frigates, two assault ships, and

at least one diesel-powered and five nuclear-powered submarines. With the addition of fuel tankers, cargo and hospital ships, the whole armada numbered some 100 vessels, all operating at the extreme end of supply lines of some 3,500 miles from Ascension Island – itself more than 5,000 miles from the UK.

Though most of the ships in the Argentine Navy were second-hand and out-of-date, they had the huge advantage of operating in home waters, and therefore close to their bases – and of course, now they had the added advantage of occupying the islands.

The main vulnerability faced by the British was in the air, where the Fleet Air Arm and the RAF were hopelessly outnumbered, if not necessarily completely outgunned. On the British side there were just 32 Sea Harrier strike planes, 18 Sea King helicopters, and 3 Nimrod early warning planes. On the Argentine side there were 68 Skyhawk bombers, 43 Mirage fighters, 10 Super Étendard carrier-based attack aircraft, 9 Canberra long-range bombers, and a total of 29 light and armed helicopters.

One of the main concerns keeping British military chiefs awake at night was that negotiations to secure a peaceful solution might be prolonged. Winter in the South Atlantic was fast approaching and, worse than that, British troops had already been on board ship for some three weeks. The prospect of having thousands of soldiers and marines on ships bobbing about in the South Atlantic while politicians and diplomats had their say was a nightmare. American Secretary of State Alexander Haig's brief but intense period of shuttle diplomacy had come to a swift end. Now, however, Haig had been brought back into action as part of another peace initiative launched by the government of Peru. That was all very well, but military chiefs of staff told politicians back home that once they were in a position to fight, they would have to fight, or the risk of disaster would increase exponentially.

While the commanders felt it was important to disembark troops as quickly as possible, they also saw it as essential before doing so for the British to limit the Argentines' ability to harass any landings or mount any counter-attack. Therefore it was vital to keep the Argentine Air Force out of the skies.

Argentina had a separate dispute with neighbouring Chile over sovereignty of three islands in the Beagle Channel which had brought the two countries to the brink of conflict four years earlier. Mrs Thatcher made an agreement with General Pinochet of Chile, under which a number of Canberra photo-reconnaissance aircraft were sent to Chile and repainted in Chilean colours, but flown over Argentina by RAF crews. (Hence, presumably, Mrs Thatcher's subsequent support for Pinochet when, in 1998, he was arrested in Britain and contested extradition to Spain on charges of torture.) Under the terms of the deal, Chile would have access to the 'product' and the aircraft would be left behind at the end of the war. In addition, SAS troops were dropped by helicopter (using Chilean bases) and observed Argentine airbases, sending messages to the Task Force on special high-speed radios when the planes took off. This avoided the necessity for the British Sea Harriers to be on the alert all the time.

Notwithstanding these secret agreements, it remained the case that the mere 300-mile distance from bases in Argentina was a significant worry, but of even greater concern was the Argentine aircraft carrier *Veinticinco de Mayo* ('25th of May').

The carrier had originally been built during World War II for the Royal Navy (in the very same yard in Birkenhead that had built HMS *Conqueror*). Originally and perhaps appropriately named HMS *Venerable*, she saw service briefly in the British fleet in the Pacific in the closing stages of the war. She was then sold to the Dutch and renamed, only in 1968 to be sold by them to the Argentines and renamed once again after the date of the Argentine revolution of 1810. (On board HMS *Conqueror*, they speculated on how marvellous it would be to sink the carrier on 25 May.)

While the 300-mile journey from the Argentine coast would at least give the Task Force a fighting chance of spotting and intercepting enemy aircraft before they could strike at British ships, the potentially closer proximity of the carrier cut down lead times dangerously. Such was the pressure to locate and put the aircraft carrier out of action, that *Conqueror*'s sister-boat HMS *Splendid*, which had left Gibraltar ahead of her and arrived in the region some days before, had immediately been tasked to search an area north-west of the Falklands where intercepted signals indicated that the *Veinticinco de Mayo* was operating.

HMS *Splendid* did indeed locate the aircraft carrier but she was outside of the Exclusion Zone and therefore not liable to pre-emptive attack. Later, to the surprise and chagrin of everyone involved, *Splendid* lost the trail and the opportunity to sink her was missed. As the moment of likely hostilities drew nearer, the pressure to find the *Veinticinco de Mayo* intensified.

The British government was acutely aware that the loss of one or both of the Royal Navy carriers, *Hermes* and *Invincible*, would have meant disaster for the Task Force and for the entire attempt to oust the Argentines from the Falkland Islands. Therefore, in conditions of total secrecy, the government ordered the deployment of a Polaris SSBN carrying nuclear weapons within range of Argentina. If all else failed, the threat of a nuclear attack on its mainland would force the Argentines to withdraw. The target would have been the Argentine military complex at Cordoba. Two of the five nuclear-powered SSNs in the region were deployed to provide protection for the Polaris boat. When asked later whether a submarine carrying nuclear missiles had been deployed in the conflict, the government responded that it never commented on the deployment of nuclear submarines, but that 'the normal deployment pattern was maintained'. This was technically true, but only because early 1982 was one of the relatively unusual periods when two SSBNs were available for patrol.*

---

* Corroboration for the British contingency plan to use the threat of nuclear weapons comes from the unlikely source of a psychiatrist who was seeing President Mitterand of France twice a week during this period. According to a memoir published ten years after Mitterand's death, the President was late for

While the search for the aircraft carrier continued north-west of the Falklands, HMS *Conqueror* was ordered to head from South Georgia towards an area south-west of the islands where the Argentine cruiser *General Belgrano* was thought to be operating. ARA *Belgrano* was a light cruiser, which had been bought from the United States in 1951. She had formerly been the USS *Phoenix*, and had also seen action in the Pacific during World War II, having survived the Japanese surprise attack on Pearl Harbor. This was a truly venerable warship: she had been launched in 1938. The vessel had been re-named after the Argentine founding father Manuel Belgrano.

We established our patrol to the south of the Maritime Exclusion Zone[said Jonty Powis]. We knew that the *Belgrano* was operating in that sector together with 2 ex-USN destroyers of the same vintage.

The group of Argentine ships was collectively known as Task Group (TG) 79.3.

Irrespective of their opinion of the military capability of these World War II ships, the job of the *Conqueror* was to locate and follow the *Belgrano*; however, the rules of engagement did not allow her to sink the cruiser. The term 'rules of engagement' is familiar to every member of the armed forces at every moment of their service. Every soldier, sailor or airman in every situation has rules of engagement controlling his or her freedom of action. This includes everyone from a lonely corporal walking down the Falls

---

his appointment with Ali Magoudi on 7 May 1982, and was in a fluster when he arrived: 'Excuse me,' he explained, 'I had a difference to settle with the Iron Lady. That Thatcher, what an impossible woman! With her four nuclear submarines in the South Atlantic, she's threatening to unleash an atomic weapon against Argentina if I don't provide her with the secret codes that will make the missiles we sold the Argentines deaf and blind.' Mitterand felt obliged to give in: 'She's got them now, the codes,' and his lament continued: 'One cannot win against the insular syndrome of an unbridled Englishwoman. Provoke a nuclear war for a few islands inhabited by three sheep as hairy as they are freezing! But it's a good job I gave way. Otherwise, I assure you, the Lady's metallic finger would have hit the button.'

Road in Belfast, to the captain of a nuclear submarine patrolling hostile waters off the coast of the USSR.

The rules of engagement in effect at the time were to become a critical element in the long-running controversy which came to dominate future discussion of the war. It was perfectly clear to everyone that the declaration of the Maritime Exclusion Zone meant that any ship found within a 200-mile radius of the Falklands would be liable to be attacked. Outside of that circle, according to the British declaration of 23 April, the situation was that an Argentine ship in a position 'which could amount to a threat to interfere with the mission of British Forces in the South Atlantic will encounter the appropriate response'. This was a loose definition, and open to a wide range of interpretations – as would later become apparent.

Friday 30 April was the day on which it seems that the British government decided it was going to war, come what may. The Task Force had arrived at the perimeter of the Maritime Exclusion Zone, which now became a Total Exclusion Zone, and put at risk of attack any ship or aircraft of any kind which might be supporting the Argentine occupation. When the War Cabinet met that morning, it was in the knowledge that the Americans had decided to 'tilt' diplomatically in favour of the British. This meant that the British would benefit from every kind of cooperation, from improved supply lines to the receipt of information from US satellites and other communications intelligence. It was a defining moment.

The War Cabinet decided on a show of force, designed to mislead the Argentines into believing that landings were about to take place, and therefore to wrong-foot their forces. Bombing raids were carried out by Harriers based on aircraft carriers, and the RAF mounted an extraordinary expedition involving Vulcans flying from Ascension. These veteran aircraft had been due for the scrap-heap but had been called out of retirement for one last act of service. The flight from Ascension involved multiple episodes of air-to-air refuelling, eventually enabling a single Vulcan to drop its payload of bombs on Port Stanley airport. Once the smoke had cleared, it emerged that a single bomb had hit its target on the runway, but this was enough to hamper the Argentinians temporarily. Also on that day, British destroyers sitting off the coast began shelling Argentine positions.

Despite these minor military successes of the day, back at fleet headquarters at Northwood, concern was still increasing about the failure to locate the *Veinticinco de Mayo*. A request was made to the War Cabinet for permission to attack the carrier anywhere she could be found. By any measure this was a big decision. Serious concerns lingered about the legality of so drastic an escalation of the conflict, and the effect of such an action on international opinion. Foreign Secretary Francis Pym and Attorney General Sir Michael Havers were among those who worried whether the proposed actions were justified in the context of the public warnings already issued. However, the perceived danger to the British Task Force was such that a change in the rules of engagement was granted.

That same evening, at 16.00 local time in the South Atlantic, *Conqueror* picked up the first signs of what would later turn out to be the *Belgrano*. She was flanked by two destroyers, but it was the oil-tanker which was also accompanying the group which made all the noise. She was detected on *Conqueror*'s towed-array sonar from a distance of around a hundred miles.

Navigator Jonty Powis: 'One dull evening contact was gained on a diesel signature where there should not have been one; in the vicinity of Isla de los Estados near Tierra del Fuego. We sprinted down the bearing for several hours, stopping intermittently to take a look on the hull-mounted sonars.'

Next morning, 1 May, Foreign Secretary Francis Pym was due to fly to Washington for further talks with US Secretary of State Alexander Haig. Before he left London he wrote a note to Mrs Thatcher in which he said that he had been speaking further to the Attorney General and giving more thought to the decision to allow the Argentine aircraft carrier to be sunk. He told her, 'I believe our position would be immeasurably strengthened if we had given a warning to the Argentine Government.' He attached a draft which he suggested could be handed to the Argentines via the Swiss. He repeated, 'I believe it would greatly strengthen our hand in dealing with criticism at home and abroad once an attack on the carrier has been carried out.' In the event, no further warning was to be given for another week.

Back on board HMS *Conqueror*, by late morning on 1 May, suspicion turned into certainty as the *Belgrano* group was sighted – in the act of refuelling at sea. The submarine's navigator resumes the story:

On achieving broad band contact and identifying three or four ships we returned to periscope depth. The control room was tense. The captain took a good look all around and announced four ships in sight. I was (and still am) a bit of a spotter of ships and so he called me to the periscope and invited me to say what I could see. There was the *Belgrano* in the act of refuelling from a commercial tanker accompanied by two destroyers, ARA *Hipólito Bouchard* and ARA *Piedra Buena* (ex USS *Bone* DD704 and *Collett* DD730).

Narendra Sethia was also among the officers who observed the Task Group that afternoon. The four ships were about five miles away, steaming along in parallel, and still hooked up together with lines and pipes for their replenishment at sea of stores and fuel.

Conqueror kept watch as the *Belgrano* finished refuelling and set off east-north-east – towards the Falklands and, crucially, in the general direction of the Task Force. What is more, later that day, at 15.55 local time, a signal was intercepted from the Argentine HQ ordering its Navy to attack the Task Force. So suddenly the *Belgrano* was not only heading in the direction of the British ships, but was also under orders to attack them if they came within range. On the other hand the *Belgrano* group was still a long way from the declared 200-mile exclusion zone, and a very long way from the nearest British surface vessel – and so it appears not to have occurred to anyone, least of all the captain of the *Conqueror*, that she presented a threat to interfere with the mission of the Task Force. Wreford-Brown reported *Belgrano*'s position, but at no time did he seek permission to attack. The absence of any zig-zagging or any other routine anti-submarine manoeuvres implied that the captain of the *Belgrano* also felt safe.

Indeed, Narendra Sethia recorded in his diary for 1 May: 'Well, they're not stupid, they spent the night meticulously paralleling the exclusion zone, about 18 miles to the south of it. They're doing about 13 knots and only the occasional radar sweep.'

Although the *Belgrano* group appeared to be ambling along quite unconcernedly, and anyway was equipped with only ancient and outmoded sonar equipment, there remained the constant possibility that *Conqueror* might be detected by one of the other Argentine submarines which had not been accounted for. Where, therefore, was the safest place from which to trail the cruiser? The answer is one that may be surprising to a layman.

To the uninitiated it at first seems counter-intuitive that the safest position from which a submarine can trail its target is directly beneath her. The target ship herself cannot hear the submarine because of the noise of her own engines and propellers. Escorting vessels which detect a noise will look across and assume that it is coming from the target ship. Therefore for many of the last thirty hours before she was attacked and sunk, the instrument of *Belgrano*'s destruction was lurking just 150 feet beneath her hull.

Back on the mainland, with the onset of hostilities, what had at first been a tentative attempt by the Peruvians to broker a cease-fire deal was gathering urgency and momentum. President Belaúnde in Lima was in constant contact with Secretary of State Al Haig in Washington, where Francis Pym was due to arrive later that same evening. However, it was not necessary for Pym to be present in Washington to ensure that the substance of the discussions was being shared with London; Haig was under the clear impression that the British Ambassador to Peru, Charles Wallace, was in the room with Belaúnde for much of the day. Haig was later asked how he could be certain that Wallace was conveying the proposals back to London. He replied, 'That's what ambassadors are for, isn't it?' Belaúnde also confirmed much later that Wallace was present, though Wallace subsequently denied having been with Belaúnde on that day, or that he had any substantive knowledge of the discussions until the following evening.

By the end of that day, 1 May, Haig wrote later, the Peruvian President 'had gained acceptance, in principle, from both parties, that is, Britain and Argentina . . . we were down to words, single words'.

If the Argentines were encouraged by the progress of the talks and beginning to believe that an all-out war was avoidable after all, their hopes would have been reinforced by what Pym had to say at a news conference in Washington that same evening. He announced that the day's military activity had been designed to 'concentrate Argentine minds' on the need for a peaceful settlement, and added that, 'No further military action is envisaged for the moment other than making the Total Exclusion Zone secure.'

What on earth can he have been thinking? Only the day before, Pym had attended a meeting of the War Cabinet which had approved the sinking of an aircraft carrier with 1,200 sailors and airmen on board. He knew that the Navy was desperate to locate and destroy her, and for all he knew just such an action might be under way as he spoke.

In any event, it seems that the day's limited military action did indeed concentrate Argentine minds on the need for a peaceful settlement because just a few hours later, at 20.07 South Atlantic time, the Argentine Navy was ordered to withdraw to home waters. The 'return to base' order was repeated in the early hours of the following morning at 01.19. At 05.00 the *Belgrano* reversed course and began to head west, back in the direction of its home port of Ushuaia.

Information gleaned from intercepted signals was routinely transmitted to *Conqueror* which, as with other submarines in the region, would come to periscope depth at intervals and raise aerials to receive traffic. Little was known about whether the Argentines were receiving intelligence information from the Soviets but, as a precaution, signals officers on *Conqueror* would routinely arrange to receive signals in the periods between the passing overhead of orbiting Soviet satellites.

'We are evidently able to intercept much, if not all, of the enemies' signal traffic,' wrote Sethia in his diary. 'The boys in Cheltenham know their stuff.'

Later it was confirmed that all signals between Argentine headquarters and her Navy's ships in the course of the war were successfully intercepted by or for British Naval Intelligence – not that all of them were instantly understood, or indeed passed on to everyone who might have made better decisions in the light of them. However, at GCHQ Cheltenham, and at Royal Navy HQ at Northwood, the British knew that the warship had been ordered back to base and that she was following orders to the letter.

By early morning on 2 May, not only was the *Belgrano* not inside the prohibited area of the Total Exclusion Zone, but she and her escorts were heading away from the Task Force. If she had not been considered a sufficient threat to justify sinking her several hours earlier when she was advancing towards the Task Force with orders to attack, now that she was under orders to withdraw and was steaming away, it is not easy to see how she can have been regarded as a legitimate target.

In London, however, nerves were beginning to jangle. The first real skirmishes had begun. While as yet there had still been no casualties on the British side, it remained the case that the enemy aircraft carrier had not been located, and for those leading the Task Force, the situation felt highly precarious. They could not find the aircraft carrier, but they did know the position of the *Belgrano* – and it now seemed possible that the two naval groups were capable of attacking in what was later described as a 'pincer movement' from the north-west and the south-west (though the captain of the *Belgrano*, Héctor Bonzo, did later question quite how they could have been making a 'pincer movement' when the 'prongs' were some 350 miles apart). While it was true that they were headed home they could, it was reasoned, turn around at any moment.

Task Force commander Sandy Woodward was so concerned that he issued his own order to HMS *Conqueror* to go ahead and sink the *Belgrano*. He said later that he knew he had no authority to do so, and that sinking the ship was outside of the rules of engagement, but that this was his way of concentrating minds back in London on what he regarded as the urgency of the situation. His order quickly countermanded, Woodward now made an urgent request to the 09.15 meeting of the Chiefs of Staff for permission to sink the Argentine cruiser. Though it plainly seemed a matter of urgency to Woodward, equally plainly it did not seem a matter of urgency to anyone else, because the Chief of the Defence Staff, Lord Lewin, agreed to take the request to a meeting of the unofficial War Cabinet at Chequers at 1.00 p.m. When she heard the request, Mrs Thatcher gathered a small group of ministers into a side room to hear what Lewin had to say. He told them that the commander of the Task Force was worried about the possibility that the *Conqueror* might lose the *Belgrano*. Lewin said later that he did not tell the meeting that the aircraft carrier and the *Belgrano* had been ordered home; even if he had known it, he would have considered this irrelevant. If they let the cruiser go, and she later went on to inflict damage on British servicemen, a decision not to act now would look and feel very bad indeed. The discussion was said by those present to have lasted for about twenty minutes, at the end of which Lewin was given the permission he had sought.

Just an hour later, the first message from Navy headquarters at Northwood was sent to HMS *Conqueror* giving her the order to attack.

It was well known on board *Conqueror* that the submarine had been having difficulties with her communications masts – in fact they ended up having to route signal traffic via New Zealand rather than directly back to the UK. To give themselves the best chance of receiving a clear signal, *Conqueror* had been running slowly at periscope depth for some time, and was seven miles adrift from the *Belgrano* group when the order finally came through. The first signal ordering the attack on TG 79.3 came in with a large chunk of it missing and much of it garbled, therefore the skipper asked for a repeat, but this also came through corrupted. It has since been reported that the request by Wreford-Brown for a repeat of his orders indicated his reluctance or disbelief in the need to carry out the attack. There is no evidence for this and it was not the impression of anyone else in the control room on that day. Since this would be the first torpedo fired by a Royal Navy vessel in anger since the end of World War II, the captain understandably felt the need to be certain of his orders. Wreford-Brown ordered Tim McClement quite literally to piece together the various bits of various signals which had come through clearly, in an attempt to produce a single unambiguous order. He managed to do so and finally the intention of the signal was clear: 'Sink the *Belgrano*.'

Anticipating the possibility of the attack order, officers on the *Conqueror* had gathered in the wardroom to discuss their options. On board the submarine they had the new Tigerfish Mark 24 Mod 1 torpedo which they had been testing on their exercises with the Americans earlier that year. The weapon had a long trailing wire which stayed attached as it left the submarine, continuing to supply guidance information. Put most generously, it was unreliable – there had even been instances of the weapon turning back towards the submarine from which it had been fired. One of the weapons ratings was later quoted as saying that in fact he had never been able to make the Tigerfish 'go bang' when and where he wanted it to.

But *Conqueror* also had on board the Mark 8 torpedo, which had originally been designed in World War I and then modified for use in World War II – so versions of it had been in service for nearly seventy years. A gyro-angled unguided diesel torpedo containing 810 pounds of high-explosive Torpex, its rugged design and reliability made it the best torpedo of its era. It had an optimum range of 1,500 yards but would run nearly ten times that far before exhausting its fuel. Unlike the Mark 24, the Mark 8 can turn only once – reducing the possibilities of failure, but making the initial targeting of the weapon even more critical. A less technical description of it might be 'a bomb with an engine attached'.

'Faced with the challenge of sinking a 14,000-ton armoured ship built in 1938 that was taking no discernible ASW [anti-submarine warfare] precautions, we made the obvious choice and plumped for the contemporaneous Mark 8,' said Navigator Jonty Powis. In other words it was a World War II target, and would be attacked with a World War II weapon.

Late that morning in the South Atlantic, the captain announced to the crew that they had orders to sink the *Belgrano* and that after lunch they would be going to action stations. This meant that every man on board would be at his post and ready to do whatever was necessary. This was something they had done countless times in exercise, but was the first time a British submarine had been on a real combat footing since 1945, and the gravity of the situation was not lost on those in the boat.

Lunch on that day consisted of roast pork with all the trimmings, followed by apple crumble and custard. Grant Louch had just come off his morning duty and tried to grab two hours' sleep before he would be called to action stations. Needless to say, he did not sleep.

'I remember it being very calm,' he recalls. 'Everyone was doing everything exactly by the book, just as we had been trained to do.'

Petty Officer Graham Libby said later, 'You think "That's never going to happen – we'll never fire." Even up to the point of firing, we never thought we would do it.'

Now closing the gap which had opened up between *Conqueror* and the *Belgrano* group, the submarine went deep and accelerated to 18 knots for periods of twenty minutes or so, then came up to periscope depth to check on the position of the target. This manoeuvre was repeated five or six times.

If there is a single skill or aptitude that every officer on board a submarine needs more than any other, it is probably that of speed and accuracy with mental arithmetic. These were days before sophisticated computers took over such tasks, and so calculations had to be done very quickly in the head or with the help of a slide-rule. In the case of firing a torpedo at an enemy ship, the variables are many. They include the distance, course and speed of the target ship (and the possibility that these might change), the angle between submarine and cruiser, and the speed and course of the torpedo. While it was ultimately the responsibility of the captain to decide the tactics and timing of an attack, it was also the responsibility of executive officer Tim McClement to ensure the optimal circumstances for firing the weapons. Everyone in the control room had his part to play, and everyone drew deeply on years of training and drills and practice. However much and for however long they had trained, all agreed later that nothing had quite prepared them for the real thing.

The submarine approached to a distance of about two and a half miles from the *Belgrano* group, and a glance through the periscope revealed that the two destroyers had moved to her starboard side. The captain therefore decided to attack from the port side, thereby minimising the possibility that the destroyers might get in the way, and putting the cruiser between destroyers and submarine as *Conqueror* made her getaway.

Just before 15.30 local time on 2 May 1982, *Conqueror* moved into position for the attack. The *Belgrano* was heading more or less due west, and *Conqueror* passed from the north-east of her, across her stern, to get into position on the port side. At thirty-second intervals the TASO, Robin L'Oste-Brown, shouted out the anticipated position of the target, so that when the submarine went to periscope depth and the captain raised the scope, he would not need to waste valuable seconds scanning the horizon. At that moment the TASO shouts, 'Should be . . .' and then the expected compass bearing to the target location.

When the captain of a submarine looks through the periscope and sees the target, his mind is working at lightning speed. Years of ship recognition and training enable him to know by rote the dimensions of the ship he is looking for. He quickly assesses the size she appears to be relative to the lens, and so can estimate the distance away. Then, taking into account the speed of the torpedo, instant calculations have to be made to ensure that moving ship and advancing torpedo will collide – preferably directly amidships of the target. Ideally the attacking submarine wants to fire three torpedoes, in a slight fan, to maximise the chance that at least one will hit the target. A three-second interval between firing would represent half a ship length of the moving target.

Wreford-Brown would have practised these mental drills so frequently in training that they came to him by instinct. Putting all that training to use in real operational conditions in the cold waters of the South Atlantic was something else. Despite the pressure of the situation, the captain never missed a beat. By now he was taking a look through the periscope every three minutes or so. He needed to manoeuvre the boat into a position about three-quarters of a mile to the south of the target, ending up on a course of 345 degrees, barely moving so that the periscope would not cause any wake as it broke the surface of the water.

With only minutes to go before the submarine went into the attack, Wreford-Brown told Sethia that he urgently needed to 'catch a trim'. This was the order to achieve as close to perfect neutral buoyancy as possible to give the submarine the best possible stability as a platform for firing torpedoes. The procedure involves decelerating to 3 or 4 knots, during which it is possible to tell whether the submarine is tending to rise or sink, and whether she is sitting level in the water. Valves are opened and closed, shifting sea-water in or out, or around the boat. When the boat is as close to stable as is achievable, and neither rising nor sinking, the trimming officer will pump out 100 gallons of water until the submarine begins to rise, then flood 50 gallons back in until it begins to sink again, to try to find the perfect median. After a few minutes Sethia was able to inform the captain that *Conqueror* was in trim.

At the chart table, Leading Seaman Derek Higgins was recording and taking account of every piece of information about the course and speed of the target so that its next position could be anticipated. 'It was my job to give the captain the course and speed of the contact between looks,' said Higgins. 'This is what we had trained and trained for and it went exactly by the book.'

With information coming at him from all corners of the control room, his mental computer working at full tilt, Wreford-Brown took a last look through the periscope and gave the order to stand by to fire.

'Do not fire.'

Everyone in the control room was astonished and there was a momentary hush. It was the voice of Tim McClement. It was his responsibility to ensure that circumstances were optimal for a direct hit, and his calculations told him that the opportunity would improve if they waited for just a few seconds. Even so, countermanding a captain – especially in so public and critical a situation – took some nerve. Wreford-Brown walked across the control room to McClement's position.

'Why the fuck not?'

'The angle is reducing,' said McClement.

In the time it took for Wreford-Brown to walk the four paces back to his position, he had worked out how best to reassert his authority over the ship's company.

'Do you mind if I fire now?' he asked.

McClement shouted, 'Carry on sir!' and again the periscope slid up into the captain's grasp and he gave the order.

'Fire.' There was no difficulty hearing the captain on this occasion. 'Fire,' he repeated and waited for a few seconds more. And then a third time: 'Fire.' It was the loudest anyone on board had ever heard him speak.

'The order was given to fire,' recalled Sethia later. 'A torpedo was discharged. A number of seconds later the order was again given, a weapon was discharged, and a number of seconds later the order was again given to fire, and a third weapon was discharged.'

'Torpedoes are usually fired from the control room,' said William Budding, who was in position in the upper torpedo compartment in the bows of the ship. 'Unfortunately, in £50 million worth of submarine, the button didn't work. So I got the order "fire by hand" so I think it was [tubes] 1, 3 and 4 and I fired them by hand.'

'All three torpedoes heard to run, sir,' said Robin L'Oste-Brown.

'The three Mark 8s were fired with an interval of 3 seconds,' said Jonty Powis later. The torpedoes would take 52 seconds to run the 1,280 yards to reach their point of impact.

During their run we continued to plot the target and when the stopwatch of the fire control officer indicated 15 seconds to first impact the captain again raised the periscope. He saw the two weapons hit, the first under the after superstructure and the second just aft of the bow.

'Orange fireball seen just aft of the centre of the target,' Wreford-Brown wrote later in his personal log. 'Third explosion heard but not seen – I was not looking!'

We all heard the bangs [said Powis], the whole boat cheered at the first, and again at the second; the third and fourth bangs with all four at a steady interval were a surprise. We afterwards decided that we were listening to the direct path and bottom bounce, which by chance arrived at the same cadence as the firing interval.

On board the *General Belgrano* they were in the middle of a watch change, so more members of the crew were up and on the move around the ship than would be usual. At the moment of impact, it seemed to those on board as though the ship suddenly stopped dead in the water, as if she had run aground.

'People in the dining hall saw a big hole open up in the floor,' said Captain Héctor Bonzo. 'In a fireball of hot incandescent air coming towards them, all they could do was to cover their faces to prevent it.'

The *Belgrano* had been hit by two of the torpedoes. The third explosion heard on *Conqueror* was initially thought to be the third weapon, but turned out to be a secondary explosion from on board the cruiser. In fact the first of the three torpedoes to be fired missed the *Belgrano*; it went on to hit one of the accompanying destroyers but failed to explode. The fourth explosion heard by *Conqueror* is thought to have indeed been an echo from the sea-bed.

There are differing accounts as to whether it was the first or second hit which caused the main damage.

Five seconds later another one strikes [said Captain Bonzo]. I opened the door and looked towards the bow and there was no bow . . . the bow was gone. The ship went completely dark, without energy, and there was a terrifying silence. Sometimes silence is a good thing, but on a warship the machine noises are a blessing. The danger comes when there is silence, because silence is death.

Now hundreds of men were scrambling to make their way to the upper decks in preparation for abandoning ship. 'The ship started to make a splitting sound, and it was as if a great hinge was making a noise, as if it was in pain.'

I was wearing a pair of earphones as ship control officer of the watch, as were several people in the sound room [said Sethia]. We will never forget hearing the sound of the *Belgrano* breaking up – the sound was like the tinkling of glass from a huge chandelier that has crashed to the ground.

Very quickly the *Belgrano* started to list alarmingly, but at first her captain thought that his ship would float. All communications had been knocked out by the blast, and so he had no way of knowing whether a distress call had been sent. There was no sign that the escorting destroyers were even aware of what had happened. Both were continuing along their previous paths. In fact, one of the accompanying destroyers signalled to its home port that the *Belgrano* had been hit but was still floating. The signal was intercepted and beamed back to Royal Navy HQ at Northwood.

Having ensured that he had hit his target, Wreford-Brown's immediate concern was to get the hell out of the area. *Conqueror* went deep and fast for a short sprint away. Their speed and the continuing noise behind them from exploding munitions meant that they could have no idea whether they were being pursued.

Within twenty minutes of the attack, the *Belgrano* was listing so severely to port that the crew could step directly from the deck into life-rafts. Captain Bonzo gave the order to abandon ship. The escape drill called for sailors to jump on top of rafts, but this was not always possible, and so many men jumped directly into the freezing water. Some bobbed up again and helping hands dragged them into life-rafts. Others did not resurface.

One of the pictures of the sinking ship taken from a life-raft shows two men still on deck. One of these two is Captain Bonzo, who was the last off his ship and had to swim to safety. The water, he remembered, was icy. 'It feels like a million needles are piercing your body at that moment,' he said later. 'You can't breathe, you cannot move, you cannot swim, it's not easy to swim with your outfit on, your pistol, your shoes.'

The attack had killed some 290 men instantly or within moments of the torpedo strike. Another 33 were to die before they could be rescued. At 17.00, less than an hour after the attack, some 800 men in life-rafts or in the water watched their ship sink into 9,000 feet of sea. By this time the two escorting destroyers were out of sight – following orders in the event of attack to run for their lives and save themselves.

After an hour the submarine slowed and returned to periscope depth with a view to checking the condition of the cruiser, and with the thought in mind that the destroyers might now be possible targets. Still at his post in the 'bandstand' as ship control officer, Sethia was among those who were feeling desperate to light up a cigarette.

As the submarine slowed and prepared to come shallow so that we could stick up a mast and send our report, the first lieutenant ordered 'One all round' and I leaned over to a shelf and took a cigarette and a box of matches. Just as I was about to light the cigarette, there was an almighty explosion and the boat shook from end to end – the front cover of a clock on the bulkhead actually vibrated loose. We presumed it was a depth-charge.

'We were confronted by the destroyers zig-zagging towards us at high speed,' said Jonty Powis:

So we went deeper and faster for longer to put distance between us and them as well as to reload. However, as there had been no sonar or radar transmissions from them even after the attack, we assumed that chance alone had sent them our way. There were a large number of bangs which we supposed were the destroyers dropping depth-charges blind.

It later emerged that the destroyers deployed no depth-charges, so the explosions heard must be presumed to have been from on board the damaged and sinking cruiser. It took a further hour of running at high speed before *Conqueror* felt her position to be sufficiently secure and slowed down once again to send her signal.

During this run to the south and east I opened up the latest copy of *Jane's Fighting Ships* and invited the captain to indicate where he had seen the weapons hit. He looked down at me with the patient look of an indulgent parent – 'I don't sink cruisers every day, pilot,' he whispered. I put the book away.

That night a South Atlantic storm blew up, and winds gusting up to 70 miles per hour with 20-foot waves tossed the life-rafts on the open sea. By next morning the gale-force winds had pushed the rafts some 50 miles from the scene of the attack, and the ferocity of the storm prevented spotter or rescue planes from taking to the air. At Argentine naval headquarters, it was assumed that the ship had been lost with all hands. Eventually a search plane spotted one raft, and then another. Suddenly the survivors heard a siren – the welcome sound of a blast from the fog-horn of one of the destroyers. Twenty-four hours after the sinking, the first survivors were picked up – the last of them were rescued half a day later. Some of the rafts were never found. In others, the occupants had frozen to death.

On board the *Conqueror* there was a range of reactions to the attack.

Some became rather introspective [said Jonty Powis], some seemed unaffected – most were pragmatic. We were at war in all but name and reasoned that the Argies would have had a go at us if they had detected our presence.

'The introverts became extrovert,' said Leading Stoker Simon O'Keeffe, 'and the extroverts became introverts.'

This was the moment for which we had all been trained [wrote Sethia], yet a moment which, I think, few of us thought we would ever encounter. Until the moment of firing, it was as if everything in our lives had been a dress rehearsal for a performance which would never happen. But at that moment our lives changed and we knew that the dress rehearsal was over.

The final entry in Sethia's diary on the day of the attack reads:

As I write, I am still overwhelmed by it all. I can hardly believe the enormity of what we have done. We can't go back and apologise now – it's too late. I wonder how many died. I wonder, even more, what the reaction will be? The lads have taken it very well – a couple were frightened outwardly, and the rest of us made do with being frightened inwardly.

News of the sinking might have been expected to be greeted with enthusiasm in Northwood. There were, however, some mixed reactions among the Intelligence staff. Some felt a sense of relief that a potential threat to the Task Force had been eliminated. Others feared the consequences of what was undoubtedly a massive escalation of the conflict. So far no British servicemen had been killed; surely now Argentina would have no choice but to react in anger.

On board the air-defence destroyer HMS *Sheffield*, Lieutenant Peter Walpole recalls that,

When I read the signal telling us the *Belgrano* had been attacked and sunk, I remember feeling a certain doom as it meant the start of a major shooting war. There had been some shooting already, but to all of us, the sinking of a major battleship or a cruiser meant that the shooting really was under way for the big ships – which meant us.

Back on the submarine, Narendra Sethia was among those who wondered what could have happened to precipitate the sudden and ruthless aggression from the British side:

I personally presumed that for some reason unbeknown to us any peace talks which may have been in progress had broken down and that therefore the government had decided spontaneously, 'Right, we will change the rules and show them.'

This was far from the case. Indeed, the Peruvians had been busy refining and re-drafting their peace proposals and were, they believed, within hours of a final formula which would have prevented an all-out war. In the event, news of the attack on the

Belgrano was conveyed to a group of Argentine generals meeting to discuss whether or not to ratify the final draft of the peace proposals being circulated by Peru. The meeting broke up in disarray. Their anger was shared by the Argentine people and anti-British riots broke out in the streets.

Less than two days later, on the morning on 4 May, two Argentine Super Étendard fighters attacked HMS *Sheffield*, killing twenty men. The war was well and truly on. BBC News reported on that day that, 'The attack follows yesterday's sinking of the Argentine cruiser *General Belgrano*.' An Argentine diplomat in the United States said the destruction of HMS *Sheffield* was 'justified after the massacre that the English have done shelling our men and our ships'.

In addition to the sudden escalation of violence in the South Atlantic, the sinking of the *Belgrano* gave the British a problem so far as international opinion was concerned. Throughout the preceding days leading up to the shooting war, the government had constantly been at pains to be precise about the legal justification for any action – notably the sinking of the *Santa Fe* during the retaking of South Georgia. Any action taken within the 200-mile radius of the Total Exclusion Zone was clearly justifiable, as was aggression against 'any vessel in a position where it might interfere with the mission of our task force in the south Atlantic'. Despite the continuing efforts of the US and Peru at brokering a peace, actions which were clearly taken in self-defence would still be seen as reasonable. Anything beyond that might well be met with condemnation by a sceptical international public. This was the very point which Pym had made in his memo written from London on 1 May after discussions with the Attorney General.

The attack was criticised as a serious escalation by Spain and Ireland, two countries with their own territorial disputes with Britain, and by a number of South American countries such as Bolivia and Venezuela. Of more immediate import to the British, however, was the question of how the action would be received by the United States and in the United Nations.

So how to justify the sinking of the *Belgrano*? It was not going to be easy. Here was an Argentine cruiser, a relic that predated World War II, with more than a thousand men on board, over 300 miles from the nearest British ship, armed with guns that had a range of only thirteen miles, and accompanied by destroyers that could fire their shells over a range of about ten miles. Not only was she headed away from the Task Force, she had been doing so for eleven hours before the attack on her, and she was under orders – which the British had intercepted and deciphered – to return to her home port. How was the sinking to be characterised as justifiable under the terms of the warnings given thus far? Clearly it was going to be important to stretch every sinew to place the action within the context of these public warnings.

These were the words used by Defence Secretary John Nott when announcing the action:

The next day, 2nd May, at 20.00 London time, one of our submarines detected the Argentine cruiser, *General Belgrano*, escorted by two destroyers. This heavily armed surface attack group was close to the Total Exclusion Zone and was closing on elements of our Task Force which was only hours away . . . The threat to the Task Force was such that the Task Force commander could ignore it only at his peril.

The words were clearly carefully chosen to fit the action as squarely as possible within the terms of the warnings issued by Britain to Argentina. The only trouble was that there was hardly anything in this statement that was true.

First, the *Belgrano* had not been detected at 20.00 London time on 2 May; she had been detected over forty-eight hours earlier and had been followed for the entire period until she was sunk. The suggestion that the enemy ship had been spotted much closer to the time of the attack gave an impression of decisions made in the 'heat of battle' which was not borne out by the facts.

Second, she was not close to the Total Exclusion Zone. At the moment she was sunk, she was well over thirty miles outside the Exclusion Zone, and had been meticulously avoiding it.

Third, the *Belgrano* was not 'closing on elements of our Task Force'. She was sailing in the opposite direction and had been doing so for eleven hours before she was sunk.

Fourth, even had the *Belgrano* turned 180 degrees and headed towards the Task Force at her top speed, she would have taken at least fifteen hours to come anywhere within range of the British fleet.

Fifth, at the time she was sunk, the *Belgrano* posed no threat whatever to the British Task Force. She was under orders to return home and anyway, was in the cross-hairs of a state-of-the-art nuclear-powered submarine which could blow her out of the water minutes after she became a threat.

Sixth, Nott's account deliberately gave the impression that the order to sink the *Belgrano* was given in the field by the Task Force commander – in the face of an imminent threat. In fact it was given in an ante-room in Chequers, at least four hours after it was asked for, and just before lunch.

Nott went on to repeat something the Prime Minister had said earlier that day about the two destroyers – that they were not attacked in any way, and indeed that they would not have been attacked 'so that they should have been able to go to the assistance of the damaged cruiser'. Leaving aside the question of how the destroyers might be supposed to know that they were free to pick up survivors without fear of being attacked, there is of course the fact that they *were* attacked. The first of three torpedoes fired from *Conqueror* had struck the *Hipólito Bouchard* and caused a deep gash in her hull, and only by chance had it failed to explode. We also know from the account by Jonty Powis that when *Conqueror* returned to the scene of the attack, it was partially with a view to sinking the destroyers.

So why all these lies at a point when the full truth must have been known? The statement by Nott was made thirty-six hours after the attack itself, and so 'heat of the battle' can hardly be a justification. All the information was available and unambiguous, and telling the truth would have been an option for the government.

It seems self-evident that John Nott's words were designed precisely to underpin the idea that the action against the *Belgrano* could be justified under the pretext that she was a threat to the mission of the Task Force. Even the phrase 'this heavily armed surface attack group' is pejorative and inaccurate, but plainly designed to justify the action.

As so often in politics and public life, it was not the original action which caused the problem, but the cover-up that followed it. There was an alternative. The government could have been open about the position of the *Belgrano* and the circumstances of the attack. The argument would have gone something like, 'sure, she was an old ship, and sure she was not attacking us at the time. However, she had previously been ordered to attack, and could well have been so ordered again. It is regrettable but we would rather be telling you that Argentineans have died than that we did nothing now and later our boys died.' To be fair, this was more or less the line taken by the military from the beginning. Lord Lewin said it, Sandy Woodward said it, and quite a few of the submariners said it too. If the politicians had also said it, or something like it, then there might have been a few complaints, but that also might well have been the end of the matter.

Instead the government chose not to tell the truth, and the necessity to stand behind John Nott's statement was the cause of months and years of unnecessary public debate and controversy. It led to the arrest and trial of a senior civil servant whose conscience forced him to act in the public interest. It also led to a loyal Navy officer being unjustly accused of theft and being driven to the edge of emotional and financial ruin. Perhaps worst of all, it led to extended and unjustified criticism of the submarine's action which was keenly felt by the officers and crew of the *Conqueror* herself.

'When we did get back,' said William Budding, 'there was a certain politician calling me a murderer. He had bloody sent me there! Typical politician.'

9

'Direct Orders from Northwood'

HMS *Conqueror* spent the next two days patrolling the area around the site of the attack. Their return to the scene was later characterised by politicians as being with a view to aiding in the search and rescue operation, though quite how a fully laden submarine could come to anyone's assistance was not explained. *Conqueror* did not interfere with the search and rescue operation, but pursued a vessel which broke off from the rescue group and steered north-east in the direction of the British ships which were gathered around the wreck of HMS *Sheffield*.

'We shadowed the ship at close range overnight and at first light closed up at action stations ready to fire and returned to periscope depth [said Jonty Powis]. Through the periscope the large red crosses on the superstructure were conspicuous. It was the auxiliary *Bahía Paraiso*, converted into a hospital ship . . . We broke off and resumed our patrol areas to the south of the islands.

Only a few days later, at 12.56 on 7 May, the company in HMS *Conqueror* learned for the first time how it felt to be on the receiving end of a surprise attack. The submarine was at periscope depth and the coxswain, Brian Moss, was scanning the horizon when suddenly he spotted a low-flying aircraft hurtling directly towards the submarine.

'We went to emergency stations and deep,' Sethia recalls, 'and the sound room locked on to what they classified as an airborne Mark 46 torpedo – heading towards us and at high speed.' Unlike the Mark 8s which *Conqueror* had used to sink the *Belgrano*, the Mark 46 used sonar to home in on its target, and suddenly the fear was that the torpedo had locked on to the noise being made by the nuclear submarine.

Instantly both Wreford-Brown and Tim McClement started their stopwatches. The time between detection of an incoming torpedo and impact could be six minutes, and this was to be a very long six minutes. McClement remembers thinking how unfair it was that he would not be able to see his son, by then nine months old. He also reflected that he had on board with him a pen which had been handed down from his own grandfather, and regretted that he would not be able to hand it on.

Sethia had been enjoying the last few minutes of rest in his bunk before going on duty, when the alarm sounded for action stations and the sudden steep incline of the submarine at a bow-down angle threw him to the floor. He struggled to his feet and headed up the incline towards the control room. When he got there he saw Wreford-Brown poised over a sonar screen on the port side, whilst every few seconds the sound room gave its updated and increasingly alarming report.

'Fast moving contact – deflection on watcher bearing zero three zero.'

The stopwatches were ticking, and with only seconds to go before probable impact from the torpedo, the captain ordered a manoeuvre which very few submariners ever experience during their service on a modern SSN. He gave the order 'full ahead'. Even when training in the submarine simulator at Faslane, the order 'full ahead' would never be given because to achieve it, the engineering department has to operate a mechanism that is known as the 'Battle Short Switch'. Operating this over-rides all nuclear reactor safety measures, which are designed to prevent temperature and pressure from exceeding their safe limits. Turning them off meant that temperatures and pressures within the reactor could rocket and lead to a reactor melt-down.

On this occasion, however, the manoeuvre appeared to be entirely justified, because the instruments soon showed that the torpedo was no longer in pursuit.

Now, though, it seemed clear that Conqueror was being

hunted in deadly earnest. The order was given to go to silent routine, which meant that those not on operational duty were encouraged to lie in their bunks rather than walk around, and all non-essential machinery was switched off. Seeing that he was not needed immediately, Sethia returned to the wardroom where the chief steward, Petty Officer Russell, had been laying the table for lunch.

We were still at a steep bow-down angle, and there were shattered plates and glasses all over the wardroom floor, chairs upside down. I looked at the bar and thought to myself, 'Since this is the end, I may as well have a drink.' I never did have the drink, but I looked at Russell who was leaning against the bar door and looking a trifle nervous, and I said to him, 'Oh shit Russ, this is it' – my words of encouragement to one of the men in my division.

One young rating had been climbing down between decks from the control room to a compartment that contained a small washing machine. Whilst everyone else was frozen still, he walked into the machinery space as if he was in a fear-induced trance and started the machine. Instantly a medical assistant who had been on the ladder leading to the compartment leapt down and knocked the young lad unconscious – the noise from the washing machine could have attracted the torpedo.

Wreford-Brown now threw the boat around from deep to shallow, to very deep, to shallow, at every angle imaginable. Sethia had a vivid mental image of the submarine zig-zagging through the water, with some lethal weapon zig-zagging behind in tireless pursuit. Every passing second could bring with it instant annihilation for the submarine and every man on board. Sethia felt his heart beating out of his chest.

After what seemed like hours but was probably only minutes, the submarine appeared to be in the clear; it felt like a very narrow escape. Dangerous though Wreford-Brown's drastic evasive actions had been, once again the captain had taken the correct decision under the most stressful of circumstances, and despite the continuing pressures, he never lost his sense of humour. On 12 May Narendra Sethia recorded in his diary:

The skipper suggested tonight that I could make some money when I leave the RN by setting up some bars and women for the Falklands garrison that will undoubtedly be established in the future – there was a deathly silence when I suggested glass-bottom boat tours of the spot where the *Belgrano* went down.

Next day Tim McClement took Jonty Powis aside and told him that he would cover his shift for him. News had just been received that Powis's wife had given birth to their daughter Megan. The day after that was Sethia's twenty-sixth birthday. At 16.00 he was summoned to the wardroom where he found all the off-watch officers gathered, and a birthday cake with candles, biscuits and a whole table covered with edible goodies.

The effect of the sinking of the *Belgrano* had been to persuade the Argentines to withdraw what remained of their surface fleet, including the aircraft carrier, back to home waters. This fact alone justified the action in the view of many. But while the elimination of the danger from major warships was welcome on board *Conqueror*, there remained the ever-present danger from the skies. Nerves were still jittery, and in the early hours of 22 May, the submarine was at periscope depth and Sethia was scanning the horizon when he spotted what seemed to be a light aircraft in the sky dead ahead. He recorded the incident in his diary.

'I slammed up the handles, went to Action Stations, down scope, twenty down, half ahead, maximum revs, 700 feet – and opened [i.e. increased speed] for an hour.'

It was a moment of high drama but after sixty minutes of running fast and deep and the chance to reflect, Sethia arrived at an alternative explanation.

After the event I felt a bit of an idiot as discussion with the skipper, and a calmer analysis, makes us think that it was probably Jupiter rising. However, at the time, and in the few seconds for which I looked at it,

I thought it just possible that it was an aircraft and didn't want to hang around to find out. They said, afterwards, that I had done the right thing and I believe I did – but it was a difficult decision.

Conqueror was continuing to have a range of problems with its communications and as part of one effort to make repairs, an aerial wire had been jettisoned and, it was suspected, become entangled around the submarine propeller. This in turn was causing problems, including a loss of speed and, worse still, a good deal of noise as the propeller rotated. The only way to address the situation would be to put a diver into the water to investigate and to attempt to dislodge the wire. But this was the South Atlantic; the sea was icy cold and there was a considerable swell. Everyone also knew that if an aircraft appeared while the diver was in the water, there would be no choice but to submerge instantly – thereby abandoning and possibly condemning the diver to death. If he was not killed in the process, he would be left in the water while the boat took evasive measures for however long was necessary – certainly hours and maybe longer. His chance of survival would be remote.

The task fell to Petty Officer Graham 'Horse' Libby who, amazingly, was perfectly prepared to go:

I was a single man. I was quite happy to go out there because I was all pumped up. We had just sunk a blooming great warship – this could be the icing on the cake, you know? It's just something exciting that I might never ever get a chance to do.

Libby and Tim McClement climbed out onto the submarine casing, with five other divers for support and back-up. All of the men were attached to the boat by life-lines, but straight away a wave swept Libby and John Coulthard into the water. Libby immediately disappeared from sight and, to his horror, McClement caught a glimpse of Coulthard lying apparently face-down in the ocean. For a moment it seemed that his life-line was not attached.

Lieutenant Narendra Sethia, August 1980.

Left to right: Andrew Walker, Lt-Cdr. J. 'Louis' Armstrong, 'The Sheik', Krishna Sethia, Roger Cullen, Captain Nick Hunt, Commander Neil Blair.

Launch of the nuclear-powered submarine HMS *Conqueror* at Cammell Laird Shipyard, Birkenhead, 28 August 1969.

Top left: Midshipman Narendra Sethia, aged eighteen, December 1974.

Top right: Commander Chris Wreford-Brown, captain of HMS *Conqueror* with Petty Officer Graham Libby, shortly after their return from the successful Operation Barmaid.

Bottom left: Tim McClement, first lieutenant of HMS *Conqueror* during Operation Corporate and Operation Barmaid.

Bottom right: HMS *Conqueror*'s navigator Jonathan 'Jonty' Powis greets his wife Margaret and newborn baby Megan at Faslane after his return from the Falklands.

Prime Minister Margaret Thatcher and Foreign Secretary Francis Pym (right) meeting US Secretary of State Alexander Haig to discuss the Falklands crisis. Later Haig wrote, 'It is clear they had not thought much about the diplomatic possibilities.'

Defence Secretary John Nott announces that British troops are established on the Falkland Islands, 21 May 1982.

The Argentine cruiser *General Belgrano*, after the attack by HMS *Conqueror*, 2 May 1982. 'The ship started to make a splitting sound . . . as if it was in pain.'

Most British newspapers accurately reflected the general public's mood about the conduct of the conflict.

Defence Secretary John Nott (left), with Lt-Gen. Sir Richard Trant (centre) and Lt-Col. Tim Donkin, describing the final assault on Port Stanley, 15 June 1982.

HMS *Conqueror* returns in triumph to Faslane after Operation Corporate. Just six weeks later she was off again on Operation Barmaid.

HMS CONQUEROR
c o BFPO Ships

FROM: Commander-in-Chief Fleet (Admiral Sir John
Fieldhouse, GCB)

TO: HMS CONQUEROR

1. The sinking of the BELGRANO was fundamental to
the success of Operation Corporate and took the
heart out of the Argentinian Navy. Your long
patrol was conducted throughout to my complete
satisfaction. Well done."

From: Commander-in-Chief Fleet
To: UK Forces in the South Atlantic

1. I have had the honour to receive the following
message from Her Majesty the Queen and pass it
to you all with pleasure:

"I send my warmest congratulations to you and all
under your Command for the splendid way in which
you have achieved the liberation of the Falkland
Islands. Britain is very proud of the way you
have served your country. Elizabeth R. "

* * * * * * * * * * *

HMS CONQUEROR
c o BFPO Ships

From: The Flag Officer Submarines (Vice Admiral
P G M Herbert, OBE)

To: HMS CONQUEROR

1. Your successful attack on BELGRANO pressed
home with determination and precision was in
the highest traditions of the Submarine
Service. The event had the immediate effect
of dissuading Argentinian Surface Forces from
taking any further part in offensive operations,
thereby preventing great loss of life, not only
to UK personnel but Argentinian also.

2. I was also greatly impressed by your determination
throughout the Patrol, and in particular your
penetration of the Gulfo San Matias.

3. You and your Ship's Company can look forward to
a very well earned rest. Congratulations on a
magnificent achievement.

* * * * * * * * *

HMS CONQUEROR
c o BFPO Ships

From: The Naval Chiefs of Staff
To: UK Forces in the South Atlantic

At this historic moment, the Chiefs of Staff send you
their warmest congratulations on the exemplary and
brilliant way you have carried out all tasks given to
you by Her Majesty's Government against very considerable
odds.

We are enormously proud of the gallantry, stamina and
professionalism shown at every stage of this operation
by the Armed Services, the Royal Fleet Auxiliary, the
Royal Maritime Auxiliary Service, the Merchant Marine
and other civilian members of the Task Force. Our
thoughts at this time are also very much with those
who have lost their lives and with those who have
suffered wounds in the service of their country.

We echo the admiration and gratitude of the Nation when
we say 'Well done'.

* * * * * * * * *

Narendra Sethia typed up some of the signals received on board HMS
Conqueror during Operation Corporate.

Richard Morley, October 1984.

Left: Labour MP Tam Dalyell arrives at the Old Bailey for the trial of Clive Ponting on charges of breaching the Official Secrets Act, 25 January 1985.

Right: Arthur Gavshon. Richard Crossman told Tam Dalyell that Gavshon was 'the only journalist I can truly trust'.

'How are things going up there?' From down in the control room, Wreford-Brown chose that precise moment to ask his first lieutenant for a progress report. For what he says was the only time, McClement chose to mislead his captain.

'According to plan sir,' he replied.

The life-line to Coulthard had not broken after all and he was pulled back on board, and Libby also now reappeared at the stern of the boat. Clanking around his body as he was buffeted by the waves was a range of tools and hacksaws which he thought he might need for the task. He edged his way around the submarine to the stern and found that the aerial wire was indeed wrapped tightly around the shaft and blades. Worse still, even though the engines were of course stopped, the propellers were still turning gently, and in danger of severing the diver's life-line back into the boat. Libby worked away with hacksaws, as speedily as he could, cutting off the wire in sections. The need for dexterity meant that he could not wear gloves, and gradually he felt his hands seize up and his entire body being penetrated by the cold. In his position back on the submarine, Tim McClement was constantly scanning the horizon for any sign of an enemy aircraft, knowing that there would be no way of getting Libby back in the boat if he had to give the order to dive. After twenty minutes, and just when his stamina was on the point of giving out, Libby declared the propeller clear and was hauled back inside the submarine. Wreford-Brown noted in his log that Libby's efforts went 'far beyond the call of normal duty' and he was later awarded the Distinguished Service Medal.

On the same day Sethia recorded in his diary, 'We also suffered our first casualty of war today when the POSA [Petty Officer Stores Accountant] Tony Coxon, fell out of his bunk and broke his collarbone.'

Now the *Conqueror* was directed to find the Type 42 destroyer ARA *Hercules* which, according to intercepted signals, was sailing south but staying close to the Argentine coast. Too close, because Intelligence reported that *Hercules* had strayed into shallow waters and had been damaged as she had run aground. On hearing this, *Conqueror* moved to the entrance of the Golfo de San Matías, a large bay which *Hercules* would have to cross to reach home. The entrance to the bay is more than twenty-four miles across, so that she could either remain inside territorial waters by staying close to the coast inside the bay, or take the risk of moving into international waters if she made a passage directly across the mouth of the harbour. Once in international waters, she would be a legitimate target for *Conqueror*. Having detected no sign of her, Wreford-Brown sought permission to breach the twelve-mile limit and go into the bay. Permission was granted by return signal – which was itself against the rules of engagement then in force, and contrary to the advice given by the government's own law officers, who had warned that incursions within Argentine territorial waters would not be justifiable under the terms of Article 51.

The change of orders presented another navigational challenge for Jonty Powis. The only charts available to him were five miles to the inch, so they had to use the echo sounder and remain in sight of the coast to keep out of trouble. It could only be a matter of time before the submarine made contact with the destroyer but, 300 miles away, in the main theatre of the war, the hostilities were reaching their climax. The best chance ARA *Hercules* had of remaining afloat was to stay out of sight in these last few days of the fighting. *Conqueror* now spent several days submerged close to the Argentine coast, providing early warning of enemy aircraft on their way to attack the Task Force, and hoping not to be in the way when returning fighters ditched undischarged weapons in the sea before coming in to land.

While the withdrawal to port of the Argentine surface ships made life less frenetic for the nuclear submarines, the same could not be said for the men and women on the surface ships, nor for the fighter pilots in the air. For them, and for the men and women back at command headquarters in the UK, the sinking of the *Belgrano* marked the beginning, rather than the end, of the real hostilities. In some ways it seemed as though the near four decades of military progress since the end of World War II had never happened, as infantrymen found themselves marching over hills and through mud to engage in hand-to-hand combat with the enemy, and warships appeared to float like sitting ducks as aircraft dropped bombs and fired missiles at them. Even today, thirty years after these events, those who were there or who witnessed the news coverage are unlikely to forget the attacks on *Atlantic Conveyor, Coventry, Ardent* and *Antelope*, and RFAs *Sir Galahad* and *Sir Tristram* in Bluff Cove. Brave men lost their limbs, or their faces, or their eyesight, or their lives, in the icy cold waters of an ocean far away from their homes.

The infantry battle for the Falklands capital, Port Stanley, began on 11 June, when units of 3 Commando Brigade launched attacks on fortified high ground around the town. Big guns on board Royal Navy ships off the coast provided covering fire. Eighteen Argentine and two British soldiers were killed in the taking of Mount Harriet, and another thirteen British were killed when HMS *Glamorgan* was hit by an Exocet missile.

The second phase of the final approach to Port Stanley took place on 13 June, when ten British and thirty more Argentines died in the battle of Mount Tumbledown. A ceasefire was declared on 14 June and later that day the commander of the Argentine garrison in Stanley, Brigadier General Mario Menéndez, surrendered to the commander of the British land forces, Major General Jeremy Moore. In addition to the 649 Argentine and 258 British dead, there were 1,188 Argentine and 777 British non-fatal casualties, many of them crippled for life.

Next day, 15 June, news came that the fighting had stopped, and *Conqueror* was ordered to give up the search for ARA *Hercules* and later told to head for home. They had been at sea for seventy-six days. 'The Ministry of Defence has sent us a food questionnaire,' wrote Sethia in his diary. 'I wrote back and told them that we've been at sea for so long that we had to eat the questionnaires.'

The trip north was largely uneventful and much of it was spent on cleaning and repairs to the submarine. Wreford-Brown and the senior officers were fully aware that their operation had made Royal Navy history, and they spent many hours ensuring that the patrol reports were in good order, and preparing for the inevitable debriefings.

When *Conqueror* reached the equator, the captain ordered that the submarine should stop and surface to enable the crew to swim. After so long cooped up in an artificial atmosphere, this came as a shock to all the senses. When the hatches were opened, a sickly, warm, salty smell invaded the boat – and initially it made some on board feel nauseous. In spite of the smells that are characteristic to the submarine, the air on board the boat is actually purer than the air outside, as it is made by an electrolyser that separates hydrogen and oxygen from sea water, and therefore has no impurities whatsoever.

'One of my strongest recollections,' recalls Sethia, 'was the smell of fresh air. What we normally regard as fresh air actually smells revolting to a submariner who has been below water for several weeks.'

With a week to go before they were due back in Faslane, supplies of food finally started to give out. There was no more tea or milk, and the crew were reduced to breaking into the ten-man ration-packs which were kept in the fore-end for emergencies. The captain expressed his displeasure that the tradition of eating grapefruit segments (or 'seggies') for Sunday breakfast had to be discontinued. They had also run out of bacon or sausages for breakfast, so instead they had to eat fillet steaks or gammon. In the period of the Falklands patrol, the officers and men in *Conqueror* got through 26,000 pounds of frozen meat, 6,000 cans of food, 13 miles of teleprinter rolls for signals, and 176,000 cigarettes.

The officers and crew of *Conqueror* continued to experience a wide range of emotions as the submarine made her way back to Faslane. Most felt that they had not asked to be in the position in which they found themselves, but since they had been, they had acquitted themselves well. There was a good deal of pride that they had done the job they had trained to do, and they had done it effectively. Among these was the executive officer, Tim McClement, who was a professional through and through, had earned the respect of those who served with him, and who went on to reach the rank of vice admiral.

Among those who struggled to come to terms with events was the TASO, Robin L'Oste-Brown. On the way home from the Falklands, he contemplated asking the captain if he could send a proposal of marriage to his girlfriend; in the event he waited and asked her on his second weekend after coming home. She said yes. He also made a decision that his future career would not be in the Navy.

The crew of the *Conqueror* had been promised a mail-drop on the way home, but one or two of the more experienced officers were sceptical. It was therefore a pleasant surprise when they successfully made the rendezvous with a Nimrod just north of the equator, which dropped no fewer than thirty-four packages containing letters, newspapers, and other essential supplies. Just one bag sank on contact with the ocean. It was only now that the crew had the first real idea just how famous they were about to be. It came as a shock. Until they saw the headlines, they had no idea of the amount of coverage there had been, and they were astounded. All of their training and service had made their default position one of total anonymity. They came and went in complete secrecy. Their operations were discussed with no one. Now letters received from family, as well as the headlines from dozens of newspapers, named their submarine and recounted their action using a level of detail with which they were totally unfamiliar. There were even pictures of the *Belgrano*, listing alarmingly in the background, while the foreground was filled with orange life-rafts bobbing precariously on the water.

The crew also received an accumulation of 'familygrams' which had been sent but not received during the course of the conflict, and which were restricted to ten words or less because of the pressure on communications. One message to Leading Seaman Derek Higgins from his girlfriend simply read: 'Your Mum says I mustn't mention sex.'

With a few days to go before berthing back in Faslane, a signal was received on *Conqueror* reminding officers and men that the operation was secret and that they were obliged to speak to no one about the mission, including family. Wreford-Brown replied to Flag Officer Submarines and pointed out that the ship's company's natural pride and enthusiasm meant that of course people would talk with their families. FOSM's response completely evaded the issue and merely re-stated 'the importance of not divulging weapon system effectiveness', and spelled out that no one was to disclose that the submarine had entered the twelve-mile limit during the hunt for the *Hercules*, nor to give any details whatsoever of the attack on the *Belgrano* itself.

There was a lively discussion on board about whether the *Conqueror* should conform with the time-honoured tradition for submarines returning from a successful engagement with the enemy: that they fly a Jolly Roger, suitably customised to reflect the characteristics of the battle. Some of those on board felt a niggling sense of disquiet about what seemed the frivolity of flying a celebration flag when they had been responsible for the deaths of hundreds of people. In the end the decision went in favour of tradition. A flag was produced featuring a dagger to signify a secret operation, two torpedoes, and a symbol for the atom because *Conqueror* was a nuclear-powered submarine. The flag can still be seen by visitors to the submarine museum in Gosport where *Conqueror*'s Tim McClement is now the chairman.

The beard-growing competition was won by a senior rating,

Chief Artificer Jack Houlding, but there was a rumour that he had cheated by shampooing his beard on the judgement day, and fluffing it all up with a comb to make it look bigger. Tying for second came the captain, Wreford-Brown, and Narendra Sethia, while Tim McClement has a certificate confirming that he had the finest moustache.

Colin 'The Bear' Way lost 32 lb in the weight-loss competition and arrived home at a trim 17 stone 2 lb.

As she approached the Gareloch, a small boat carrying Navy brass came out to meet the submarine. Sethia was surprised to receive a package containing fresh strawberries, a gift from the man who had been due to replace him before the war. Mike Screech had originally done his submarine-supply training on HMS *Dreadnought*, but had more recently been assigned to a frigate. In the next few days he would do a brief hand-over with Sethia, who was at last able to begin his much-delayed return to civilian life.

The conquering heroes had been warned to expect mayhem on the docks as they arrived, and so it proved. A flotilla of small boats accompanied the submarine as she approached Faslane, and some of them were in danger of being swamped by the wash from the submarine as it manoeuvred its way through the Rhu Narrows. What seemed like a thousand flashes went off from cameras recording the return of the victors, and the *Conqueror* was escorted by tug boats which saluted her with water-cannons. William Budding was standing right behind his captain, Chris Wreford-Brown, when a group of people on shore came into view holding a huge banner which read, 'Welcome home Chris'. Budding shouted out at the top of his voice – 'Who the fuck's Chris?'

Robin L'Oste-Brown was met by his parents and girlfriend, and did not know who to hug first. Jonty Powis got the chance to say his first hello to his seven-week-old daughter Megan. Grant Louch was also met by his parents and his fiancée, whom he later married. They all had dinner together on that evening but were unable to celebrate because he was due back on duty the very next day. On the dockside to meet Tim McClement was his wife, who suggested that they might celebrate his return and then go shopping for her birthday which was the following day. McClement explained that birthday shopping was out of the question; his duty required him to attend a meeting about *Conqueror*'s programme for maintenance and repairs.

There was a barrage of questions from waiting journalists, most of them of the irritating 'How does it feel?' variety. Ever diffident and self-effacing, Commander Wreford-Brown plainly knew that he would be obliged to answer some questions. As part of an interview for television, he was asked to give the reason why he had sunk the *Belgrano*. His answer was formal, professional, unambiguous and entirely true.

'I had been watching the *Belgrano* for a few hours beforehand,' he said, 'and under direct orders from Northwood, I went in and attacked her.'

With those words, the captain unwittingly set off a train of events which he is very unlikely to have predicted. For his remarks were naturally reported in the newspapers and were duly read by the Honourable Member of Parliament for Linlithgow, Tam Dalyell.

10

The Story Travels

An old Etonian and former Scots Greys officer, Tam Dalyell cut an unlikely figure for a Labour MP. Universally known as Tam, he is actually the 11th Baronet, Sir Thomas Dalyell Loch, and has lived for his entire life in a seventeenth-century Scottish pile surrounded by 200 acres of parkland called 'The Binns'. Tam had studied history and economics at Cambridge, where he had also been chairman of the Conservative Association. He joined the Labour Party after the Suez Crisis in 1956 and was elected as a Labour member, initially for West Lothian, in 1962. With his impeccable manners and soft Scottish accent, Tam gained an early reputation for his campaigning zeal and tenacity.

Dalyell had held reservations about the Falklands War from the very beginning. He had not been called by the Speaker George Thomas in the Commons debate on Saturday 3 April, but on the following day had made a public statement that the sending of the Task Force was 'the most ill-conceived expedition to leave these shores since the Duke of Buckingham went to La Rochelle in 1627' (in which the unhappy Duke lost 4,000 of his force of 7,000 men). Dalyell's concerns had been heightened when he attended a lecture given to MPs by the commander of the Task Force, Sandy Woodward.

Until now, however, his doubts had been largely about what he felt was the precipitous rush towards the use of force to eject the Argentines. On hearing the words of the captain, his ears pricked up. '. . . under direct orders from Northwood,' Wreford-Brown had said, 'I went in and attacked her.'

That was not what MPs had been told by the Defence Secretary in the House of Commons.

'I made it clear yesterday,' John Nott had said two months earlier on 5 May,

... that every action by our forces in the South Atlantic is taken within strict political control and authority. The actual decision to launch the torpedo was clearly one taken by the submarine commander, but that decision was taken within very clear rules of engagement ... As I made clear yesterday, we regarded the *General Belgrano* as a threat to our forces ...

In fact, of course, Wreford-Brown had never sought permission to sink the *Belgrano*, because at no time had he felt that the ship was an imminent threat to any part of the British Task Force. Had he at any time had that suspicion, he could and would have sought permission to sink her, or indeed would have been within his authority to launch an attack on his own. He did neither.

'In my experience,' said Dalyell later, 'small inaccuracies are often part of larger ones, and seemingly small lies are part of larger lies, and don't you think it's important that in the biggest military action since the Second World War, that we should have the truth?'

The discrepancy between what John Nott had announced and what the captain of the submarine now clearly stated, was enough to set Dalyell off. From that day onwards he began a campaign of questioning which irritated the government to the point of exasperation, and it is fair to say equally vexed a good many on his own side too. But Dalyell was not a man to let a matter as trivial as being insulted by other MPs put him off. A parliamentary old-stager, he had the scent in his nostrils that Members had been deceived, and he was not going to let up before the whole truth came out.

All that was in the future. For now the crew of the *Conqueror* had returned to a heroes' welcome at their base, and were given leave to return to their homes.

Now technically a civilian, Sethia was preoccupied with his plan to set off around the world in that small yacht with his friend

Bones. The navigator from the *Conqueror*, Jonty Powis, was happy to let him take away a number of charts which would otherwise have been destroyed, and in common with just about every other serving officer, or indeed employee of any company, he also helped himself to one or two other bits and pieces which technically belonged to his employer. These included a water-proof hold-all, two unmarked ledgers, and a copy of *The Sailmaker's Handbook*.

After a day or two catching up with friends in Faslane, Sethia travelled down to Hamble to make final preparations for his delayed trip across the Atlantic. There was much to do before they would be ready to leave; preparations to be made and old friends to say goodbye to.

Such had been the publicity and interest arising from the sinking of the *Belgrano*, that Sethia wondered whether his diary might eventually become the basis for a book. He discussed the matter with his friend Simon O'Keeffe, because his father Timothy was a publisher. Sethia said that he planned to start writing a manuscript on the trip around the world, and would send a draft of the first few chapters when he could.

Back at the submarine, there were all the routine jobs to be done following an extended operation at sea. The on-board logs, including the signals logs and the control room logs, were stowed away in a locker in the control room. The routine was that they would wait until they had a bundle of six monthly logs, before sending them to the Ministry of Defence Record Depository in Hayes. Since only three months had passed since the last six logs had been bundled together and dispatched, it would ordinarily be the beginning of October before this next batch was due to be sent off.

On 8 August 1982, just over a month after his return from the war, Sethia and his friend Bones set sail in their tiny boat from the Hamble. There to see him off were some sixty of his friends. If he was slightly disappointed by a lower than expected turn-out of comrades from the submarine, it was quickly explained that the crew had been called urgently, and were off for another 'sneaky'. So much for their extended leave.

In the course of the next three months, he and his friend drank and smoked and blagged and bummed their way via Alderney down the coast of France and Spain to Gibraltar where they arrived on 19 September. There they had supper in 'Strings' restaurant, returning for the first time since July the previous year, on the night before *Conqueror* set off for its failed attempt at Operation Barmaid in the Med. They remained in Gibraltar for a week, visiting old haunts, and eventually talked their way into the Royal Navy base, HMS *Rooke*, where Sethia put four phone calls, twenty gin and tonics and forty cigarettes on his mess-bill at Faslane.

'Very naughty,' wrote Sethia in his diary, 'However, I behaved in a very officer-like fashion and no one suspected. Must do this more often.' Sethia had written down his genuine mess number – Faslane 656 – and the bill eventually went to the wardroom there where his old comrades had a smile and were glad to pay it.

Sethia and Bones continued sailing down the coast of Africa, with stop-overs in Casablanca and Safi before making for Lanzarote and the final landfall before their voyage across the Atlantic to Barbados. They had their last sight of land on 12 November – and made fifty miles on day one, eighty-four miles on day two, and counting . . .

Meanwhile, the war had been won and the nation was still enjoying the after-glow of the victory. The Prime Minister's stock had bounced from an historic low, and surveys now showed that 70 per cent of people approved of her handling of the conflict. On 12 October, she took the place which was usually reserved for Her Majesty the Queen at a victory parade for the Task Force organised by the City of London. This was perhaps the first sign of what later became a frequently satirised aspect of Mrs Thatcher's premiership – that at some level she felt she actually was the Queen. (Why is Margaret Thatcher like a pound coin?

– Because she is thick, brassy and thinks she's a sovereign.) It would be another seven years before she amazed the world by announcing in the royal first person plural that 'We have become a grandmother'; for the moment, she counted herself as merely the spokesperson for the nation.

'We, the British people, are proud of what has been done, proud of these heroic pages in our island story, proud to be here today to salute the Task Force. Proud to be British.' But some people were more proud of the work done by the armed forces than they were of the work of their government.

Tam Dalyell spent a good deal of the parliamentary summer recess that year priming his guns for what would be a determined assault on the government over the circumstances of the sinking of the *Belgrano*. A number of journalists had been busy comparing the official account of events, as recounted in Parliament, with the stories told by various military chiefs who had been in the South Atlantic, and there seemed to be important discrepancies.

Among them was the key question of the direction in which the *Belgrano* had been travelling at the time when she was attacked. Thatcher and Nott had both told MPs that the *Belgrano* was 'closing on elements of the Task Force, which was only hours away'. The first salvo, therefore, in what was to become Dalyell's persistent and tireless campaign, came on 29 November 1982:

General Belgrano: Mr Dalyell asked the Secretary of State for Defence what course the *General Belgrano* was steering when she was torpedoed.

By convention, parliamentary answers are usually short and to the point. In this case the total true answer could have been '280 degrees' (which is just north of west and in the direction of the Argentine coast). To have answered so simply and briefly would have been to concede without qualification the point that the *Belgrano* was heading home, and not sailing towards the Task Force as had been asserted by the government. So the answer instead consisted of 161 words, the last of which were '280 degrees'. The rest of the ministerial reply included an unusually long narrative which once again sought to shoe-horn the circumstances of the attack so that they would fit into the definition of a threat to the Task Force.

While setting straight the record on one inaccuracy in the government's account, the statement gave birth to another by stating that 'Throughout 2 May the cruiser and her escorts had made many changes of course.' This was plainly intended to give the impression that, while the *Belgrano* was sailing away from the Task Force at the moment of the attack, she may have been approaching the Task Force before the attack, and could at any time have turned towards the Royal Navy ships from her current course. In fact there had not been 'many' changes of course by the *Belgrano* group throughout 2 May; there had been two. One was the reversal of course following the order to return to base, and the second was a minor change from 270 degrees to 280 degrees just before the attack.

The same deception was repeated a number of times over the following weeks, by both John Nott and the Prime Minister. In all cases, the alleged zig-zagging was cited as evidence that the *Belgrano* could at any time have turned towards, and become a threat to, the British Task Force. This was despite the fact that the *Belgrano* had been sailing in the opposite direction consistently for a period of eleven hours.

Throughout the following months, as Narendra Sethia and Bones were watching dolphins and being haunted by hump-back whales, back in Westminster, Tam Dalyell was returning again and again to the subject of the sinking of the *Belgrano*. He raised it every time there was a chance to ask a parliamentary question; he made speeches about it in debates on any topic, no matter how tangentially related; he asked dozens of written questions of each of the Defence ministers and of the Prime Minister.

His questions covered every aspect of the sinking, including the time the *Belgrano* was first detected, her course and speed,

The Story Travels

the interception of orders to Argentine ships to return to base, the location of the attack. Sometimes the answers were misleading, sometimes they were incorrect, sometimes they were 'economical with the truth' and sometimes they were downright insulting. When Dalyell managed to get an adjournment debate on the subject in May 1983, this is what he was told by the Minister of State in the Foreign Office, Cranley Onslow:

The Hon. Gentleman's behaviour in these matters begins to cast grave doubts on his mental stability. He seems to have an obsession or a fixation of which he cannot rid himself. He comes back time and time again. However often he is told that he is wrong and shown the facts, another invention creeps into his mind and inflames his imagination or a journalist eggs him on and off he goes again. The Hon. Gentleman can return to the subject as often as he likes, and I dare say he will, but he will not alter the facts. The facts are as he has been given them.

In reality, almost every 'fact' presented by the government to justify the sinking was untrue.

Much of this uplifting debate had been going on in Parliament and in the broadsheets and, apart from the odd insult to Dalyell from the tabloids, discussion of his campaign was largely confined to the chattering classes. Until, that is, the general election campaign of May 1983, when the Prime Minister appeared on BBC *Nationwide* in a programme featuring questions put to her live by members of the public.

Diana Gould was a teacher from Cirencester in Gloucestershire who had studied the Antarctic at university and had a long-standing interest in the Falklands. She had followed the government's statements about the sinking of the *Belgrano*, and contrasted them with the accounts which were being so painfully extracted point by point by Dalyell and in a number of books by journalists. When she heard that the Prime Minister was due to appear on *Nationwide*'s election call programme, Mrs Gould wrote in and was duly invited to appear on the show. From her neat and conservative appearance, she might easily have been

145

mistaken for a supporter of the Tory government. She was not – two days before she was due to appear, she had telephoned Tam Dalyell and asked him for a full briefing on all the known facts about the discrepancies between the Prime Minister's account of events, and the other evidence. Mrs Gould's contribution to the programme was from the BBC's Bristol studio.

'Mrs Thatcher, why, when the Argentine battleship *Belgrano* was outside of the total exclusion zone and actually sailing away from the Falklands, why did you give the order to sink it?'

'It was not sailing away from the Falklands,' Mrs Thatcher cut back decisively, 'it was in an area which was a danger to our ships and to our people on them. In an area where we had warned, at the end of April, we had given warnings that all ships in those areas which presented a danger to our ships, were vulnerable . . .'

'Mrs Thatcher you started your answer by saying that it was not sailing away from the Falklands. It was on a bearing of 280 and it was already west of the Falklands, so I am sorry but I cannot see how you can say that it was not sailing away from the Falklands.'

Mrs Gould persisted and the Prime Minister, clearly rattled, started treating Mrs Gould as though she was an idiot, then attempted to patronise her, and then could not remember her name. It was a debacle, towards the end of which Mrs Thatcher launched what was plainly intended as the decisive salvo.

Mrs Thatcher: 'Mrs Gould, when the orders were given to sink it, when it was sunk, it was in an area which was a danger to our ships. Now, you accept that, do you?'

Mrs Gould: 'No, I don't.'

When the presenter Sue Lawley intervened to ask Mrs Gould what she suspected was the motivation for the sinking, Mrs Gould was clear. She claimed that the sinking 'was in effect sabotaging any possibility of any peace plan succeeding, and Mrs Thatcher had fourteen hours in which to consider the Peruvian peace plan that was being put forward to her'.

Mrs Thatcher: 'One day, all of the facts, in about thirty years time, will be published.'

It has since been claimed that the 'facts' to which Mrs Thatcher was referring were that, following the signal which had been sent to Argentine ships to return to base, yet another signal had been intercepted some hours later which had ordered the ships to resume the attack on the Task Force. This has been taken by some to be a further justification for the sinking. However, others who have made a close study of the circumstances surrounding the military action doubt that this 'attack' signal ever existed. If it did exist, it is hard to see why it was not called in evidence of justification at the time. In the meantime, however, the valiant Diana Gould was not letting go.

Mrs Gould: 'That is not good enough, Mrs Thatcher. We need . . .'
Mrs Thatcher: 'Would you please let me answer? I lived with the responsibility for a very long time . . . Those Peruvian peace proposals, which were only in outline, did not reach London until after the attack on the *Belgrano* – that is fact . . . I think it could only be in Britain that a Prime Minister was accused of sinking an enemy ship that was a danger to our Navy.'

In the green room after the show Mrs Thatcher's husband Denis and her other advisers knew that it had been a disaster for the Prime Minister. Denis told the editor of the programme, Roger Bolton, that his wife had been 'stitched up by bloody BBC poofs and Trots', and remarked that the BBC was run by 'a load of pinkos' which, in those days at least, probably had an element of truth to it. In a poll for the *Radio Times*, the interview was rated as the ninth best of all time. You can still watch it on YouTube.

If the Prime Minister's opponents hoped that the suggestion that she had precipitated an unnecessary war might sway the election against her, they were to be disappointed. In the space of just over a year, the Conservative Party went from being less popular than the newly formed SDP–Liberal alliance, to a famous and landslide victory in the general election of June 1983 – a victory which was generally attributed to public approval of Mrs Thatcher's handling of the Falklands crisis.

Meanwhile Narendra Sethia was blissfully unaware of any aspect of the controversy which was bubbling away back in the UK. He and Bones had spent the last few months before the British general election smuggling wine, which they bought at a dollar a litre in Martinique, a French possession, and sold for rather more in the British territories of St Lucia and elsewhere.

We fetched up in Antigua for the annual Race Week which has many wild parties and, recalling that my father had told me that it was very important to dress correctly and speak good English, Bones and I donned black tailcoats, white evening shirts and bow-ties, and called ourselves 'Bones & Seth – Vintners'. We rowed around English Harbour, Antigua, in our eight-foot plastic dinghy, accosting multi-million luxury yachts and attempting to sell them 'some fine wines'. We sold all of it.

At the time they were using pieces of four-by-two as paddles as their oars had been stolen in Portugal and they could not afford replacements.

By May 1983, the two adventurers found themselves in St Lucia. They had the equivalent of £4 between them, no bank accounts, no credit cards and no rich parents. One afternoon, they were wondering whether to go to the supermarket and buy some bread and cheese, or whether to go to nearby Pat's Pub for happy hour. There was a party at Pat's Pub, and among those present were three of the shareholders of Trade Wind Yacht Charters, who let it be known that the company was in dire straits and needed help. Once again, Sethia put on his best 'retired British Navy officer accent and manners'. Next day, he and Bones were both offered jobs. Sethia was asked by Trade Wind Yacht Charters to deliver a 44-foot racer-cruiser to Martinique to have some canvas work carried out, and Bones was asked to skipper one of their 47-foot yachts to the Grenadines with some guests aboard.

Bones was an infinitely more experienced and skilled yachts-man than Sethia, but ironically his boat hit a rock and he lost his job and re-located to the British Virgin Islands. Sethia sold his share of their jointly-owned yacht to Bones for £1,000 and managed to get to Martinique and back to St Lucia without breaking anything.

Back in the UK, Mrs Thatcher's success at the polls did not spell the end of the controversy over the sinking of the *Belgrano*, which continued to hound her. Thanks to Tam Dalyell, Diana Gould, and a number of distinguished journalists including Richard Norton-Taylor and the late Paul Foot, the campaign to get to the truth of the sinking was now gaining momentum rather than diminishing. Among the increasing number of those watching the exchanges between Opposition and government were, of course, the officers and crew of the submarine, and among that number was one Leading Stoker Simon O'Keeffe. Simon was getting more and more heartily sick of hearing the lies being told by the government about the circumstances surrounding the operation, of which he had been a part.

Just a matter of days after the clash between Mrs Gould and the Prime Minister, and the successful re-election of the latter, Simon and his wife took a holiday in the West Indies. There he met up with his old friend Narendra Sethia. Sethia told O'Keeffe that he had been as good as his word and had started work on a book about their experiences in the Falklands War; he would be glad to have the opinion of O'Keeffe's father on whether it was publishable.

Photocopying was not an easy matter on St Lucia, and Sethia was not happy to give O'Keeffe the original manuscript of his first draft of the book, so the two men agreed that O'Keeffe would take custody of Sethia's diary from the *Conqueror*, and would show it to his father as an example of the style and likely content of the book. Simon packed it in his luggage for the long trip back to London where, over the next few months, the row over the sinking of the *Belgrano* showed no sign whatever of fading away. Week by week, Tam Dalyell and Labour's Shadow Defence spokesman, Denzil Davies, were winkling out new and different aspects of the differences between real events and the government version of them.

Then one morning, in the autumn of 1983, Simon O'Keeffe phoned the House of Commons and asked to speak to Tam Dalyell. There was no immediate reply and so he left a message asking the MP to return his call. Later that day, Dalyell picked up a pink note from the lobby. He did not recognise the name, but returned the call anyway. O'Keeffe told Dalyell that he had been watching his campaign to get to the truth of the sinking of the *Belgrano*, and that he had some information which he might find helpful. Dalyell asked what kind of information it might be, and O'Keeffe replied that he had served on the submarine which sank the *Belgrano*.

That was enough. That same evening, Dalyell was due to appear as a guest on a radio programme at BBC Broadcasting House in Portland Place, and so he asked O'Keeffe if the two men could meet after the recording. They duly met and spoke for a few minutes, during which O'Keeffe told Dalyell that he had personal knowledge that much of the government account of the sinking was untrue. O'Keeffe did not believe that the cruiser had been a threat to the Task Force, and told Dalyell that the officers and crew on board the submarine had been surprised when they received the order to sink her.

After a few minutes of conversation, O'Keeffe reached into his bag and produced a hardback notebook, A4 size, full of hand-writing. He handed it to Dalyell. This, he told him, was a contemporaneous diary which had been kept by an officer from the *Conqueror*. In it were recorded many of the details of the times, locations and orders which Dalyell had been trying to tease out of the government. Dalyell realised straight away that this could be dynamite. Immediately he asked O'Keeffe if he could photocopy the diary. O'Keeffe agreed and the two men climbed into a black taxi which took them directly back to the House of Commons where Dalyell went in search of a photocopier.

Thirty years later, the two men have generally very similar memories of the meeting; however, their memories and accounts differ in one important respect. Dalyell believes he is perfectly clear that he asked O'Keeffe whether he had the permission of the author of the diary to hand it over to him, and that O'Keeffe confirmed that he had. O'Keeffe is equally clear that he did not tell Dalyell that he had the permission of the author. He was giving the information to Dalyell entirely of his own volition.

Whichever memory is accurate, it is common ground between them that Dalyell undertook to keep the identity of the author confidential. The two men parted company and Simon O'Keeffe went home and waited for the sound of the explosion.

Tam Dalyell was thrilled by the new turn of events. Naturally he turned straight away to the entries for the days preceding the attack on the *Belgrano*, and there it was – confirmation that the enemy ship had been detected long before the time stated by the government. Confirmation that she was sailing in the opposite direction from the Task Force. There were expressions of frustration that the submarine was not allowed to attack the *Belgrano* because she was outside of the Total Exclusion Zone. There was also a vivid and graphic account of the attack, including a reference to returning to the scene with the thought in mind of making a further attack on the destroyers.

One of Tam Dalyell's first actions was to reach for the telephone to call his old friend Arthur Gavshon. Dalyell had first come across Gavshon when the MP had been Parliamentary Private Secretary to the former Labour Housing Minister Richard Crossman. Dalyell used to stay during the week at Crossman's house at 9 Vincent Square, and Gavshon was a frequent visitor. Crossman had once told Dalyell that Arthur Gavshon was the only journalist whom he could truly trust.

Gavshon richly deserved the reputation. He had been born in Johannesburg of Jewish parents who had come originally from Lithuania. His first proper job in journalism had been as parliamentary correspondent of the *Express* in Cape Town and he also edited a magazine called *Libertas*, which was one of the few publications to campaign in favour of the embryonic struggle against apartheid. After World War II, he was offered a temporary job as a sub-editor with the Associated Press, which was to be his employer for the next forty years. He came to London, and quickly gained sufficient respect for his accuracy and integrity that he could have private off-the-record interviews with Anthony Eden, Harold Macmillan, Alec Douglas-Home, Harold Wilson and Ted Heath among others.

Gavshon specialised in national and international politics and diplomacy, and had written a well-reviewed book about the circumstances surrounding the death in a plane crash of the Secretary-General of the United Nations, Dag Hammarskjöld. Now Dalyell tried to persuade Gavshon to turn his mind and his journalistic expertise to the sinking of the Argentine cruiser *Belgrano*. At first Gavshon was reluctant; the litany of deception by the government was shocking, but much of it had already been revealed by other journalists. It was only when Dalyell told Gavshon that he had just returned from a visit to Lima, where he had learned much more detail about the Peruvian peace plan, that Gavshon's journalistic instincts began to twitch. When Dalyell also revealed that he had just been handed the personal diary of an officer from on board the submarine, Gavshon could resist no longer.

Gavshon was intrigued by the possible reasons for the catalogue of prevarication and deception. He thought it unlikely that the motive for all this deceit was merely the wish to establish the legality of the attack. He began to be much more interested in the allegation which had been circulated, and repeated by Mrs Gould on the *Nationwide* programme, that the *Belgrano* had been sunk in order to scupper the Peruvian peace plan.

He realised straight away that half of the story he needed to tell could only be found in South America – one of the few parts of the globe where he did not have first-class contacts of his own. But he knew a man who did. Desmond Rice was an oil executive who had worked in Argentina, spoke fluent Spanish, and had access to a whole range of politicians, diplomats and industrialists at the highest level. Gavshon immediately contacted him and the two men got to work.

11

The Crown Jewels

In March 1984, a new appointment was made to a key post in the Ministry of Defence – that of head of DS5. DS5 was the group within the Ministry which ensured that sensitive military operations were given approval by the relevant politicians. The name of the man appointed was Clive Ponting.

Ponting had joined the civil service in 1970 as an assistant principal – in his own words, 'the conventional way for a budding mandarin to start his career'. He climbed the ladder steadily and by September 1981 he had been promoted to assistant secretary, a position just four rungs away from the highest ranks in the service. He was still only thirty-five years old. Despite his steady rise, Clive Ponting was a rather unusual mandarin. For a start he was a grammar school boy, educated at Bristol Grammar, and he had studied history at Reading University and UCL, not Oxbridge. If all that was not bad enough, he had also recently developed an interest in Buddhism – not, he explained, that there was 'one particularly blinding moment, but the more I read about it, the more I found myself sympathetic to that point of view'. He was not your average Sir Humphrey.

When he arrived at his office as the head of DS5 in the Ministry of Defence in Whitehall, Ponting was surprised to find no fewer than four telephones on his desk. One was for ordinary phone calls, another was a direct line to members of his staff, and the other two were secure phones for making calls in which the conversation would be classified as secret. A commonplace later on among creatures as lowly as Labour MPs, the requirement to carry a 'bleeper' at all times in case of emergency marked him out in those bygone days as a member of an exotic species.

Within just two weeks of taking up the post, Clive Ponting found himself in the sixth floor office of Michael Heseltine, who had been appointed Defence Secretary just over a year earlier. Heseltine was seen as a long-term rival of Mrs Thatcher, and perhaps eventually a candidate to succeed her. He had not hitherto shown conspicuous interest in the Falklands in general, or the sinking of the *Belgrano* in particular, but now he was instructing his civil servants to compile a complete dossier of the circumstances. Downing Street and his department were under a continual bombardment of questions from Dalyell, and now also from Labour Defence spokesman Denzil Davies. Heseltine said he wanted to get to the bottom of the matter. No one knew for sure why he initiated the full report, but he was said to have remarked that 'I want to be quite sure that there isn't a Watergate in this somewhere.' The statement begged the question, if this was a Watergate, who was the President Nixon who might end up having to resign? If there was scandal, Heseltine wanted to know about it.

Ponting was given the task of producing a complete narrative of the matter, and he was to be allowed just a week to do so. He immediately called for all the signals which had been sent and received to and from Northwood, and he contacted the Foreign Office to request copies of all telegrams relating to the Peruvian peace plan. His primary task seemed to be to produce a chronology detailing the events in the South Atlantic and aligning it with events on the diplomatic front, in an attempt to ascertain whether there was any truth in the increasingly noisy allegation that the sinking had been a deliberate means of scuppering the peace proposals.

Ponting saw no reason at the time to call for any of the documents or logs from the submarine itself, and did not do so. Not the captain's log, not the signals log, not the control room log.

His request for relevant information from within his own ministry and the Navy produced an avalanche of material. His request to the Foreign Office produced precisely two telegrams. One had come from Washington and one had come from Peru, and both were marked as having been received late in the evening of 2 May (after the sinking of the *Belgrano*), and gave the 'first indications' of the Peruvian peace plan. Ponting was not able to glean any further information about the telephone calls which had certainly taken place between Washington and Lima, or indeed the conversations which had taken place face to face between Alexander Haig and Foreign Secretary Francis Pym. Later the government altered its description of these telegrams from the original 'first indications' received about the Peruvian peace plan, to 'first authoritative indications' – a distinction which experienced Whitehall watchers felt was highly significant.

Ponting's eventual report was some twenty-five pages long, and was given a top secret classification, Top Secret/Umbra/HVCCO – (Handle via Communications Intelligence Channels Only). Only six copies were made. In a conversation much later with Tam Dalyell, a senior civil servant referred to Ponting's document as 'the Crown Jewels'. The name stuck.

Now that the department had compiled what seemed to be a comprehensive chronicle of events, attention turned to how to deal with two letters which had been received asking questions about the action. While hitherto the campaign to wrest the truth from the government had been carried out more or less entirely by Tam Dalyell acting alone, now it was taken up by the Shadow Cabinet. Of the two letters received in the Ministry, one was from Dalyell and the other from Denzil Davies.

Davies's letter asked one simple question: had the *Belgrano* first been detected on 2 May, as had been reported by John Nott to the Commons, or some forty-eight hours earlier, as had reportedly been said by the captain of the submarine, Christopher Wreford-Brown?

Dalyell's letter contained nine questions, and by now it was clear to Ponting and the others that the Linlithgow MP had access to some very detailed and very accurate information. What they did not know, at the time, was that Dalyell had been carefully studying the hand-written diary kept on board the *Conqueror* by Narendra Sethia. By this time, Dalyell also had the benefit of all the new information which had been acquired by Arthur Gavshon and Desmond Rice in their recently published book, *The Sinking of the Belgrano*. The book was the first comprehensive effort to pull together all the diverse threads of the diplomatic and military activity, and it added up to a devastating blow-by-blow destruction of the government's account of events.

Ponting was summoned to a meeting in Heseltine's office which was called to discuss how to deal with these latest questions. It was attended by Heseltine himself, by his Private Secretary, Richard Mottram, the Permanent Secretary in the department, Clive Whitmore, and John Stanley, the junior minister and a former PPS to the Prime Minister. Stanley's main reason for living seemed to be to protect and support Mrs Thatcher who, he told Ponting, 'is too good for this country. The country does not deserve such an outstanding person. She is the greatest leader this country has been privileged to have this century, and that includes Winston Churchill.'

Also in attendance was the First Sea Lord, Admiral Fieldhouse, who had been Commander-in-Chief Fleet, based at Northwood, during the Falklands campaign. Fieldhouse had to leave the meeting early to fly off to America, but before he left he raised the extraordinary fact that someone in the Ministry had altered his official account of the sinking, by changing the date when the *Belgrano* was spotted to 2 May. No one present admitted to having any knowledge of it, and for the time being the matter passed without discussion.

The group then proceeded to go through the various options on how to deal with the questions from Davies and Dalyell. Not having been involved with any of the decisions himself, Heseltine seemed to be in favour of giving as much information as possible.

John Stanley was vehemently in favour of saying as little as possible, and giving as a reason that the material was classified.

Ponting pointed out that this latter course would be difficult for two reasons: one was that the material was not classified, and secondly that, if it was, it would be difficult not to prosecute the various naval officers who had talked openly about it – whose number included the captain of the submarine, Commander Wreford-Brown, and the Chief of the Defence Staff, Admiral Lord Lewin.

The meeting eventually broke up after three hours with a general agreement that the best policy was to be as open as possible, and Clive Ponting was asked to prepare a response from the Prime Minister to Denzil Davies. He spent the weekend being called backwards and forwards to the Ministry, in and out of meetings, where every nuance of every possible aspect of every answer was analysed and debated. Eventually he produced a draft which admitted for the first time that the *Belgrano* had been spotted far earlier than had previously been stated. His draft was sent to Number 10 for ratification, and was sent on to Davies, under the PM's signature, more or less as Ponting had written it. However, Ponting noted that a sentence had been added to his original stating that 'I have only been able to do this now as, with the passage of time, those events have lost some of their original operational significance.' So yes, all this time the government had been lying, but only because the interests of national security forced it to do so.

Now Ponting was told to turn his attention to answering the longer and more detailed letter from Tam Dalyell to Michael Heseltine. In it, Dalyell was asking for full details of the course, speed and position of the *Belgrano*, the precise time when she was first spotted and when she was attacked, and also for details of the various changes of course which had been plotted in the hours between. As well as giving the lie to the government's account of when and where she was located and sunk, he was of course also attempting to get at the truth behind the government's assertion that there had been 'many changes of course' on the day of the attack – which itself had been intended to give the impression that the *Belgrano* might have turned to attack the Task Force at any time.

Ponting's draft reply pointed out that much of this information had now been given by the Prime Minister to Denzil Davies but, in the new spirit of openness, he went on to give the minimum of information consistent with the known facts about the positions, course and speed of the *Belgrano*, and her changes of course. Ponting submitted his draft and expected it to be sent to the MP with few or no amendments. When he eventually saw the reply sent by Heseltine to Dalyell, he was astonished.

Thank you for your letter of 19th March asking some questions about the circumstances surrounding the sinking of the *General Belgrano*. Since you wrote this letter, you will have seen the Prime Minister's letter to Denzil Davies of 4th April and you have yourself had a further round of correspondence in your letter of 5th April and the Prime Minister's reply of 12th April. There is nothing I can usefully add.

'I had never come across anything so blatant in my fifteen years as a civil servant,' Ponting wrote later. 'It was a deliberate attempt to conceal information which could reveal that Ministers had gravely misled Parliament for the previous two years.'

This sequence of events threw Clive Ponting into a crisis of conscience. He was neither a leftie nor a radical, but he did have a firm belief that democracy depends on the government telling the truth, and being accountable to Parliament. All of his training in the civil service had taught him that, whatever else happens, Parliament must not be deliberately misled, and if it is misled inadvertently, then the first possible opportunity should be taken to set the record straight. Here was a group of ministers who had systematically misled Parliament for a period of two years since the sinking of the ship, and were seeking still to do so. He felt unable to be a party to such a cover-up, and so he took the first step along a path which would lead him eventually to the dock of number two court at the Old Bailey.

On 24 April 1984, Clive Ponting wrote a note to Tam Dalyell:

Dear Mr Dalyell,

For what I hope will be obvious reasons I cannot give you my name but I can tell you that I have full access to exactly what happened to the *Belgrano*. You have probably seen by now that Michael Heseltine has not answered any of the questions that you posed in your letter in March. This was against the advice of officials but in line with what John Stanley reccomended [*sic*]. None of the information is classified and to get answers you should put the questions down as PQs. In addition you might like to consider another linked question. Did the change in the rules of engagement on the 2 of May refer only to the *Belgrano*? Or did they go wider? When were the rules of engagement changed to allow the attack on the *25th De Mayo* was this on the 2 May or was it earlier? If so when? You are on the right track – keep going.

Upon receiving the anonymous note, Dalyell did as advised and tabled the original enquiries from his letter as Parliamentary Questions, and these again came to Ponting for a draft response. Ponting drafted replies on behalf of Defence Minister John Stanley, but the Minister was saved from having to decide whether to send them because on the same day as they were due to be tabled, Dalyell was suspended from the House of Commons for calling the Prime Minister a liar.

The transcript from Hansard is worth reproducing at some length, not only because it is entertaining, but also because it exemplifies so much of the debate which was going on every time Dalyell seized on even the most remote opportunity to raise the matter.

Mr. Dalyell

Asked the Secretary of State for Trade and Industry whether he will seek to follow up the initiatives of the then Minister of State, the right hon. Member for Enfield on his trade mission to Argentina in August 1980, after the re-establishment of civilian government in Argentina.

Mr. Tebbit

I presume that the hon. Gentleman is referring to my right hon. Friend the Member for Hertsmere (Mr. Parkinson) who, as Minister for Trade, visited Argentina in August 1980. There are no specific trade initiatives outstanding from that visit.

Mr. Dalyell

Since, according to the *Financial Times* of 12 August 1980, the right hon. Gentleman congratulated the junta on approaching its economic problems along the same lines as the Prime Minister's government, and since the right hon. Gentleman let the cat out of the bag on 'Panorama' by revealing that he knew about President Belaúnde's peace plans, with the clear implication –

Mr. Speaker

Order. This is a trade matter.

Mr. Dalyell

– with the clear implication that the Prime Minister was lying –

Mr. Speaker

Order. The hon. Gentleman will have to withdraw that word.

Mr. Dalyell

By implication, it is a matter of fact, not supposition –

Mr. Speaker

Nevertheless, the hon. Gentleman has been here long enough to know that he should not attribute lying to any right hon. or hon. Member.

Mr. Dalyell

By implication, what the right hon. Gentleman –

Mr. Speaker

Order. The hon. Gentleman knows exactly what I am getting at.

Mr. Dalyell

The proof is here. I have the text of the Prime Minister's –

Mr. Speaker

Order. I say to the hon. Gentleman, who is a very experienced Member, that this takes up time out of questions and he must withdraw that word.

Mr. Dalyell

Could we return to this at 3.30 pm, Mr. Speaker?

Mr. Speaker

Yes, in the interests of time.

Mrs Kellett-Bowman

He has to withdraw it now.

Mr. Tebbit

Since the hon. Gentleman cannot even get his facts right concerning the constituency that my right hon. Friend represents, it is unlikely that he would have his facts right, or even be able to regain his manners, during the next 20 years.

Mr. Dalyell

On a point of order, Mr. Speaker.

Mr. Speaker

It is not a point of order. Will the hon. Gentleman now please withdraw the remark that he made about the Prime Minister?

Mr. Dalyell

On a point of order, Mr. Speaker. First, I was chided by the Secretary of State for getting the name of the constituency wrong, which is an attack on the Table Office. I have spoken in the constituency of the right hon. Gentleman –

Mr. Speaker

That is as may be. We can deal with that aspect later. I must ask the hon. Gentleman now to withdraw his remark about the Prime Minister.

Mr. Dalyell

On a point of order, Mr. Speaker. [HON. MEMBERS: 'No.']

Mr. Speaker

I ask the hon. Gentleman to withdraw that remark. I shall deal with the points of order afterwards.

Mr. Dalyell

I said that by implication the Prime Minister was lying, and there is proof and evidence for it, because she told –

Mr. Speaker

Order. I am going to say to the hon. Gentleman – I very much regret this – that if he persists in refusing to obey my order I shall be forced to take other action, which I do not want to take. Will the hon. Gentleman withdraw that remark?

Mr. David Winnick (Walsall North)

rose –

Mr. Speaker

Order. I shall be forced to take other action if the hon. Gentleman does not withdraw. I do not want to do that. Will the hon. Gentleman please withdraw the remark?

Mr. Winnick

On a point of order, Mr. Speaker.

Mr. Speaker

Order.

Mr. Dalyell

There are references that I can give from Hansard which, by implication from what the right hon. Gentleman said –

Mr. Speaker

Order. I am interested, not in the implications, but that the hon. Gentleman should withdraw his remark, in which he accused a right hon. Member of lying. That is language which, as the hon. Gentleman well knows, is not tolerated in this place. I must ask the hon. Gentleman to withdraw what he said; then we shall move on to another point of order.

Mr. Dalyell

By implication, what the right hon. Member for Hertsmere (Mr. Parkinson) said suggests that the Prime Minister was lying.

Mrs Kellett-Bowman

Name him.

Mr. Speaker

Order. I must say to the hon. Gentleman – I should be grateful if he would help me – that if he persists I shall be forced to name him, and that is something that I should have the deepest reluctance to do. I ask him to withdraw his remark that the Prime Minister was lying. We shall go on to another point of order afterwards. I am not prepared to have any further arguments. This is his last warning.

Mr. Dalyell

It is the right hon. Member for Hertsmere who has implied this. That greatly saddens me.

Mr. Speaker

Order. I give the hon. Gentleman one more warning. [Interruption.] Will he withdraw that remark, please?

Mr. Dalyell

It is a matter of fact.

Mr. Speaker

I name Mr. Tam Dalyell and ask the Leader of the House to move the appropriate motion.

Motion made and Question put: that Mr. Tam Dalyell be suspended from the service of the House.– [Mr. Biffen.]

The House divided: Ayes 196, Noes 33.

It reads like something out of a Gilbert and Sullivan libretto, doesn't it? Dalyell's suspension from the House of Commons for five business days had the effect of postponing the need for a final decision on how to answer his nine questions. During that period, John Stanley continued to argue that the government should refuse to answer on the grounds of national security, even though he had been assured that none of the information which had been requested was a matter of national security.

Eventually Heseltine responded to Dalyell to the effect that, since the MP's entire purpose was to prove that the Prime Minister knew about and intended to scupper the Peruvian peace plan, and since this was not true, there was no point in continuing to respond to his detailed questions. He went on to say that there would be 'nothing to be gained' by doing so. Certainly it was true that the government had nothing to be gained by telling the truth so late in the day; whether or not Parliament had anything to be gained by hearing the truth was still to be discovered.

Now it was the turn of the House of Commons Foreign Affairs Select Committee to take the stage. The Committee decided to embark on its own inquiry into the relationship of the sinking of the *Belgrano* to the Peruvian peace plan. Having taken evidence from Francis Pym and from Baroness Young, who was Minister of State at the Foreign Office, the committee sought detailed information about the various changes in the rules of engagement which had led to the sinking of the Argentine cruiser. Once again the Ministry of Defence was thrown into something close to panic. Having registered his dissent from the wishes of ministers once too often, Ponting was now bypassed and one of his colleagues, Michael Legge, was asked to draw up a memorandum proposing how to deal with the Committee's inquiry. Legge's paper, sent to John Stanley's office on Friday 6 July, recommended that the Ministry should not provide the Foreign Affairs Committee with the information they had requested. The note argued that the rules themselves were classified, and that anyway providing them would be a complex and time-consuming exercise. In addition:

. . . a full list of changes would give more information than Ministers have been prepared to reveal so far about the *Belgrano* affair. For instance, the list of changes in the period 20th April–7th May would show that the engagement of the Argentine aircraft carrier *25th de Mayo* outside the total exclusion zone was permitted from 30th April, and that the change on the 2nd May was not restricted to *Belgrano*, but included all Argentine warships over a large area. It would also reveal that whilst the public warnings and ROE changes for the MEZ and TEZ were simultaneous, there was a delay until the 7th May before the appropriate warning was issued of the 2nd May change.

For Clive Ponting, this was the last straw. Already he had been seriously unhappy about the deceit and prevarication in relation to questions being asked by Tam Dalyell. It now seemed that withholding information which a parliamentary Select Committee was perfectly entitled to have was taking things a step too far. It was plainly preposterous to withhold the information on the grounds that it was classified – the Foreign Affairs Committee quite frequently saw classified material. It was also absurd to argue that it would take too long to assemble the information – all of it was readily available from Northwood from where all changes in the rules of engagement were transmitted to the Task Force. The real reason was that to give the list 'would give more information than Ministers have been prepared to reveal so far . . .' and this, for Ponting, was unacceptable.

Ponting spent the weekend of 14 and 15 July contemplating what to do. His training as a civil servant urged upon him his loyalty to ministers and to the department. On the other hand, he did not feel that he could remain silent while ministers deliberately misled MPs. It seemed to him to be a breach of the trust upon which our democracy depends. If honest men stand by and allow Parliament to be deceived, the whole system breaks down.

The possibility that what he was contemplating might lead him to face prosecution under Section 2 of the Official Secrets Act was of course not far from the front of Ponting's mind. On the face of it, leaking confidential information without authorisation was as clear and simple a breach as could be imagined. However, over that weekend, Ponting remembered a passage in a book he had recently read entitled *Your Disobedient Servant* by Leslie Chapman. The book included a note from the Treasury to the Commons Public Accounts Committee stating that, 'if a civil servant gave factual information without authorisation', there would be no breach of the Official Secrets Act 'if the sole publication were to the Committee of the House since the publication would in that event amount to a proceeding in Parliament and would be absolutely privileged' – in other words, would be exempted from the terms of the Act.

At no point did Ponting consider leaking information to the press. His entire concern was about the misleading of Parliament, and so it was Parliament which ought properly to be alerted to what was going on. He contemplated sending information to the Chairman of the Foreign Affairs Committee, Sir Anthony Kershaw; however, much of the detail and the significance of individual answers was quite complex, and it would not be easy for anyone other than an expert to understand all of the nuances. Ponting decided that the only person who would really 'get it' was Tam Dalyell himself.

On Monday 16 July, Clive Ponting kissed his wife Sally goodbye as usual, struggled through the commuter traffic to work as usual, and when he got there he did something which would alter the course of the rest of his life. He made a copy of the letter which he had originally drafted in response to Dalyell's list of questions, and took a copy of the memorandum which had been written by Michael Legge giving the excuses for not providing the FAC with what they had asked for. He put them in an envelope and addressed it to Tam Dalyell at the House of Commons.

Needless to say, Tam Dalyell was immediately aware of the significance of what he had been sent. He had of course been on the receiving end of the prevarications and cover-up for a period of two years, and had been subject to wide-ranging abuse for his trouble. Here for the first time was evidence that the mistreatment of Parliament went much further than routine discourtesy or dissembling. What he now held in his hands was clear evidence of a deliberate policy within government to keep the facts from elected members of the House of Commons.

Dalyell felt that he had no alternative but to draw the matter to the attention of the Chairman of the Foreign Affairs Committee, Sir Anthony Kershaw. The entire purpose of the Select Committee system is that it remains independent of government, and represents the Commons in its dealings with government departments and ministers. Dalyell fully expected Kershaw to share every iota of his own indignation, to alert the rest of the members, and then to drag Heseltine in front of the Committee to explain this extraordinary breach of parliamentary procedure. Kershaw instead did something else. He went to see Heseltine in his private office and gave him the documents which had been leaked to Dalyell.

Heseltine called in the Ministry of Defence police and immediately there was an inquiry into the source of the leak. It did not take a genius to work out the answer. Very few people indeed had been privy to the documents which had been sent to Dalyell, and only one of them had protested orally and in writing about the need to give more and better information to Parliament. Within days of the leak investigation getting under way, Ponting was called to see the inquiry team. Those involved in the following conversations gave conflicting accounts of what happened next – but it was Ponting's clear impression that if he resigned there and then, that would be the end of the matter. He readily agreed, and before he left the building he was told to come back the following week to sort out some administrative details.

On the following Monday, the second Permanent Under-Secretary at the department, Sir Ewan Broadbent, went to visit Heseltine at his home in Oxfordshire. He told his Secretary of State that the head of DS5, Clive Ponting, had confessed to his responsibility for the leak. He had not given his reasons for doing so, though it was known that he had recently gone through a difficult patch in his private life, 'in the course of which he had become a Buddhist'. The MoD Police, he told Heseltine, were not recommending prosecution – on the grounds that there had been no breach of national security, and no leak outside Parliament.

Despite this, Heseltine declared himself to be in favour of a prosecution, but said he would leave the matter to the Attorney General, Sir Michael Havers. One day later, Ponting was called to see the Head of Personnel at the Ministry, Richard Hastie Smith, who told him that there had been a change of heart in the department. His resignation was now not going to be accepted after all, and instead he would be suspended without pay while it was decided what further action might follow. Action followed quickly. Within a few days, police arrived at Ponting's house and took him to Cannon Row police station where he was finger-printed, photographed, charged and given bail. That same evening a reporter from the *Daily Mail* arrived at the front door of his house to ask Ponting's wife Sally how she felt about the fact that her husband was in trouble with the police. On the following morning Ponting appeared at Bow Street Magistrates' Court to secure an extension of his unconditional bail.

Tam Dalyell was in his bathroom at 'The Binns', shaving with a cut-throat razor, when he heard on BBC radio that a senior civil servant had been arrested for allegedly leaking confidential information to a Labour MP. The shock nearly caused him to cut his own throat. He was appalled by what Kershaw had done. While he considered what the best course of action might be, he went to his constituency surgery and declined to respond to the many enquiries from the press.

On 13 September, the day that Ponting was due to appear again before Bow Street magistrates, an item in the diary columns of the *Guardian* newspaper detailed a meeting of Whitehall information officers at which Mrs Thatcher's gung-ho press secretary, Bernard Ingham, was reported to have said that the government was 'quite set' on the prosecution, and that he hoped that 'an appropriately severe member of the judiciary would be on hand to hear the case'. Ponting's solicitor, the radical lawyer Brian Raymond, surprised everyone at the hearing by asking that reporting restrictions should be lifted. He then handed a copy of the article to the bench and said, 'If what is said is correct, and the Prime Minister's personal press secretary has asked for this matter to be listed before a severe judge, it constitutes a serious interference with the process of justice.' Ingham later apologised and said that he had been 'joking'.

12

'Why the Hell Did You Do That?'

Narendra Sethia was settling in to his new life in the West Indies. He had secured a job as a manager in a the Trade Winds yacht charter company in St Lucia, and spent the days working very hard on building up the business, and the evenings with friends sitting on the veranda and watching the sun go down. He had received back through the post the original diary which he had entrusted to Simon O'Keeffe in order to get his father's opinion; the envelope had included a note from Simon with the words 'My father thought it was very well written'. He took this to be at least reasonable encouragement, and began to consider more seriously the idea of editing the classified material in the diary and turning it into a book for publication. With this in mind, he wrote to the Ministry of Defence on 15 February 1984 indicating his intention to do so, and three weeks later he received a standard reply at his address on the island.

Three months later, in May, Sethia needed a character reference in order to renew his work visa on the island, and his thoughts turned to his old friend, Wreford-Brown's predecessor on *Conqueror*, Richard Wraith, now commander of the 3rd Submarine Squadron in Faslane. Wraith had of course commanded the *Conqueror* on the attempt to use the 'Barmaid' equipment in the Mediterranean, and he was known to regret that he had not still been on the submarine when she had gone to war.

Sethia telephoned his former boss in Faslane and Wraith readily agreed to provide the reference. Just before they said goodbye, Wraith said: 'So who has been writing to the *Guardian* then?'

The remark took Sethia by surprise and all he said was 'Not me', but failed to ask the reason for the question. However, over the following weeks, Sethia paid more than his usual scant attention to the radio news, and heard a number of references to a diary written on board the *Conqueror*. Then, during the summer, Sethia heard from another friend from the Navy that extracts from a diary – allegedly written by someone on board *Conqueror* – had been used the previous April in an episode of BBC's *Panorama* programme and repeated in the *Guardian*. The friend did not think that the words quoted sounded like Sethia's style. In any case, Sethia knew that his diary had been shown only to two people, and was now safely back in his possession, so there was no question that it could be his.

Nevertheless, week by week, there were continuing reports of the controversy. Sethia read about the efforts of the Labour MP Tam Dalyell to stir up trouble and felt angry that what had been achieved in the South Atlantic was being used for political ends. He thought little more about it and concerned himself with the charter company.

Then, in September, Trade Winds sent him back home to Britain on business, and so Sethia looked forward to the opportunity to meet with some old friends. He was staying with one of them, Emma Field, at her family home in Sussex, when his eye strayed to the front page of her father's copy of *The Times*. His attention was grabbed when he read the words '*Conqueror*' and '*Belgrano*'. He turned to the article and was amazed to find that he was reading extracts from a diary which he immediately recognised as his own.

'He appeared to be very shocked and upset,' said Emma. 'He took me outside because we were with my father, and told me what he had just seen in my father's copy of *The Times*.'

Straight away Sethia telephoned Simon O'Keeffe to ask what on earth was going on. O'Keeffe replied that he would prefer not to speak on the telephone, and suggested that the two men should meet. A few days later, on Thursday 20 September, Narendra Sethia and Simon O'Keeffe sat across the table from each other in the Dolphin Hotel in Old Portsmouth High Street. Sethia had asked Emma Field to accompany him, to be a witness to whatever was said. Sethia demanded an explanation and O'Keeffe – rather shame-facedly – admitted that one year earlier he had taken the diary to the House of Commons and shown it to Tam Dalyell.

Sethia was aghast at what he felt was a complete betrayal of trust. 'Why the hell did you do that?'

O'Keeffe explained that he felt that what they had done on the *Conqueror* had been used by the government for political ends. Week in, week out, he had read lie upon lie from the Prime Minister and Defence ministers, and had felt heartily sick about it. He had had in his hands the evidence which could put the record straight, and so he had taken Sethia's diary to show to Dalyell.

Sethia's indignation was complete. Or at least he thought it was until O'Keeffe went on to admit that he had allowed Dalyell to take the diary away in order to photocopy every single page of it. Now indignation was not quite adequate to express Sethia's feelings.

Many thoughts ran through Sethia's mind. Among them was the fact that the leaked extracts had contained some operational details which he would have edited if intended for publication. Their leak to the newspapers might well lay him open to difficulties under the Official Secrets Act. Also in his mind was the question of what his mates from the submarine would be thinking; already his former captain had wrongly come to the conclusion that Sethia had deliberately leaked his diary. Not least of his concerns was that any value that the diary might have had as the source of a book he might write was now diluted, probably beyond recall. Taking all this into account Sethia wrote again to the Ministry of Defence on 9 November stating that in view of all the controversy, he was abandoning his plan to write a book. He received a reply stating that they believed his 'decision not to publish is well-founded'.

13

'Belgrano Sensation'

It transpired that the only concession won by Sir Anthony Kershaw in exchange for grassing up Clive Ponting had been an undertaking by Michael Heseltine to come down to the Foreign Affairs Committee to give evidence. Heseltine was facing the prospect of an uncomfortable time, as the list of government lies, evasions, half-truths and distortions was a lengthy one. However, at the last minute, circumstances came to his rescue and he was spared the detailed post-mortem.

By an extraordinary coincidence, on the very day that Heseltine was due to appear before the Committee, the *Daily Mirror* broke a story under the headline '*Belgrano* Sensation'. For once the hyperbole was entirely justified. It said that the control room log from on board the submarine had disappeared. The news story stole the show.

Heseltine later reported to an astonished House of Commons that it had just been discovered that indeed it was true – the control room log from on board the *Conqueror*, for the period that included the sinking of the *Belgrano*, was missing. This was the log-book which was filled in daily by the officer of the watch, and kept in the control room, which contained details every hour of course, engine speed, depth, and a range of other operational and household matters on board the submarine. Each volume covered an individual month, and twice a year a bundle of six volumes would be sent to the Royal Navy Record Depository in Hayes. They were primarily the responsibility of the navigator, and their security level was 'Confidential'. The missing logs covered a period from April to September 1982, but had only been found to be missing when a civil servant in Heseltine's department went in search of one of them to check the answer to a question raised by an MP.

Instantly Opposition spokesman Denzil Davies speculated that there were only two possible reasons why such a log could have gone missing: one was a complete lack of professionalism on the part of the Royal Navy, and the other was that it had 'disappeared because it contained information embarrassing to the government'. Needless to say, Heseltine rejected the latter interpretation, but nonetheless said that he had set up a board of inquiry to find out what had happened.

News of the missing log-book served only to add further fuel to the fire already burning passionately inside Tam Dalyell, and his conviction that he was on the verge of exposing a national scandal. He was undoubtedly indignant about the misleading of Parliament, but more than that he was angry about the loss of life – Argentine and British – which he passionately believed had been unnecessary.

'No *Belgrano*', he reminded MPs and journalists time and time again, 'no *Sheffield*, no *Antelope*, no *Ardent*, no *Atlantic Conveyer*. No Bluff Cove. No Goose Green.'

Dalyell was determined to keep the spotlight on the discrepancies between the government's account of the sinking and the truth as revealed in the diary of the *Conqueror*'s voyage. With help from his old friend Arthur Gavshon he had already achieved a great deal in keeping the issue in the public eye. His constant badgering of Mrs Thatcher and other ministers had been reported conscientiously in the broadsheets and, much to the annoyance of the government, an episode of the BBC's *Panorama* series had been devoted to the subject. The book by Gavshon and Rice had been a best-seller, and was still in great demand. Now they were looking for a new means to keep the issue in the public consciousness, and they had one further card to play.

Simon O'Keeffe is clear that when he took Sethia's diary to the House of Commons to give to Dalyell, he told Dalyell that the diary had 'come his way' and he gave no indication that he had the authority of the author to hand it over. That was not how Dalyell remembered it. He believed that the author of the diary was aware of the use which was being made of it, and he now decided that further momentum could be given to the issue by revealing the source of all the information which had been used so effectively to undermine the government's version of events.

Dalyell met with Gavshon to try to decide the best course of action. Since *Panorama* had already given coverage to the issue, the natural choice was to go to the rival programme on ITV.

Produced by Granada Television and based in Manchester, *World in Action* had been ITV's flagship current affairs programme for twenty years. Far more tabloid in its approach than *Panorama* or other traditional current affairs series at the time, *World in Action* had a reputation for fearless investigations, and especially for challenging the establishment whenever the opportunity presented itself. In recent times the programme had threatened the very existence of Granada when a court ordered *World in Action* journalists to reveal the identity of a 'mole' who had leaked internal papers belonging to British Steel. The company had shown that it would rather close down altogether than reveal a source, and the reputation of the current affairs series was riding high. A former editor of *World in Action*, Gus (later Lord) MacDonald, summed up the programme's philosophy with a phrase which tripped neatly off the tongue – 'Our job is to comfort the afflicted, and to afflict the comfortable.' Successive Conservative governments regarded the *World in Action* team as dangerous subversives, which was a badge they wore with pride.

Arthur Gavshon was able to tell Dalyell that he had already been contacted by a member of the *World in Action* production team who was interested in the story, and it was agreed that Gavshon should go back to his contact and set the ball rolling.

*

At this point, a character makes an appearance into the story who, if this was a work of fiction, would seem too far-fetched to be plausible. Richard Morley was not an inch below six feet six tall, and was thin beyond all reason, with pointed features and hollow cheeks. Considering also his body-language and eccentric manner of dress, it might not be too melodramatic to describe his appearance as Mephistophelian.

Morley was to hit the international headlines some years later when he waged a high-profile public campaign to prevent a young boy whom he had brought to Britain from Nepal from being deported. These days, for reasons best known to himself, Morley calls himself Daijhi, and perhaps the least controversial way to describe what happened later is to quote directly from his website www.daijhi.com.

In 1984, he [Morley/Daijhi] fell seriously ill whilst trekking near Daulaghiri. A policeman, Basu Khadka, ran for 3 days to the nearest telephone in Jomson and called for help. It was a gesture that Daijhi never forgot. He offered a reward but the man refused any money. Worried about his own health, Basu asked Daijhi instead to care for his youngest son should anything befall him. And so a promise was made that shaped the destiny of everyone concerned.

A few years later Basu died and Daijhi kept his word. He returned in 1990 to search for the boy and, after a two-month trek, he eventually found Jayaram Khadka working in a Bakhtapur restaurant. The boy recognised him from a photograph his father had once given when explaining how a tall Westerner would rescue him one day. Jayaram knew that Daijhi was to be his adoptive father and so he promised to be a dutiful son to him. His new father promised in turn to care for him as his own son and the pact was sealed in a simple exchange of blood from their fingers. The spoken language was difficult between them and it was gesture that could not be mistaken by either.

Jayaram was taken to England for his education but the British government stubbornly refused to recognise his adoption. Because they would not let him stay, ironically he couldn't leave Britain either. Daijhi appealed against the decision on compassionate grounds but the legal process dragged on for years during which all chance would be lost if Jayaram ever left the country.

Their story made headlines around the world. This was no ordinary immigration dispute where the State could claim a possible cost to public funds. Fortune had smiled on Daijhi, and although he had been very poor as a young man, by 1995 he had built a very successful company.

Glossy magazines pictured the once poverty-stricken youth from the Himalayas now the son and heir to a wealthy family with a large historic estate in the heart of England. TV films portrayed the dramatic mountainside rescue and the romantic integration of a simple mountain boy into sophisticated British society. Newspapers and TV broadcasts all over the world covered the twists and turns of a story that held intensive media attention for two years. Youth magazines featured Jayaram as an icon for young girls; the tabloid press looked for sensation and portrayed the whole thing as a cult. Senior politicians from every political party were questioned on their views. The Immigration Tribunal recommended a residence visa. In a national radio poll, 80 per cent of the listeners voted that 'Jay should stay'. Even the High Court criticised Home Secretary Michael Howard on his decision. It was just before the 1997 General Election but still the government refused to give way. Then came the vote.

The Conservative Party had not suffered such humiliation at the polls for 150 years. 18 years of continuous government with a massive majority in Parliament was reduced to a broken party with barely enough members to fulfil its function as the opposition. Journalists explained the general opinion that the Party had seemed to lose human compassion. The new government certainly acted swiftly. On his first day in office, Labour Home Secretary Jack Straw reversed Howard's decision and Jayaram was finally granted residence. The whole process had taken seven years.

It is hard to know what to say.

However, all this was some way in the future. For the moment, Richard Morley was making himself known to journalists who were interested in the controversy which was now raging about the missing control room log-book from the *Conqueror*. Morley contacted the *Observer* newspaper and the *World in Action* TV programme, and told journalists that he knew the identity of the person on board the submarine who had stolen it.

Morley raised suspicions from the outset. Leaving aside his unusual appearance, his demeanour and behaviour were 'cloak and dagger' to a theatrical degree. Everything he said seemed to be in some kind of code. He peered around corners to see if he was being followed. He used euphemisms to avoid speaking a word with a military connotation. He had at one time been arrested, he said, as a suspected spy for East Germany and had been ruthlessly interrogated by agents of British Intelligence before being released. These were paranoid times, and Morley behaved like a paranoid within them. He insisted that he would not reveal the name or location of the officer but would, if terms could be agreed, personally lead the newspaper and the TV programme to meet him.

Suspicions were raised still further when, upon further enquiry, it became clear that the journey to meet the officer would be a long one – but Morley would be no more specific than to reveal that it would involve travel to another continent. Also, although he was a very close friend of the officer, he could not guarantee that the man would speak to journalists when he was finally contacted, because at the moment he had no idea that Morley was coming.

I had been a producer on the *World in Action* team for two years at this point, and was one of a number of people who had remained interested in the fall-out from the Falklands War. I met Morley in the *World in Action* office in Upper James Street in London.

'How do you know that he stole the control room log?' I asked him.

'Because he told me that he did.'

'How did he do that?' I asked. Needless to say, I was hoping that the answer might be 'in writing' so that I could ask to see the evidence.

'On the telephone,' was the reply. Morley explained that he had not used the words 'log-book' because MI5 would be bound to be listening, and the words 'log-book' would trigger recording devices. 'I asked him if he had the "written material" and he said that he did.'

'So how do you know he was talking about the log-book and not something else?'

Morley could only reiterate that he was certain that his friend was talking about the control room log.

One of the many things feared by investigative journalists is being led up the garden path, and there was much about Richard Morley which made me uncomfortable. Though there seemed to be no reason to doubt that he believed what he was saying to be true, the danger was that we were going to be led on an expensive and time-consuming wild-goose chase halfway round the world, for the purposes of reuniting Morley with an old mate who would have no idea what he was talking about. Morley was not asking for payment, but clearly his expenses would have to be met.

Meanwhile I was remaining very close to Arthur Gavshon and Tam Dalyell.

I had originally made contact with Arthur Gavshon when his book had first been published. He and I had met at his home in Highgate, and had hit it off. When Arthur called me at my home one Saturday and told me that he and Dalyell had decided to disclose to me the identity of the author of the *Conqueror* diary, I knew a scoop when I heard one. Extracts and snippets from the diary had been quoted throughout Gavshon's book, without naming the source, and had been used as background material with which to harry the government throughout Dalyell's campaign. Every journalist in Britain was interested in knowing more about the author, and here it was being handed to me on a plate.

Arthur was probably the very opposite end of the spectrum of the human species from Morley; short, slight, considered and restrained, and certainly not a man given to drama or paranoia. So when he told me that he did not wish to say the name on the telephone, I asked no questions but prepared to travel to London for a meeting. I took the train from Manchester that afternoon.

Arthur lived with his wife Audrey in a huge and rambling detached house, set back from a quiet road in Highgate. The house told you everything you needed to know about the couple; they had brought up their three daughters in it; it was full of books;the walls were covered with original works by artists, all of whom they seemed to know personally; and every piece of furniture was covered with the hair from two huge dogs on which both of them doted.

When I arrived at the house that Saturday afternoon, Arthur was clearing away leaves in his beloved garden and his dogs were running free in the grounds. Even if you were willing to brave the walk, it was never possible to get from the front gate to the front door without being covered in muddy footprints. Like most dog-lovers, Arthur and Audrey found this charming.

Arthur invited me in, made me a cup of tea, puffed on his pipe, and told me how and why he and Tam Dalyell had come to the decision to hand me this coup. He was completely frank. They had deliberately been letting the story trickle out gradually, and the time had come to give it a further shove. He and Tam were relying on me, he said, to find the best way to give a suitably high profile to this revelation.

He went on to tell me that all they had was a surname and a location – which Tam had written down on a slip of paper shortly after his meeting with Simon O'Keeffe. Only when I thought I might take a seizure from the unbearable anticipation did Arthur slowly get up and walk over to his desk, and open up his notebook. He turned a few pages and extracted a loose slip of paper, which he walked across to hand to me. I glanced at it and saw just three words.

'SETHIA. ST LUCIA.'

That was all. Arthur did not know whether Sethia was a Christian name or a surname, and Tam had written down that the author now lived on the island of St Lucia. Arthur had also had the foresight to ask Tam Dalyell to write a short note by way of introduction, which I could hand to the author of the diary as evidence of my bona fides if I was ever to meet him.

Within an hour I was on the phone to a travel agent, booking my flight for the next day – Sunday 18 November 1984. Before I boarded the plane I made a phone call to Richard Morley to ask him if the name of the man he was claiming had possession of the control room log was Sethia. He confirmed that it was.

I arrived at the airport in St Lucia, collected my suitcase, and walked out into the warm tropical sunshine. Instantly a dozen taxi-drivers began squabbling over me, several of them trying to grab my bag to secure the fare. As I had no idea where I wanted to go, I was hardly in a position to negotiate.

'Take me to the biggest hotel on the island,' I said.

He looked puzzled.

'There is only one hotel on the island.'

We drove for what seemed to be many miles between high-rise banana plantations and eventually reached what looked from the outside like a prison complex. Big iron gates were opened by uniformed security men, and the taxi carefully steered a route between the holiday-makers. I paid a small fortune to the driver, retrieved my case, and went in to the reception. Fans were whirring and cicadas were chirruping and now I felt like a character out of Graham Greene.

'Can I have a single room please?'

'Do you have your reservation?'

'I have no reservation.'

'We have no rooms.'

Yes, it turned out that this was the only international hotel on the island, and they were fully booked. Not a room or bed to be had. Consternation. The manager was called. Eventually a poor housekeeper was turfed out of her accommodation and made to share with a colleague, and I was allocated the cupboard in which she usually slept.

I started to ask if anyone knew a British former naval officer with a name that sounded like Sethia and who may have been in the Falklands War. It is a small island and within a few hours I had a clue that someone answering that description was working at a yacht charter business called Trade Winds and operating out of an office on another part of the coast. Next morning I called a cab and was driven through more miles of banana plantations, eventually emerging at a tiny village called Rodney Bay. It took no time at all to learn that what had been described as an office was in fact a metal cargo container with doors opening out onto the harbour.

I skirted the edge of the metal container and walked around to the front. Inside I could see a desk and a chair and some shelves and odds and ends. Sitting at the desk was a young man with black hair and a black beard. He seemed to be of Asian origin. He was speaking on the telephone and had a very cut-glass English accent. I nodded a greeting and watched him for a few minutes while he finished his call. Only then did I realise that I had come all this way, but had not rehearsed what I would say as an opening gambit.

'Mr Seethia?' I had mispronounced it.

Sethia's heart missed a beat (he told me later). He could tell from the lack of suntan that his visitor was a new arrival to the West Indies, and from the formal manner of the introduction, he assumed that I was from the Ministry of Defence.

When he identified himself as Mr Sethia, I handed him the letter from Tam Dalyell which Arthur had given me. On the envelope were the words 'House of Commons' and it carried a large and splendid red wax seal. Sethia looked puzzled, but he opened and read it.

House of Commons
London SW1A 0AA

Dear Mr Sethia,
I feel I know you from your elegantly written and moving diary. Equally you will know that I have been extremely discreet for over two years.

There followed some kind words about me, after which Dalyell simply said:

'. . . any help you give him would be a great service.
  With good wishes,

Tam Dalyell.

I told Sethia that I was a producer from the *World in Action* TV programme in the UK and that I wanted to ask him some questions about his diary. Immediately he was very courteous, but said that he hoped I would understand that he did not have a high opinion of journalists in general, partly because of what he felt had frequently been the misreporting of events in the Falklands. Since I had come all this way, however, the least he could do was to buy me a beer. He did and we sat in the brilliant sunshine on the veranda and chatted.

My first big surprise was to hear from Sethia that he had never authorised Simon O'Keeffe to show or give his diary to Tam Dalyell, and had only discovered long after the event that he was the source of so much of the information which had been used to wrong-foot the Prime Minister. He had given the diary to Simon simply so that he could show it to his father to see if he felt it could be the basis for a book. Sethia was angry and embarrassed about the uses to which it had been put by others.

My spirits began to sink. This man was plainly a loyal retired Navy officer who had played no willing part in trying to under-mine the government's account of the action in which he had been involved. When I reached into my bag and produced a photo-copy of a few of the pages from his hand-written diary, I could see that Sethia was shocked. As well as containing a lot of classified operational information about life on board the submarine, the diary also included a great deal that was private and intimate, and very unlikely to have been intended for wide circulation.

As a journalist working on a programme like *World in Action*, you get to meet a lot of crooks and liars. Mostly they are surprisingly easy to spot. Sethia struck me as a highly intelligent and straightforward man and I believed what he was telling me. His responses to all my questions about the war were direct: either he would answer, or he would not answer, but he did not seem to be devious or dissembling. I hesitated but decided to put my cards on the table.

'I thought you might like to give me the control room log from the *Conqueror.*'

For the second time, I could see that Sethia was genuinely shocked by what I was saying. However, he retained his composure. 'I don't have the log,' he said, 'I never have had it.' He asked me why I thought he might.

'Do you know a man called Richard Morley?' Sethia said that he did. In 1977, he told me, he had been a sub-lieutenant-under-training on a Type 12 frigate called HMS *Brighton*. Morley was one of the junior watch-keeping officers. The two men got on reasonably well because, unlike some of the other officers, Morley was unconventional and was regularly in trouble. One day, for example, when 'blowing soot' out of the boiler rooms, he had turned the ship the wrong way so that rather than carrying the soot away, the wind dumped it all over the ship's decks. It was the kind of thing that appealed to Sethia's sense of humour.

'Is there any reason why Richard Morley would be telling people that you had stolen the control room log?' I told Sethia that Morley had approached both *World in Action* and the *Observer* with the story that he knew who had stolen the log, and had been offering to escort journalists from either organisation to find the thief. Sethia seemed to be genuinely confused. He knew Morley as a practical joker – perhaps he just wanted to visit his old friend at the expense of some gullible journalists?

I asked if Sethia had ever discussed his diary with Morley – perhaps there had been some confusion caused by the reference to 'written material'. Sethia did not think he had. Morley had been among the friends he had telephoned when he arrived back at Faslane after the war, but Sethia could recall nothing in the conversation which might have been construed as suggesting that he had stolen the control room log. It was a mystery to him.

All this time my over-riding ambition was to try to persuade Sethia to come back to England with me so that we could make a programme based on his recollection of the sinking of the *Belgrano*. The fact that his diary flatly contradicted the government's account of the action was still big news, and it would be a coup for whoever located and interviewed the author. It occurred to me that by suggesting that Sethia was the culprit who had also stolen the log-book from the submarine, Morley might unwittingly have done me a favour.

'One way or another,' I said to Sethia, 'it is beginning to seem as though your name is about to be associated with the loss of the control room log.' I told him that if he was willing to come back to England with me to participate in the programme, he could also take the opportunity to clear his name.

Sethia said he was tempted by the offer but wanted a few hours to think about it. He invited me to dinner with some of his friends that evening, and we all got along well. Next morning he told me that he would come back to the UK with me to make the programme on the understanding that he could set the record straight. However, he had a few business matters which had to be cleared up, and so would not be able to travel until the end of the week.

My horror at being forced to remain on a beautiful Caribbean island for a week with a major scoop in the offing and nothing to do but to keep an eye on my interviewee can only be imagined. However, I remained concerned about Richard Morley. If he did bring another journalist to St Lucia, my exclusive story might suddenly have to be shared.

Sure enough, next day Sethia told me that he had heard from several members of his family that Richard Morley had been in touch with them, and had been leaving increasingly bizarre messages. Sethia's mother had received a telegram from Morley at her home in Barbados saying that it was 'imperative that he does not speak to others'. Other messages contained warnings that Sethia was in 'great danger', and that he should 'go to ground', and especially that he should not speak to any reporters. In none of the messages did Morley indicate that he was trying to bring one with him. My sources back in London let me know that David Leigh of the *Observer* had decided to take Morley at his word, and was planning to accompany him on a trip to locate the thief. However, it was becoming obvious from his ever-more-frantic questions to Sethia's relatives that Morley did not know exactly where his old friend was.

Sethia learned from messages left by Morley with friends that he had travelled to Amsterdam with Leigh, and that they were preparing to leave for Martinique. He and I speculated on what this could mean. Perhaps Morley knew only that Sethia was in the West Indies and so was closing the gap pending answers to his various enquiries. Or maybe Morley knew that Sethia was on St Lucia but had not been able to fly there directly, and was therefore travelling via Amsterdam and Martinique. This seemed less likely. Even so, Sethia and I worked out that even if Morley and Leigh were to fly directly to St Lucia, they would arrive after we had returned to London.

I had then, and still have now, great respect for David Leigh, but at this point he was competition. I got a number for him in Amsterdam, called and spoke to him. I said that I could not say how or why I knew it, but that if he made the trip he was currently planning, he would be wasting his time. He was competition for me and I was also competition for him, so naturally he did not believe me. Despite my very best efforts, he assumed that I was merely trying to put him off the scent, and I failed to convince him.

In common with a large number of submariners before and since, Sethia knew Morley as someone who enjoyed a practical joke. He strongly suspected that this was what was going on here, but he was angry that his former colleague and friend had been circulating a suggestion that he was involved in a criminal act which could land him in prison. What if Sethia had stolen the log, as Morley appeared to believe? Wouldn't Morley's betrayal be likely to lead to Sethia's arrest?

By now he was also beginning to get fed up with the increasingly hysterical messages being left with his various friends and relatives. Both of Sethia's brothers, Babulal and Krishna, were surgeons and their addresses were therefore registered with the General Medical Council, though one brother had recently moved house and had not yet informed the GMC of his change of address. Morley suggested that this had been part of a deliberate subterfuge to cover tracks that might lead to Narendra.

Sethia was also angry that at no point had Morley revealed or sent a message that he was bringing David Leigh with him. He decided to play a practical joke of his own which might teach Morley a lesson. He telephoned a girlfriend who lived in Miami and asked her to tell callers that he was staying with her, but that he was not home at that moment. He then told his friends and family to give her telephone number to Morley or any reporters who were trying to get in touch with him. By now it was time for us to pack our bags and catch a plane back to England.

Before we left St Lucia, Sethia decided to call Morley and invited me to listen to the conversation. In it, Morley made no mention of the log-book, either by name or any of his other euphemisms. He also gave no indication to Sethia that he was bringing a journalist to see him. Indeed, nothing in the conversation provided corroboration for the story he had earlier told me. It reinforced my earlier concerns.

It later emerged that Morley and Leigh landed in Martinique, where Morley made increasingly frenzied attempts to contact Sethia. Eventually he received the message that Sethia had gone to stay with a girlfriend in Miami. At this point Leigh was becoming more and more impatient with Morley and decided that they should split up. Leigh arrived at the girlfriend's house in Miami, only to be told that Sethia had recently left for Pasadena! Now in a terrible temper, and with his deadline fast approaching, Leigh returned to London to write a story headlined '*Conqueror* Officer's War Diary Revealed'. The newspaper was not yet quite ready to name Sethia, but clearly identified him as a former officer from the *Conqueror* who had retired in 1982 and was 'running a business in the Caribbean'. The newspaper printed extended passages from Sethia's diary, and in that and subsequent editions indicated that he had indeed taken documents from the *Conqueror*.

Meanwhile, Sethia and I had exchanged the tropical sunshine and balmy breezes of St Lucia for the cold and rain and howling winds of Manchester. We had become friends in the few days that we had been together, and so I asked him to stay at my house in Heaton Moor. If I am honest, I also knew that a good many journalists were looking for him, as well as perhaps the Ministry of Defence. I wanted to get my interview in the can before events might intervene.

Sethia proved to be a very good interviewee. He was calm and composed, and with his black moustache and beard, he looked the part and had the authority of a Royal Navy officer. When he said that he did not believe that the *Belgrano* was an imminent threat to the Task Force, it carried weight.

Sethia re-affirmed that the *Belgrano* was outside the Total Exclusion Zone when she was attacked, and that therefore would have been entitled to feel safe. He thought the Argentines should have been given a specific warning, and deeply regretted the loss of life. By now he had been publicly accused of stealing the control room log from the *Conqueror*, and so I asked him directly on camera if this was true. He replied that it was not. I asked if he had any knowledge of what had happened to it, and he replied that he did not.

The interview safely recorded, Sethia and I sat down to discuss what he should do next. Aside from his anger and astonishment that the *Observer* had accused him of theft and had quoted from his diary without permission, Sethia was preoccupied with one line from the story: the 'head of naval security has been questioning the officer's friends as to his whereabouts'. Sethia had given the MoD his current address in St Lucia some months earlier when he had notified them of his intention to write a book. There was no mystery as to his whereabouts, but the hint of a manhunt by security forces appeared to give credence to his presumed guilt.

Later that day Sethia spoke to his older brother and was told that Babulal had received a call from the Director of Naval Security, Rear Admiral William Lang. By chance, Babulal had once dated Lang's daughter, and now Lang said that he was trying to contact Narendra. Sethia returned the call to Lang at his home. The two men had a friendly and casual chat and agreed to meet at the MoD the following Thursday.

Before he left Manchester, I arranged for Sethia to meet a group of people of whom he knew almost nothing, but who knew his most intimate thoughts and feelings through having read his personal diary. The meeting was arranged at a hotel owned by a CND activist, Lee Chadwick. Attending were Tam Dalyell, Arthur Gavshon, and the Professor of Peace Studies at Bradford University, Paul Rogers. Despite the events of recent days, Sethia was still very much a loyal retired naval officer, and so this was unusual company for him.

Dalyell seemed to be genuinely surprised and upset when he learned from Sethia that he had not given permission for his diary to be handed over. The MP was adamant that the person who had brought it to him had assured him that he had the author's permission to do so. He, in return, had remained discreet about Sethia's identity. Initially he had given Sethia's name only to Arthur Gavshon, and only then in conditions of great secrecy. Gavshon had used Sethia's diary as one source for the book he had written with Desmond Rice, which had played such a huge part in fuelling the long-running controversy. Although the diary had not been overtly identified in the book, Gavshon was also upset at having unwittingly reproduced parts of it without the author's permission.

As Sethia listened to this group's apparently encyclopaedic knowledge of the events surrounding the sinking of the *Belgrano*, he felt even more deeply disturbed about the discrepancies between the official account of the action and his own knowledge of the truth. The errors and omissions were not, for the most part, matters affecting national security – with which Sethia would have had total sympathy. Instead they concerned only events which could be politically embarrassing to the government. Sethia felt that he was getting a crash course in how the government conducts its business. Later that week he was to learn even more.

For the previous three weeks, the board of inquiry into the loss of the control room log had been doing its work. It had interviewed nearly every one of the officers and men from on board the submarine who had had contact with the log-book. When Narendra Sethia found himself standing to attention in the office of the Director of Naval Security at the Ministry of Defence at 4.30 on Thursday 29 November 1984, the conclusions of the board of inquiry had already been written.

Admiral Lang was wearing a civilian suit and the Navy commander sitting next to him had pen poised, ready to take notes. On the desk in front of them was a thick file in a red folder which is the standard colour for 'Top Secret' material. Lang opened it and, to Sethia's amazement, produced a complete copy of his diary.

'Do you recognise this as your diary?' he asked.

He handed over the photocopied pages. Each of them had been stamped 'Top Secret Umbra'. Sethia was amazed that his collection of mostly highly personal notes had been given so sensitive a security classification. He acknowledged that the diary was his.

Lang's next question came as no great surprise. Had Sethia stolen the control room log? Sethia replied that he had not. Lang then returned to the diary and began flicking through the pages. Sethia assumed that Lang would be concerned about him having recorded the submarine's depth, course and speed, all of which could theoretically be of value to the enemy. The next question therefore surprised him.

'Who is P?'

Sethia thought for a moment. Then he remembered. It was an initial that he had used when referring to a naval friend who had been on leave when the submarine had departed for the South Atlantic. Lang's next question took Sethia totally by surprise.

'Do you realise that homosexuality is illegal in the Navy?'

Sethia could only stare back in amazement. He felt himself begin to tremble with anger. Without looking up, Lang read from the diary: 'I keep having nightmares about the food running out and daydreams about P. Can't help myself.' Now Lang looked up at Sethia: 'Did you have a homosexual relationship with P?'

The commander stopped taking notes and glanced at Sethia, who continued to sit in silent disbelief. Was he really sitting in the Ministry of Defence, two years after having left the Navy, being asked if he was homosexual? Even if the suggestion had been true, what on earth could this have to do with the Director of Naval Security or the matter in hand? Finally Sethia was sufficiently in control to trust himself to speak.

'I wish to go on record that I resent that question and find you rather disgusting. As far as I am concerned, the interview is over.' The commander turned to Lang, eyebrows raised, but the Director of Naval Security seemed unable to look Sethia in the face. Sethia remained where he was, still utterly furious.

Lang pressed a buzzer under his desk and the meeting was interrupted by another man dressed in civilian clothes. Lang introduced him.

'Mr Sethia, this is Detective Chief Superintendent Hardy. He will be continuing this interview.'

With a glare at Lang and the commander, Sethia left the office without speaking further, and a few minutes later found himself in a car being driven by another policeman who was introduced as Detective Sergeant Mike Ashdown. Sethia's afternoon of surprises was not over. These men were from the Serious Crime Squad, and they were driving him to New Scotland Yard.

It seemed to Sethia that Hardy's approach was far more professional than that of the Director of Naval Security and it was immediately apparent that the detective was a good deal more experienced at putting people at their ease. Hardy asked Sethia a lot of questions about his diary, and also directly whether he had stolen the log-book from HMS *Conqueror*. Sethia found it rather undermining when Hardy reached into a file and produced the actual copy of the Official Secrets Act which Sethia had signed. Hardy reminded Sethia that merely recording classified information in his diary was technically a breach of the OSA, and the former officer admitted that he knew this to be the case.

Although the experience was far from comfortable, Sethia was feeling confident of his ground. He knew that technically he should not have kept a diary, but he had frequently written it directly under the gaze of the submarine captain, and he could scarcely be in trouble merely for that. He knew that he had played no part in having elements of it leaked to MPs or to the press, and if called upon to do so, he could prove it. He also knew that he had not stolen the log-book from the *Conqueror*, and he felt confident that sooner or later this would also be proven.

But the conversation then took a surprising direction.

Hardy drew attention to a section of Sethia's diary in which he admitted to taking away a number of charts which would assist him on his proposed sailing trip around the world. Sethia's mind began to race over what could be coming next. There must be very few Navy sailors anywhere in the world who could put hand on heart and say that they had never at some time taken any item of service property for their own use. In the case of charts, it had infuriated a lot of service personnel that relatively expensive navigational charts which had gone out of date and therefore were of no further use to the Navy had routinely been burned rather than sold off cheaply to people who could make use of them. There was nothing secret or classified about them – they were merely navigational charts of the sea-routes of the world. This being so, Sethia had been glad to accept a number of them from the friendly navigator on the *Conqueror*.

The line of Hardy's questioning, however, seemed to indicate that this was being regarded as a far from trivial offence, and that there was a distinct possibility that Sethia might find himself being prosecuted for removing Ministry of Defence property. Still relatively naive as he was at this point, the possible significance of this was not yet clear to Sethia.

The interview lasted for two hours, during which Sergeant Ashdown wrote page after page of Sethia's statement and required him to sign each one. It was 7.00 p.m. when finally he was allowed to leave New Scotland Yard.

Sethia had taken the opportunity of the unexpected visit to London to arrange to meet Emma Field. He had been at her parents' house when he had first discovered that his diary had been leaked to the press, and she had accompanied him to hear O'Keeffe's confession that he had handed Sethia's diary to Tam Dalyell. Emma had been due to attend a private dinner party in the back room of a Thai restaurant in the Fulham Road, and so she took Sethia along with her. Also in the party was a man whom Sethia later remembered as a 'very large, very friendly, very black Nigerian'. The man developed an instant fancy for Emma, and over the course of a long and drunken evening, took to leaning across to Sethia to whisper conspiratorially to him the details of his amorous intentions towards her. It was all light-hearted fun and everyone had a pleasant evening.

It was only five days afterwards that Sethia learned that this Nigerian, who was a former church minister and now a law student, had later been arrested by the police and taken into custody to be questioned about his conversation with Sethia. He was shown a seating plan of the restaurant and asked to confirm where everyone had been sitting. Clearly someone, somewhere, suspected that Sethia was passing military secrets to the enemy. Sethia was horrified.

On the following day, Friday 30 November, Michael Heseltine was in a position to report to the House of Commons the results of the board of inquiry into the missing log-book. The interview with Sethia must, therefore, have been its very last act before finalising its report. Heseltine talked MPs through what the inquiry had determined to be the range of possible solutions to the puzzle.

There are several possible causes for the loss. Loss in transit between the submarine and the Ministry of Defence records office at Hayes, mishandling at Hayes, and dispatch to an incorrect address are all considered to be unlikely. Indeed, there is no proof that the logs ever left HMS *Conqueror*. Before the ship's company moved out of the submarine for the refit, a considerable amount of material, which was no longer required, was placed in bags and incinerated in Devonport dockyard. The possibility that the logs were inadvertently destroyed at this time cannot be ruled out. They could also have been mishandled and put in an unmarked or incorrectly addressed envelope or left in a locker which has since been disposed of; deliberately and unlawfully destroyed, although there is no evidence to suggest this; or removed as souvenirs or for their assumed political or financial value.

In a nutshell, after three weeks in which the inquiry had interviewed just about every officer and rating on board the submarine whose job involved going near the control room log, the inquiry was evidently no wiser about what had happened to it. Heseltine continued:

I have referred the matter to the Director of Public Prosecutions and I understand that he has asked the Metropolitan Police to conduct an investigation.

Hence, presumably, Sethia's interview the previous day with Hardy and Ashdown.

In view of all the publicity there had been in the press and on TV involving Sethia's diary, Heseltine was then asked whether the officer in question was a suspect, and whether any prosecution was envisaged under the terms of the Official Secrets Act. Heseltine replied that:

A copy of a diary which apparently was kept by a member of the crew of HMS *Conqueror* is in the possession of my Department. The diary contains classified information and it appears that its contents have been communicated to persons not authorized to receive such information. This constitutes a *prima facie* breach of the Official Secrets Acts. In the circumstances of this case my Department considered that it was a matter for reference to the Director of Public Prosecutions.

All this seemed irregular to say the least, and perhaps shambolic would be a better description. For those who understood all the implications, the most startling thing of all was Heseltine's revelation that the board of inquiry had reported that 'It is clear that the logs were compiled and probably remained on board the submarine until October or November 1982.' Since Narendra Sethia had left the *Conqueror* for the last time in July 1982, and the missing logs had remained on board the submarine until October or November 1982, on the face of it, it was not possible for him to have stolen them. Sethia had left the submarine before the log-books went missing. And since this finding of the inquiry must surely have been available to Admiral Lang when he had interrogated Sethia on the previous day, perhaps it is unsurprising that the Admiral had spent so little time on the subject of the missing log. He was asking Sethia whether he had taken the control room log even though he must have known that it was all but impossible for him to have stolen it!

The board of inquiry had strained every sinew to try to find a way to make it possible to pin the blame on Sethia. Their full report, released to this author under the Freedom of Information Act twenty-eight years after it was produced, identifies a total of five officers and crewmen of the *Conqueror* who could conceivably have taken the logs or otherwise been responsible for their loss. The report goes through the possible culprits one by one, and attributes various degrees of possibility that each individual stole it. These include the captain, Wreford-Brown; the XO, Tim McClement; the navigator, Jonty Powis; and Petty Officer William Guinea, who was responsible, under Powis, for sending off the logs. Surprisingly, those interviewed did not include Sethia's replacement as supply officer on *Conqueror*, Mike Screech. By the time of the inquiry Screech had gone on to his next posting and, despite the fact that he had access to, and sometimes made entries into the control room log, was never asked if he knew about its whereabouts.

When it considers Narendra Sethia the report markedly departs from the very formal style which characterises the rest of the text. With the implied distaste which has been perfected over centuries of report-writing and minute-taking in Whitehall, it says of Sethia that it was 'well-known that he had a flair for journalism. He also kept a very detailed narrative-type diary during the Falklands campaign.' If a flair for journalism did not, in itself, tell the reader all he or she needed to know, worse was the come. 'Sethia also embellished the logs with cartoons and drawings which may have increased the log's souvenir value, especially to Sethia himself.'

So not only was Sethia a budding journalist, he was also an artist. It was practically time to reach for the manacles, and clearly this is what would have happened, but for the irritating detail which followed.

Had the logs April to June '82 only disappeared, Sethia would have been considered a most likely suspect. However [and you can almost smell the disappointment], he left the Navy in August 1982 and access to the July to September '82 logs would have been difficult unless they were passed on by a member still serving on the *Conqueror*.'

Aha – there was hope yet! Indeed, here is the *coup de grace*:

... 'Sethia was known to have more contact with junior rates than is normal. The possibility of there being two separate losses [April–June and June–September 1982] is considered remote. It is considered unlikely that he actually removed the logs himself. But his further involvement, including the possibility that he has them now, cannot be ruled out.'

All of which may explain why Sethia's every move while in London was being watched and reported on, as was every move made by those he met.

On Sunday 2 December 1984, Narendra Sethia sat down with his friend Emma for a farewell breakfast at the Grosvenor House in Park Lane. In front of them were the newspaper headlines. '*Conqueror* Diarist in Yard Quiz' was the *Observer* headline. 'Writer of *Belgrano* diary is questioned at Yard' reported the *Sunday Telegraph*. There were others in similar vein. Sethia sat quietly and wondered how, merely by keeping a personal diary and speaking honestly about its contents, he had managed to find himself in the centre of a national controversy. He ate very little breakfast and that afternoon took the flight back to St Lucia.

Meanwhile, I had been hard at work at Granada Television in Manchester, putting together the episode of *World in Action* in which Sethia was due to appear. It was a rare and genuine old-fashioned scoop. Everyone was talking about the author of the *Conqueror* diary, and here he was in the flesh. The programme reconstructed the events involved in sinking the *Belgrano*, and Sethia's interview was put into context by interviews with Professor Paul Rogers from Bradford, Arthur Gavshon and Tam Dalyell. On that occasion, no one from the Navy or the government would agree to be interviewed.

After the broadcast, the Chairman of the Conservative Party, John Selwyn Gummer, wrote a letter of complaint to the Chairman of the Independent Broadcasting Authority, Lord Thomson. In it he said that 'the main thrust of the programme was to depict Government Ministers as acting deceitfully and/or foolishly over the sinking of the *Belgrano*,' and that 'In fact there is not a scintilla of evidence to support these contentions.' Some months later I produced another programme on the subject, this time reporting the main finding of the House of Commons Select Committee in which the Labour group described the sinking as 'a hasty and unjustifiable decision to risk many lives and a possible disaster, in order to ensure the life of an administration which was itself palpably negligent', and even the Conservative group concluded that, 'As a result of the approach adopted by Ministers, the House remained for too long in ignorance of information which members were perfectly entitled to request . . . to that extent the House was misled.'

Back in St Lucia, Sethia received a number of supportive and sympathetic letters from his former colleagues from the submarine who had assumed that he had been disloyal, but had only fully understood the truth of his position when the *World in Action* programme had been broadcast. He shrugged his shoulders and wondered if now he would be allowed to get on with the rest of his life.

14

'There but for the Grace of God'

Opinion among those who took an interest now divided sharply between those who approved of the government's actions in the Falklands and regarded its critics as disloyal or subversive, and those who felt uncomfortable about the growing evidence that the official version of events had been distorted. The next significant episode in the contest between them was to be the trial of Clive Ponting under Section 2 of the Official Secrets Act. The case was due to come to court at the end of January 1985, and the actions of the prosecution suggested that its strategy was to paint the defendant as a traitor who was trying to thwart the legitimate objectives of the democratically elected government.

If Ponting was to argue a case that Parliament had been deceived, he needed to be able to contrast the statements that had been made by the government to MPs with the chronology as he had collected and presented it. His defence team therefore requested that his report on events surrounding the sinking of the *Belgrano* – the so-called 'Crown Jewels' – should be made available as evidence. Shortly before the trial began, it was announced that, such was the sensitive nature of some of the material, parts of the trial would have to be held 'in camera' – that is to say, away from the press and the public and behind closed doors. This of course heightened the impression that Ponting was a spy who had leaked classified information which could endanger the state, rather than a whistle-blower who reacted against the misleading of elected representatives in a democracy. Furthermore, individual members of the jury would also need to be vetted, thereby adding yet another layer to the intrigue.

At this stage, the only element of the 'Crown Jewels' which could conceivably be regarded as sensitive was the information regarding the timing of the interception and receipt of Argentine signals. It was no secret that we were able to read such signals – courtesy of Ted Rowlands MP in the House of Commons debate of 4 April 1982. Similarly the content of the intercepted signals could scarcely be secret – presumably the Argentines already knew what they had said and when they had said it. Perhaps knowledge of the speed of receipt and decoding might give succour to the enemy. For this reason, Ponting's defence team suggested that sensitive information of this kind might be summarised. It was a price worth paying to remove the taint of treachery which an in-camera trial would otherwise conjure up.

In the House of Commons, Liberal Leader David Steel asked the Prime Minister: 'Last October, in the committal proceedings against Clive Ponting, the Prosecution reported that no national security had been damaged by his actions. In view of that, why is he subject to the East European-type secret trial now?' It was a good question, and was followed by a good answer.

'The full trial starts on Monday and the matter is sub-judice,' replied the Prime Minister. 'The courts are independent of Parliament and must remain so.' The careful observer of events over the following weeks might have wondered.

The trial got under way in court number 2 of the Old Bailey at 10.30 on 28 January 1985. The two weeks of argument would come down to a question of how the 'interests of the state' should be defined. Were the interests of the state to be considered to be 'the interests of the government of the day', as the prosecution suggested, or should the jury accept a wider definition, in which the interests of the state are represented by Parliament and society as a whole? And, specifically, if a government decided to mislead Parliament, was a civil servant who leaked the fact to MPs a traitor or a hero? Day after day, reports of the case filled the national and international news headlines.

Back in St Lucia, and busily running the Trade Winds yacht charter business based at Rodney Bay, Narendra Sethia was doing his best to put behind him everything to do with the *Belgrano*, the diary, and the British press. Sitting watching the waves ripple gently into the harbour just a few yards from his office was a good way to do it. The icy waters of the South Atlantic and the bleak winter days in London both seemed a world away.

In spite of himself, he could not help but take an interest in the prosecution under the Official Secrets Act of a Whitehall civil servant for having leaked classified material. He considered the case in relation to his own situation. There was no doubt that Sethia's diary contained material which was every bit as secret and sensitive as the material leaked by Ponting to Tam Dalyell. There was equally no doubt that as a Navy officer, he had every bit as much duty to comply with the OSA as did a senior civil servant. Sethia had not leaked the material, but even keeping a diary was technically an offence, and handing it over to be shown to someone not authorised to see it seemed to offer a cut and dried case to an unsympathetic prosecutor or his political masters. When he tuned into the BBC World Service and heard the daily reports of the unfolding case against Ponting, Sethia's thoughts were simply, 'There, but for the grace of God, go I.'

In the Old Bailey in London, the prosecution had put its case in full and the defence was coming to a close. It was Friday 8 February, and on the following Monday the judge would complete his summing up and the jury would go out to consider its verdict. As he heard the news reports of the progress of the case, it seemed likely to Sethia – much as it did to Clive Ponting – that the former civil servant was destined for a prison sentence.

Despite the heat of the day the thought made him shudder and, just as he did so, he looked up and saw two men walking towards his office. He had a brief hallucinatory moment as he realised that he had seen them before. It was none other than Detective Chief Superintendent Ron Hardy and Detective Sergeant Mike Ashdown from the Serious Crime Squad. Both men had broad smiles on their faces, but Sethia thought they also looked embarrassed.

He wondered whether he had been premature in counting his blessings at not standing in the same place as Clive Ponting was currently standing. Had these two men come to arrest him? His mind quickly went over the questions of jurisdiction and extradition, and he realised that he did not know the answers.

The three men chatted for a few minutes about the flight and the weather, and then the visitors got down to business. Hardy reminded Sethia that he was still under caution from their last meeting the previous November, and began to ask a series of questions about his diary. How had it come to be written? How did it come to have been leaked? Where was it now?

As a matter of fact, at that moment the original diary was beneath the desk in front of Sethia, about four inches from his ankle; however, the last thing he wanted to do was to hand it to Hardy and Ashdown. He therefore told the two men that he had become so sick and tired of the whole saga that he had taken a boat out one day and thrown the diary into the sea.

'Who was with you at the time?' asked Hardy.

'I was on my own,' replied Sethia. The former Navy officer strongly doubted that the policemen believed him, but at that point there was little that anyone could do about it.

Hardy mentioned the control room log-book only briefly, and when Sethia repeated his denial that he had stolen it or knew of its whereabouts, the detective gave no indication of suspicion or disbelief. Indeed, Hardy must undoubtedly have read the same report which had earlier gone to Heseltine, which concluded that it was all but impossible that Sethia could have stolen it.

At this point, Hardy asked Sethia again about some admissions that had been made in the diary about having removed a number of trivial items of Navy property from the submarine. All the time the conversation seemed to Sethia to be remarkably casual and friendly, especially considering that the two men had travelled

5,000 miles to talk to him. Sethia was still wondering what the point of the exercise would turn out to be, when Hardy paused and put down his notebook.

'Seth, do you know what would really be helpful?' he said. 'If you had any of these bits and pieces with you, and you handed them over for me to take back to England. It would show that you had been trying to cooperate which would be useful for you. Do you have any Ministry of Defence property on the island? After all,' he said, 'you wouldn't want me to get a search warrant.'

Sethia needed no further persuasion. Leaving the two coppers on the scorching hot veranda sipping beer, he set off on the two-mile drive to the company storeroom to see whether he had anything which had originally belonged to the Royal Navy. After an exhaustive search he found three unclassified charts of northern Spain, a copy of *The Sailmaker's Handbook*, two unmarked ledgers, and an orange plastic waterproof holdall used by the RAF for dropping mail to the submarine. He put them in the car and returned to give them to Hardy and Ashdown. They seemed delighted.

I told Hardy that I could not recover the charts that I had appropriated from the submarine because subsequently I had given them to the owner of the Charthouse Restaurant and they were now varnished onto the table tops – so Hardy and Ashdown accompanied me to the restaurant so that they could inspect the table tops and ensure that they did not contain classified entrées.

All good-humoured stuff, so much so that the three men agreed to meet that night in a local bar for a few drinks, during which Hardy told Sethia that not for a moment did he think that he had stolen the control room log; indeed, he was heartily sick to death of the whole inquiry. He had come, he told Sethia, specifically at the request of the Director of Public Prosecutions.

What Hardy did not tell Sethia was that earlier that evening, he had returned to room 6 at the Halcyon Hotel in the north of the island and placed a call to the Chief Crime Correspondent of the *Mail on Sunday*. Chester Stern had recently been recruited to the newspaper from his job as head of the Press Bureau at New Scotland Yard. Stern had already heard that Hardy was off on a trip to St Lucia, but until his home telephone rang that evening, he did not know the reason.

'Do you know where I am?' asked Hardy.

'Yes I think I do,' said Stern.

Stern says that Hardy wanted to tip him off to the fact that he had interviewed Narendra Sethia, and that he had recovered what he described as 'certain navigational documents and equipment'. Stern asked if by 'navigational documents' Hardy was referring to the control room log. Hardy replied that he did not want to use those words, but would prefer to stick with the phrase 'navigational documents'.

Stern went to work on the Saturday morning and informed his editor, Stewart Steven, of the conversation. Naturally Steven wanted to know whether the control room log had been seized or not, and instructed Stern to call Hardy back. Stern telephoned Hardy at his hotel, and asked the detective directly whether he had recovered the stolen control room log. Hardy would neither confirm nor deny the specific question. However, he repeated that he had recovered 'naval navigational documents' and told Stern that he had enough evidence to recommend to the DPP that Sethia should be prosecuted for theft. Stern is clear that he gave Hardy many opportunities to steer him away from the allegation that he had recovered the control room log, but that he did not do so. Stern wrote the story in the same ambiguous terms in which it had been conveyed to him, only to have his editor, Stewart Steven, re-write it under Stern's by-line, as if the material recovered from Sethia did include the log, which was not what Hardy had told Stern.

Next day, Sunday 10 February, the day before the jury in the Ponting trial was due to consider its verdict, Sethia woke at 7.00 a.m. and turned on the BBC World Service.

Scotland Yard has confirmed that two detectives have flown to the West Indies in connection with the search for the missing log-book of the submarine HMS *Conqueror*, which sank the Argentine cruiser *General Belgrano* during the Falklands War; and there are reports this morning that the log-book may actually have been recovered.

Alarmed and confused, Sethia immediately telephoned friends in England who read out that morning's newspaper headlines. '*Conqueror* Log Seized' screamed the *Mail on Sunday* headline. 'The log, and other papers described as "navigational books" have been recovered and will be returned to London in the next few days.' '*Conqueror* Log: Yard men fly to the Caribbean' announced the *Sunday Telegraph*. Most of the national newspapers carried stories in a similar vein, a number of them indicating that the log had indeed been recovered.

Now very angry, Sethia telephoned Hardy at the Halcyon Hotel. The policeman claimed to have no idea how the story came to be leaked in such a way, and assured Sethia that he personally had nothing to do with the allegation that he had removed the log. Chester Stern later signed an affidavit confirming that he had obtained most of his story from the detective.

Sethia went into his office where the phone was ringing off the hook with calls from reporters, and later that day a film crew from ITN landed on the island. One of the company's sports reporters, Jeremy Thompson, had been on shift on a quiet Sunday and had been ordered onto the plane. Thompson found Sethia at the Charthouse Bar close to Reduit Beach in St Lucia, and recorded an interview with him in which he denied any knowledge of the log-book. Cameraman Ronnie Carrington shot footage of two policemen looking out of place and not quite sure what they were doing on a sun-drenched island. Neither detective would agree to be interviewed on camera, but Hardy gave an off-the-record briefing to Thompson in which he confirmed that he had obtained nothing of any significance from the submarine, and that this trip was merely for the purposes of 'routine questioning'.

Mindful of his day job, Thompson had just enough time for a social meeting with the legendary St Lucian and West Indian cricket commentator Reds Perreira before flying to Barbados to get his report on the satellite to make his deadline.

As Sethia parried the calls from friends, relatives and reporters that day, he wondered what on earth had persuaded Hardy and Ashdown to come all this way, at the expense of the taxpayer, to go through the motions of asking some questions about the control room log. What could possibly be the point of this anxiety to repossess some junk which had been taken from the submarine? And why come now, with no warning?

Then light dawned. The following day in London the jury in the trial of Clive Ponting under the Official Secrets Act was due to be sent out to consider its verdict. The headlines were now full of another 'traitor' to the government being brought to book. If anyone had suspected the government of 'losing' the log-book because it contained information embarrassing to its account of the sinking of the *Belgrano*, their suspicions were laid to rest – at least for the moment. The thief had been found. He was hiding on a tropical island thousands of miles away.

The *Mail on Sunday* could not have made the government's case more lucidly if it had been dictated by Bernard Ingham:

Previous suggestions that the log-book, which mysteriously disappeared, had been sold to the Russians can now be discounted. So can the idea that it was spirited away by Royal Navy officers because it would prove embarrassing.

The newspaper went on to debunk the line taken by the conspiracy theorists:

The implication of the[ir] story was clear; Whitehall was engaged in a massive cover-up on the true direction and position of the *Belgrano* when it was attacked – and the Terms of Engagement under which the *Conqueror* operated were not those officially published at the time. If there were variations between what Ministers and officials had been saying and what has actually occurred, the one place to establish this absolutely would be in the log.

Now that the log had been found, in the possession of a disenchanted former Navy officer, any suspicion of a government cover-up could be discounted.

It followed that Ponting's claim that he was simply exposing material which was embarrassing for the government, was spurious: there had been nothing to hide. At the Old Bailey a disloyal civil servant was being taught a lesson, and on the other side of the world another subversive was being brought to justice. Her Majesty's Government was dealing with all the traitors in one go. The effect on the Ponting jury had no doubt been carefully calculated.

Back in Britain, in some quarters it took only a day for the penny to drop. On page 2 of the *Daily Mirror* the following morning, under a comment piece about Mrs Thatcher headed 'The Wasted Years', was an article headlined '*Belgrano*: Wild Goose Chase'. The author reported Narendra Sethia as saying that he was mystified as to the reasons why the police wanted to see him, and denying that he had the log let alone that it had been seized from him. Chief Superintendent Hardy was also quoted. 'I am not prepared to discuss what, if anything, we have recovered. I am here at the request of the Director of Public Prosecutions.' The *Daily Mirror* reporter (just as a matter of interest) was Alastair Campbell.

Back at the Old Bailey, by fair means or foul, Bernard Ingham's prayers for a 'hanging judge' could scarcely have been better answered. From the very start Mr Justice McCowan could hardly have made it more clear that he had Clive Ponting pegged. Had he left any room whatever for doubt, it had been closed during his summing up on Friday.

'The defence accept that the evidence is all one way,' said the judge, 'that he was not authorised to make the disclosures. There is only one ingredient to dispute: "duty in the interests of the state".'

This referred to Ponting's case that by leaking the information to Parliament, he was following his duty as a civil servant to act in the interests of the state. Therefore the question was whether the interests of the state were represented by Parliament, or by the government of the day. Mr Justice McCowan's view was clear:

Interests of the state, I direct you, means the policies of the state as they were in July 1984 when he communicated the documents, and not the policies that Ponting, Tam Dalyell, or any of us, think they ought to have been – the policies laid down for it by the recognised organs of government and authority.

Put even more plainly, it was the judge's view that if it was government policy to lie wholesale about a given event, or to slay the first-born of every household, then it was the duty of the civil servant to keep quiet about it unless authorised to make the facts known.

The only consolation for Ponting's team was that the judge's rulings throughout, and the summing up in particular, had been so one-sided that if necessary they would give ample grounds for appeal.

That Monday morning, 11 February, the judge completed his summation with a series of clear and unambiguous reminders to the jury that Ponting was as guilty as hell and it was their job to find him so. He sent them out mid-morning to consider their verdict, leaving Ponting and his lawyers to pace the corridors and wait for his fate to be determined. He had little doubt of what the verdict would be, and had arrived at court that morning with his pockets stuffed full of toiletries and writing implements which he would need when sentenced to prison.

Then, at 2.00 p.m., the court bailiff came to find him and said that the jury had returned. He just had time to give his wife Sally a goodbye kiss, and was taken back to the dock. The clerk of the court stood up and asked the foreman of the jury if they had reached a verdict.

'Yes.'

'And is it the verdict of you all?'

'Yes.'

The clerk read the charge aloud and asked, 'Do you find the defendant guilty or not guilty?'

'Not guilty.' There was a gasp in the courtroom, followed quickly by cheering and clapping from the public gallery. Ponting was awarded costs and left the court with Sally and his defence team to celebrate.

We may never know what effect the judge's summing up had on the jury in the Clive Ponting trial. Nor are we likely to know how they were affected by the headlines over the weekend about the control room log-book seized by Scotland Yard detectives who had flown halfway around the world in pursuit of it. What we do know is that the intentions behind both acts back-fired. It is one of the great things about the jury system that, just now and again, 'twelve good men and true' will not be pushed around – the more they feel that they are being pressured by the authorities to think in a certain way, the less likely they are to think it. The verdict they were being pushed into by the government and the prosecution could scarcely have been more clear, and the jury refused to accept it.

'An incredible day that started in the depths has ended in the heights,' wrote Ponting later. 'We have won a tremendous victory and the jury has made an historic decision in favour of democracy.'

15

The Iron Lady

For all of Tam Dalyell's campaigning, the success of the book by Gavshon and Rice, the valiant work of Diana Gould, and the efforts by Clive Ponting and others to get at and to reveal the truth, no one was ever able conclusively to prove that the War Cabinet knew about the Peruvian peace plan when the order was given to sink the *Belgrano*.

US Secretary of State Alexander Haig was angry and frustrated that his peace efforts had come to naught, and appeared for some time to be encouraging the notion that the plan was further advanced than perhaps it was; in addition to which, in his later accounts he got some crucial times wrong by a factor of twenty-four hours.

The British Ambassador to Lima, Charles Wallace, who was at various times said by President Belaúnde of Peru and by others close to the negotiations to have been part of the discussions over the weekend of 1 May, vehemently denied that he had been there.

Foreign Secretary Francis Pym had flown to Washington on 1 May, and arrived with enough time to be able to give a press conference, but claimed not to have checked in with Alexander Haig who had been conducting the negotiations with the Peruvian President all that day.

Chief of the Defence Staff Lord Lewin, who addressed the sub-group of the War Cabinet which approved the sinking, was adamant that there was no discussion or knowledge of the peace plan when the decision was made.

Though it seems unlikely that the two telegrams which the Foreign Office sent to Clive Ponting were the sum total of all relevant transatlantic calls or messages that weekend, no one has ever come up with any firm evidence that the government knew that the plan was as far advanced as has subsequently been claimed. (The government claimed that these telegrams were the first 'authoritative' information on the peace plan – a clear indication that there had been other, less formal, indications earlier.)

None of that, however, is the real point. The point is that, if ministers and civil servants and diplomats and Cabinet members were not aware of the progress and status of the Peruvian peace plan, and how close it had come to an agreement which could stop the bloodshed, they should have been.

Through no fault of her own, Great Britain had been dragged into an anachronistic colonial dispute about a set of islands of which the British people knew nothing and – until they were taken over by the neighbouring country – cared not at all. The invasion should have been foreseen, but it was not. Diplomats and civil servants and politicians were culpable, and vulnerable, and they knew it. The invasion had been a dreadful humiliation for a Prime Minister who was already deeply unpopular. Throughout the run-up to the conflict, she must have had those portentous words of Enoch Powell in the 4 April House of Commons debate ringing in her ears.

The Prime Minister, shortly after she came into office, received a soubriquet as the 'Iron Lady'. It arose in the context of remarks which she made about defence against the Soviet Union and its allies; but there was no reason to suppose that the Right Hon. Lady did not welcome and, indeed, take pride in that description. In the next week or two this House, the nation and the Right Hon. Lady herself will learn of what metal she is made.

The Prime Minister knew, as did everyone else, that her premiership and probably the survival of the government itself depended on the way that she conducted the conflict against Argentina. Was she, or was she not, the Iron Lady? A compromise which involved mutual withdrawal of all forces, with perhaps an interim administration, and a panel of countries to monitor the peace – any fudge or formula short of total victory and restoration of sovereignty, would not be enough.

After the publication of Gavshon and Rice's book, *The Sinking of the Belgrano*, Admiral Lord Lewin agreed to meet the two authors in order to tell them of what he regarded as the many inaccuracies and misunderstandings in their text (there turned out to be precious few, and all of them arguable). When asked about his impressions of the possibility of a negotiated settlement which would have prevented war in the Falklands, he said:

I was convinced at that stage [round about 23 or 24 April] that we were dealing with a government in Buenos Aires who could not agree to a settlement which would keep them in power and would keep Mrs Thatcher in power ... From my point of view that was the end of the negotiations ... What I want to convey is the feeling in the War Cabinet and certainly in the military, by 25th and 26th April, that a negotiated settlement was not on. There was no way you were going to get a settlement which would keep both governments in power, and it was unthinkable that the Conservatives should settle for something that would mean they would be defeated in Parliament and would have to go to a general election.

It could scarcely be clearer. It was unthinkable that the Conservative government could agree to anything which would necessitate going to the country to fight an election which they would certainly lose. So ultimately it was not about sovereignty, nor was it about the freedom of British subjects to choose their own destiny, nor was it about the survival of soldiers and sailors and airmen and islanders. It was about the survival of Mrs Thatcher's government, and its members were convinced that the Argentines would not agree to a solution which would keep it in power.

By the beginning of May, therefore, there was no reason why Foreign Secretary Francis Pym would feel that he should rush to the State Department when he arrived in Washington to see if there was any way to avoid war. There was no reason for British Ambassador to Peru Charles Wallace to be on duty at the Presidential Palace in Lima to monitor President Belaúnde's hour-by-hour negotiations with the junta. No need for the Foreign Office to be straining every sinew to update themselves on a regular basis so that the meeting in a side-room called to decide whether to sink a ship with a thousand men on board should be aware of the progress of peace talks. 'There was no chance of a settlement which would keep both governments in power.'

In her memoirs, *The Downing Street Years*, Lady Thatcher recalls and quotes Enoch Powell's words, and adds the following footnote.

Later, when the war was won, Enoch Powell returned to the subject in a Parliamentary Question: 'Is the Right. Hon. Lady aware that the report has now been received from the public analyst on a certain substance recently subjected to analysis and that I have obtained a copy of the report? It shows that the substance under test consisted of ferrous matter of the highest quality, and that it is of exceptional tensile strength, is highly resistant to wear and tear and to stress, and may be used to advantage for all national purposes.' Ian Gow had the two quotes printed and framed for me as a Christmas present in 1982; they hang still on my office wall.

16

'Unquantifiable Damage'

The Clive Ponting case was not the last time that a jury would hear many of the same facts and the same arguments about the sinking of the *Belgrano* and its aftermath. In the week after the Old Bailey verdict, in St Lucia, Narendra Sethia was bombarded with phone calls and messages from friends and former comrades who now assumed from what they had read in the newspapers and heard on the radio that he was a thief. It was clear to Sethia that he had been libelled, and he was far from happy about it.

Defamation is a fascinating area of the law and one which my experience of working on *World in Action* had taught me a little about. When we were trying to assess the risk that someone we were making a programme about might take an action for defamation against us, the lawyers would always ask us the same question: 'Is he rich?'

If the answer was yes, then extra caution was always advisable. If the answer was no, our lawyers worried rather less. For the fact is that defamation is a difficult and expensive thing to prove, and for the ordinary individual to take on a national newspaper or a national broadcaster, with all their resources and well-oiled and geared-up machines, is a formidable prospect.

That said, it is an unwise journalist or editor who under-estimates the power of an individual with a genuine sense of injustice. It would be impossible to count the number of occasions when 'little people' who feel they have been wronged have risked everything they own to take on giants. Usually it does not work out and they lose their shirts as well as their reputations, but sometimes it does.

When Narendra Sethia called to ask me if I thought he should take an action for defamation against the *Mail on Sunday*, the *Observer* and the BBC, one thing I knew about him was that he was not rich, and so I advised him against it. He would be in for a long and expensive battle against wealthy adversaries, who would have no scruples in the way they contested his action. Even publishers with integrity, such as those of the *Observer* and *Guardian*, tend to circle the wagons when under attack in the courts. It was true that the merits of the specific allegation should be open and shut: the articles and news items had effectively accused him of having stolen the control room log-book, and he had not done so. On the other hand, the room for muddying the waters was as wide as the Atlantic. He had, after all, technically broken the Official Secrets Act by keeping the diary and by allowing Simon O'Keeffe to show it to his father who was not authorised to read it. He had also, again technically, stolen a few items of Royal Navy property – namely the obsolete charts, the waterproof bag and other bits and pieces which had been returned to Hardy and Ashdown. 'OK', the newspapers would be bound to argue, 'so maybe he did not steal the control room log, but clearly he was a thief, and clearly he broke the Official Secrets Act, and so since he is the kind of character who could easily have stolen the log-book, what harm had they done by reporting that he had stolen it?'

In common with most people who know more about what is right and wrong than they do about the finer points of the law, this argument did not wash with Sethia. He felt that he had been wronged, and was determined at least to get a correction and an apology from those who had libelled him. He instructed a solicitor, Philip Lucas, who duly wrote to the *Mail on Sunday* and other newspapers on the Tuesday following publication seeking a retraction in the edition of the paper on the next Sunday. He also invited proposals for damages. In the next few days there followed a flurry of letters and phone calls, culminating for the time being in a holding reply from the *Mail on Sunday*: 'I understand that the police officers concerned in the enquiries are still in the West Indies . . . I regret therefore that the time limit you have imposed is an impossible one.'

Clearly the newspaper was still hoping against hope that Hardy and Ashdown would come up with something in their investigations which would justify its sensational claims. It was not to be. Hardy and Ashdown could not have expected to find the control room log on their trip to the West Indies, and had returned from their holiday at the taxpayers' expense with a few unclassified charts, a tatty bag and a copy of *The Sailmaker's Handbook*. However, they had achieved the objective that the DPP had actually sent them for – to create the smoke which it was hoped would divert the Ponting jury. They had made the smoke and got the headlines, but the jury was not fooled.

The mere fact that their story was not true did not deter the *Mail on Sunday*. Their defence consisted utterly predictably of accusations that Sethia had broken the Official Secrets Act by keeping a diary and allowing it to be shown to an unauthorised person, and that anyway he was a thief because he had stolen property of the Royal Navy, for example 'charts, nautical almanacs, torch batteries, a waterproof bag, stationery and a flag'.

The decision by the *Mail on Sunday* to resist Sethia's demands for an apology and retraction left the former officer with a difficult choice to make. He could either tell all his friends and colleagues that he had been defamed but could do nothing about it, then try to forget the whole thing; or he could sink every penny he had, and every penny he could raise from friends and supporters, into a fight for justice. Sethia thought nothing of risking everything he owned; he had shown on a number of occasions that he had little interest in material possessions, and he owned very little anyway.

As well as the *Mail on Sunday*, Sethia had also commenced an action against the *Observer* – both for breach of copyright by having reproduced large sections of his diary without permission, and for defamation in accusing him of stealing the control room log. On 29 December 1985 he wrote to Arthur Gavshon to describe the tactics being employed by the newspaper.

I have recently passed through the 'threat' stage of 'if you do not withdraw your proceedings, we shall print more that will expose you' and to this I have replied in certain Biblical, reproductory terms. So, now they have progressed to the 'long drawn out' stage of attempting to drag the case on to the extent that I shall run out of funds to fight for what I believe is just – or, rather, against their own injustice. I shall not be deterred and am even preparing my old suits for sale to Oxfam.

Notwithstanding the improbability that Oxfam would be interested in buying his second-hand suits, Sethia was in a fix. He did, however, have friends and supporters. Despite having been a working journalist all of his life, Arthur Gavshon was keen to give Sethia whatever assistance he could. After all, Gavshon had used Sethia's diary as a source for the book he had written with Desmond Rice, which had been highly successful. He met Sethia when he came to England for the *World in Action* programme, and had been horrified to learn that the officer had never given permission to have his diary exposed in public. The two men had become friends and had stayed in touch.

Gavshon's feeling of guilt was further exacerbated by the fact that he had given Sethia's diary to the *Observer* in the first place. According to a detailed file-note he made at the time, he had handed the diary to a journalist on the paper, Andrew Wilson, on the understanding that it was merely to be used for checking some facts, and not copied or otherwise reproduced. When the *Observer* had gone ahead and printed extracts, Gavshon had called Wilson to protest, but had received no reply. However, he was sent a cheque by the *Observer* for £200 which, he assumed, was a token payment for the help and advice he had given to *Observer* journalists. Instead it was later claimed by the newspaper to be a payment for publishing the extracts from Sethia's diary.

It was part of the *Observer*'s case that Sethia had willingly given his diary to Gavshon and others for publication, and so could hardly complain that the newspaper had run with it. Sethia had to ask Gavshon to provide a statement confirming that he had not handed over his diary, and that he had no prior knowledge that it would be used by Gavshon in his book. Gavshon had no choice but to comply, and thus became a reluctant participant in the dispute.

On the morning of Tuesday 14 May, Gavshon received a visit at his home in Highgate from the Managing Editor of the *Observer*, Magnus Linklater. Linklater wanted to make an off-the-record offer to Sethia, in the hope of avoiding what he said was bound to be an expensive and damaging legal action. He said he did not wish to make the offer through lawyers, because he did not want 'the other side' to think that the *Observer* was weakening. He sought Gavshon's assistance in passing on his proposal to Sethia and his lawyer. In essence the offer was of a printed correction accepting that the paper was wrong to have stated that Sethia had removed the *Conqueror*'s log from the submarine, and a token payment for a technical breach of copyright. However, there would be no apology, no damages, and no contribution towards Sethia's costs. Gavshon was so uneasy about the visit that, as soon as it was over, he made a detailed note of the conversation. He wrote that he had been left with the impression that the alternative to acceptance was 'that the paper would contest the action with all the vigour at its disposal. That would mean a lot of people getting hurt, myself included. He [Linklater] volunteered the information that what he said was exercising pressure on me. To this I replied that it was not pressure he was trying to exercise but that he was threatening me. After briefly discussing the meaning of the word "threatening" he acknowledged that in fact this is what he was doing.'

Gavshon's note of the meeting continues: 'In discussing how the *Observer* intended to contest the action Linklater said the paper would go to the point of using "that despicable little character, Morley" as a witness . . . his version of Sethia's character and past would be extremely damaging.'

The newspapers were not content merely to try to exhaust Sethia's resources by extending the proceedings for as long as possible. They also used another weapon in the armoury of the well-heeled Goliath in contest with the individual David, by applying to the court for security of costs. The argument goes that if a penniless individual sues a newspaper or broadcaster, loses the case, and costs are awarded against him, then the publisher has little chance of recouping the costs it has incurred in defending the action. This applies especially when the plaintiff lives abroad and is potentially beyond the reach of the civil courts.

While the courts decided whether or not to uphold the request, Sethia's lawyers advised him to prepare for the worst. He had already been told that an unsuccessful action could cost him the best part of a quarter of a million pounds; Philip Lucas had purposefully not asked him how he planned to find this money if his action was not successful, but there was no way of ignoring this demand for security of costs by the newspapers. If granted, he would be required to put some £40,000 on deposit into court. He would have the money returned to him if he won, and would lose it if he did not. That was now an academic consideration, because having scraped the proverbial barrel in order to keep the main action going on a week by week basis, finding another £40,000 was way beyond his resources.

Once again Sethia was faced with the prospect of having to give up an action against an injustice which had wounded him deeply. Finally, on 12 April 1987, he wrote a round robin letter to as many friends and supporters as he could think of, asking them to come up with £1,000 each. The money would be paid into court, where it would earn interest, and be returned directly to the donors, including that interest, after his victory. In the event that he was not victorious Sethia offered to guarantee, through his lawyers, that the money would be repaid from his own resources over a specified period of time.

It is a difficult thing to write and ask for this contribution but, two and a half years on, it now seems that unless I am able to find this money, I shall have no alternative than to drop these litigations. The newspapers will emerge victorious in the knowledge that the small man in the street is unable to fight the might of the press. I would very much appreciate it if you could help. Would you please let me know if you are able to (and don't feel bad if you are not).

Perhaps Sethia had let his friends off the hook too easily, because just a dozen people put up the money. Happily the courts decided not to grant the newspapers' claim for security of their costs and, with a lot of faith and goodwill from his friends and lawyers, Sethia was able to press on with the action.

As the two sides squared up for battle over the following months, it became more and more clear that the newspapers would be relying heavily on the evidence of Sethia's diary itself. Not only was the very existence of the diary a *prima facie* breach of the Official Secrets Act, but, in the supposed privacy of its pages, Sethia had admitted to having taken the various bits and pieces from the submarine, and also a range of other youthful exploits which (in a perfect world) he might have preferred not to be revealed in open court. However, the newspapers had a problem – which is that the Ministry of Defence had declared the diary to be 'Top Secret' and would not allow any part of it to be used in the trial. On 2 May 1986, Defence Secretary George Younger signed an affidavit:

The production of Lieutenant Sethia's diary to persons not authorised to receive it would be likely to cause unquantifiable damage by reason of the disclosures involved. Additionally, such disclosure would clearly damage the operational capability of nuclear submarines at present in commission and thereby the national security of the United Kingdom.

In the same affidavit, Younger declared that even parts of the diary which covered non-operational matters should be withheld because, when taken together with other intelligence which might have been obtained by a hostile power, they might form an overall picture which would be damaging.

Needless to say, this development was received very badly by lawyers acting for the newspapers and, after further entreaties, Younger softened his position. Indeed, Younger softened his position not once, not twice, but three times, and each of them to the benefit of the newspapers. By the time the trial came around, the copy of the diary which would be available to the court was so full of deletions that the jury could have been forgiven for thinking that Sethia's sole purpose in writing it was to endanger the national security of the United Kingdom.

At every turn, it seemed as though the government was doing everything possible to assist the newspapers, and everything possible to obstruct Sethia. Perhaps it was understandable that the government would be displeased with someone whose diary had fuelled the extended controversy and embarrassment they had suffered over the sinking of the *Belgrano*. On the other hand, their behaviour seemed more sustained and systematic than would ordinarily be justified by what had taken place. Only then did it occur to Narendra Sethia that the government might be concerned that he intended to use the cover of court privilege to talk about Operation Barmaid, the highly-secret attempt to capture a Soviet towed-array sonar.

The more he thought about it, the more it seemed to Sethia that this might be the answer. Whereas the details of the Falklands operation were a matter of some political embarrassment, and anyway were now four years and a general election in the past, the sensitivities surrounding Barmaid were every bit as sharp as they had been in 1982. Accordingly, Sethia wrote a letter directly to the Prime Minister at Downing Street, reassuring her that it was absolutely not his intention to reveal what he knew about the top secret operation, and that his case was entirely about what had happened as a result of the missing control room log. Sethia received a non-committal answer, but thereafter his legal team felt a distinct lifting of the obstructive attitude by the MoD.

The *Mail on Sunday*'s libel had been the most egregious, and so it was their case which took the lead, while the others lined up behind. They included the *Observer* (for libel and breach of copyright), the *Sun* (for libel), the *Guardian* and *Washington Post* (for breach of copyright) and the BBC (for reporting and repeating the libels from the various newspapers).

The case against the *Mail on Sunday* and its Crime Correspondent Chester Stern eventually was heard at the Royal Courts of Justice in October 1987, two and a half years after Sethia's first letter seeking a retraction. In between the work he had to do to prepare to defend his reputation in the British courts, Sethia had found time to build up the yacht charter business in St Lucia, and had married his girlfriend, Sally Webster, at a ceremony in Brixton Registry Office. Sally was in court to support him, and their friend Emma Field also attended as a witness.

The trial judge was Mr Justice Boreham. Representing Sethia was Patrick Milmo QC, assisted by the Hon. Andrew Monson. Representing the defendants was Michael Hill QC (whose obituary in August 2003 described him as 'particularly devastating in cross-examination, when he missed nothing; he never gave up on a point, never took a backward step'). Andrew Caldecott QC was also in the newspapers' corner.

The case lasted for twenty-one days, during which no journalist or editor from the *Mail on Sunday* appeared in court. Chester Stern was relieved not to be required to give evidence, and thinks that this was because he would have had no choice but to blame the inaccuracies in his piece on the re-write by his editor, Stewart Steven. Steven had already famously been taken in by a couple of hoaxes in recent times, and is unlikely to have relished the idea of being identified as having fallen for another.

Richard Morley was asked by Associated Newspapers to be available to them each day of the trial, and was accommodated in the Waldorf Hotel for the duration. The reason he believed that his former friend had stolen the control room logs, he told the defence team, was because on his return to Britain after the war,

Sethia telephoned to tell him that he had. He claimed that the two men had discussed Sethia's intention to write a book and that Sethia had boasted of having taken some logs from the submarine to help him make his recollections more accurate. Morley also claimed that he had spoken openly to friends and others about the fact that a log from the submarine was missing some time before Heseltine had announced the fact. If Morley had indeed known and spoken about the missing log before its loss had been announced, how else could he have known about it unless Sethia had told him? There seems to be no doubt that Morley genuinely believed that what he was saying about Sethia was true. However, despite the fact that this story would have been persuasive if it was believed, and that self-evidently there must have been witnesses to whatever Morley had said to friends and others on the subject before November 1984, in the event the newspapers decided not to call him to give evidence. To this day Morley has no idea why this might be.

At one time it seemed that the newspaper might allege that Sethia had authorised me to use classified material from his diary in the episode of *World in Action* in which he had also appeared, and I was asked by Sethia's lawyers to come to court to refute the claim if it was made. It was not, but I was there to hear some of the evidence given by Sethia himself. Normally strong, confident and robust, he looked like a man who had just been through a horrible traffic accident. After an extended battering by lawyers representing the newspapers, Sethia was asked by his own lawyers what had been his reaction when reading accusations that he was a thief and a liar, and of having them read in front of his wife and family. He choked back tears and could only reply, 'I was very upset sir.'

Mr Justice Boreham was about as transparently on the side of Narendra Sethia as Mr Justice McCowan had been on the side of the prosecution against Clive Ponting. When Michael Hill asked Sethia about his habit of referring to junior ratings by their first names, Sethia responded that in a submarine this was not at all unusual. A former wartime Air Force officer himself, Justice Boreham helpfully interjected, 'Exactly, just like an aircraft bomber's crew!'

At the end of the trial, the judge took the defence case point by point and subtly but effectively blew it out of the water. Twice the jury came back and asked for guidance on what should be the level of damages, and twice the judge was obliged to say that he could not assist them. However, he did take the opportunity to point out that they were at liberty to take into account the conduct of the newspapers during the trial. The defendants could have come to court and fought the case purely on the truth or otherwise of what they had originally claimed. Instead they had come to court and compounded their original error by taking every opportunity further to blacken Sethia's character.

You are entitled to take into account, for instance, the fact (for fact it is) that at the behest of the Defendants, Mr Hill had to call him a liar in front of his wife and in front of you and me, and anybody else, the ladies and gentlemen of the press – perhaps, most of all, his wife.

The jury awarded Narendra Sethia damages of £260,000.

The *Mail on Sunday* immediately demanded that all of the money should be held by the courts, pending an appeal, while Sethia's barrister took the line that a successful claimant should not be denied the fruits of victory. Mr Justice Boreham agreed with Milmo, and Sethia was given £160,000 immediately, with £100,000 being retained by the courts.

In November 1988, a year after the trial, and whilst the *Mail on Sunday* appeal was in motion, Sethia was ambling around the lower Annapurnas when he received a call from his solicitor, who was afraid that an appeal judge might well award a much smaller sum and was advising him to settle. Sethia preferred not to refight old battles. He agreed to repay £40,000, and the £100,000 held by the court was also returned to the newspaper, making his final settlement from the *Mail on Sunday* £120,000 of the £260,000 originally awarded.

The day after the verdict against the *Mail on Sunday*, Sethia filed suit against the *Sun*. They had printed just one paragraph, stating that a former Navy officer who now lived in the West Indies was to be prosecuted for theft. This case sat quietly whilst they observed the *MoS* test case, and after the *MoS* verdict they agreed to an out-of-court settlement of £15,000. The *Observer* paid Sethia £40,000.

Sethia dropped the action against the *Guardian* for copyright infringement and, once again through the good offices of Arthur Gavshon, was eventually paid $1,000 by the *Washington Post* for breach of copyright. In June 1989 the BBC made a declaration in court and paid Sethia £7,500, bringing his total damages for defamation and compensation for copyright breaches to £182,500.

Asked by a newspaper what he felt about the settlements, Sethia said:

I'm delighted it's all over. I went through four years of pain, threats and anguish to clear my name. Friends said it would be a long, bloody fight – and it has been. I know it's difficult to assess how much a reputation is worth but a lot of people will still always believe that I stole the log-book because that was reported in the newspapers and they will not have read of my successful actions.

17

Operation Barmaid – Last Orders

So – if Narendra Sethia did not steal the log-book from the control room of the *Conqueror*, who did, and why? The mystery remained. Neither the Ministry of Defence board of inquiry, nor Scotland Yard's finest, had come up with a definitive answer.

It seems unlikely that the control room log was deliberately 'lost' by the government because it contained information which contradicted the official version of events in the South Atlantic; the same information was contained in a number of other logs and official records, and none of those had been lost or stolen. The episode showed every sign of becoming one of those frustrating enigmas to which we never find the answer.

Then one day, just a few months before Sethia's libel case was due to come to court, I received an invitation to Narendra Sethia's wedding. He and I had kept in touch since the programme, and I was delighted to hear his good news and very pleased to have the chance to see him again. I was happy to accept.

The wedding was a lovely occasion. It took place at the Brixton Road Registry Office and was followed by a lunch for family and friends at the Bombay Brasserie. Being something of a showman, Narendra was dressed in full traditional Indian costume. The bride, Sally Webster, also looked very happy and very beautiful.

Later that day I found myself in a nearby public house with several of the former crew of the *Conqueror*. Inevitably the conversation eventually turned to the Falklands War and some strong opinions were expressed about the controversy that had raged after hostilities had ended. Politicians were not held in especially high regard and nor, it is fair to say, were journalists.

226

However, since I was a friend of Narendra's, the company seemed willing to make an exception for me.

When the conversation reached the topic of the control room log and what had happened to it, I felt sure that I saw some knowing looks among those present. Needless to say I pressed for more information. No one seemed to know for certain what had actually happened to the missing logs, but over the course of an hour or so, the feeling emerged that their disappearance was nothing to do with the sinking of the *Belgrano*.

'If it had been about the *Belgrano*,' said one of them, 'then ask yourself why six months of logs would have gone missing.'

'We left Faslane for the Falklands in April and were back by July, so why would anyone need to lose the logs up until October?'

It was a good point. Why would anyone wanting to 'lose' embarrassing information about the *Belgrano* also 'lose' the logs for the three months following the war? For the first time, it occurred to me that perhaps what was being hidden was not to do with the war, but with what came after it . . .

One way and another, in the course of the remainder of that evening and after some other enquiries in the following days, I learned about Project 2000 and Operation Barmaid. I learned about the beginnings of the project in June 1980, and the two stealthy attempts which had been made by *Conqueror* to obtain a towed-array from AGIs in the North Atlantic and in the Mediterranean.

Then I learned about what had happened to the submarine shortly after she had returned to Faslane at the end of the war: the real secrets of the *Conqueror*.

The Falklands War, remember, had been a temporary diversion from the main purpose of *Conqueror* and other boats in the nuclear submarine fleet – which was locating, tracking and generally monitoring the enemy's nuclear warfare capability. The entire programme of activity – Operation Holystone – was carried out in continual consultation with the Americans, and the sudden loss of a significant part of the NATO submarine capability while the British had been otherwise engaged in the South Atlantic had been a cause for grave concern – especially in the Pentagon. The desire to obtain an example of the towed-array being used by the Soviets had not gone away with the war, and indeed had increased with the passage of time. Now the Falklands War was over, and the pre-existing imperatives clicked back into place.

After their return to Faslane on 13 July, the crew of the *Conqueror* had been sent home to recuperate. They had been at sea for more than fifteen weeks, at a state of high alert for most of it, and there is no doubt that they needed a break. The whole mission had also exacted a toll on the submarine itself: there had been a series of problems with communications systems throughout, and there was a long list of repair and refurbishment jobs to be done. In addition to the practical tasks, there was a vast amount of administration to be caught up on, reports to write, records to update, basic stores to replenish. Taken together with the need to give the officers and men time to absorb the enormity of the actions in which they had been involved, no one on board was surprised to be told that it would be at least two months before they would be called upon again.

But it was not to be. Later that month of July 1982 new intelligence reports were received that two Polish AGIs were using towed-array sonars in the North Atlantic. *Conqueror* was still one of the designated submarines for carrying out 'sneakies', and anyway had been especially fitted with the Barmaid equipment designed for severing the towing-cables and retrieving the array. All thoughts about the recent operations in the Falklands were put to one side, and a request went from the head of Naval Intelligence to DS5 for political clearance to carry out an operation to try to capture the longed-for apparatus.

In the world of international politics, these were never less than sensitive times, but this moment was especially so for a range of reasons. The Americans had been reluctant to take sides in the Falklands War, preferring to try to maintain the cordial relationship they had enjoyed with Argentina. Eventually they had 'tilted' in favour of their oldest ally on 30 April and their assistance with intelligence and logistics had been invaluable and probably critical. The opportunity for the British to do some-thing on the Cold War front line which would be valued by the Americans was therefore an important one, not to be missed if at all possible.

On the other side of the coin, it was not known how much help, if any, had been given by the Soviets to the Argentines. Though the politics of the two countries could scarcely have been more different, there is an old adage that 'my enemy's enemy is my friend' and there had been frequent rumours during the war of the possible presence of Soviet submarines in the South Atlantic. Certainly, as we have seen, *Conqueror*'s officers would routinely calculate the times when Soviet satellites were due to pass overhead before raising communications masts or surfacing.

Against this background, it would not be a good moment for the UK to find itself at the centre of another international controversy. Nevertheless, the head of DS5 went through his usual procedure of seeking clearance from the Foreign Office and the Defence ministers. Both felt that the possible prize of capturing the towed-array would be worth the risk. The matter therefore went before the Prime Minister. Still on a 'high' following the military victory in the Falklands, and always anxious to please her American allies, Mrs Thatcher gave the go-ahead. The crew of the *Conqueror* were called back to the boat for an expedition in the first half of August. They were informed that they would be heading for Gibraltar.

'Suddenly we were back and doing the thing we had really been trained for,' said one of those who had been summoned, 'chasing Russians. And this operation in particular was special to us because we had been rehearsing for it for more than two years.'

In the small hours of the morning on 12 August 1982, *Conqueror* slipped out of its base at Faslane for what would be one of the most sensitive and dangerous missions in the entire history of the Cold War. Fitted to the outside of the bows of the submarine were the Barmaid pincers which, if it proved possible to get close enough, would be used to cut the cable of the towed-array system being used by one of the Polish spy-ships. The two previous tentative efforts had been useful practice, and now they felt match-fit from their experiences in the war. On board the submarine there was a sense that this time they would be successful.

'Submariners on any boat develop an unusual sense of loyalty and teamwork,' said one senior officer, 'but the team-spirit and fellow-feeling among the crew of the *Conqueror* after what they had been through in the South Atlantic made this a very special unit indeed.'

The usual complement of a hundred or so officers and crew included four skilled and specially-trained divers, one of whom was Graham Libby, who had distinguished himself so remarkably in the South Atlantic. Once the AGI had been located and the cable had been cut, it would be their job to ensure that it was secured to the exterior of the submarine so that it could be carried back to friendly waters. The task they faced was a challenging one. As they knew, the towed-array would be attached by a steel cable three inches thick, and might be as much as 3,000 yards long. Towed-arrays used by the US and UK were designed to have neutral buoyancy – they would neither sink to the depths nor float to the surface if left unsupported. However, it was not known whether those used by the Soviets were designed in the same way. If the captured array was heavier than water, once detached from the towing vessel it would immediately begin to sink to the bottom of the ocean. As before in the attempts in the Barents and the Mediterranean, the contingency plan, should they be unable to manhandle it into position or, worse still, they were spotted and pursued, would be to allow the dislodged towed-array to sink to the sea-bed and to mark the position with an eye to later retrieval.

'We knew from dealing with arrays on our own boat that they were awkward buggers to manhandle,' said a young officer from *Conqueror*, 'and we would be trying to do it in hostile waters.'

The early morning sun was still just below the horizon when *Conqueror* slipped its lines. The huge fin and the long, dark whale-shaped body of the boat slid quietly through the cold waters of the Gareloch. It would have looked majestic and effortless as it moved out into the deeper waters of the loch, but the giant craft had to be extremely careful in the narrow sheltered waters of the Clyde estuary. A nuclear submarine has only one main propeller so is difficult to manoeuvre normally in a tight space. It also has a piece of equipment known as an 'egg-beater', which is a small propeller on the end of a long shaft which can be lowered into the water and then trained through 360 degrees to provide pull in any one direction (an egg-beater is a puller rather than a pusher). A tug was also on immediate standby to offer assistance in negotiating the tight turns should it be necessary.

Standing on the bridge were the skipper, Christopher Wreford-Brown, the executive officer, Tim McClement, and the navigating officer, Jonty Powis. A navigating officer can spend many hours in advance planning for entrance or departure from harbour. His job was to call out a count-down to the next course change: '20 seconds to wheel-over ... 10 seconds to wheel-over ... new course zero three zero now ... now ... NOW!' – and the manoeuvres needed to be accurate to the second. All orders were given from the bridge and piped down to the control room, where the harbour stations officer of the watch acknowledged and responded.

Despite the fact that these were their most familiar waters, exiting the Gareloch always demanded particular care. There is a very narrow gap just south of the submarine base, near Helensburgh, known as the Rhu Narrows, where there is no room for

SECRETS OF THE *CONQUEROR*

the smallest error. HMS *Conqueror* needed at least thirty-eight feet of water when in trim, and more than one submarine has ended up grounding there.

Once out of the Gareloch, the submarine threaded its way on the surface at 6 knots towards open water, passing the holiday resort of Gourock from which a ferry service sailed to Dunoon – useful for submarines which could from time to time carry out dummy torpedo attacks on the ferries. It was not unknown for ferry passengers to catch sight of a periscope breaking the surface – excited passengers could sometimes be seen pointing and waving back at the submarine – but on this occasion *Conqueror* passed by undetected.

Passing the entrance to the Holy Loch, a US ballistic missile submarine base until 1992, the boat was soon able to increase speed to 10 knots as it entered the wider waters of the Firth of Clyde, leaving the island of Arran to starboard. It was from Arran that potential submarine captains would set off each day for the gruelling sea phase of the 'Perisher' course for designate commanding officers.

Conqueror increased speed once she was clear of Arran and entered the North Channel between Ulster and Scotland, with the Mull of Kintyre and Islay to starboard. Now the submarine was driving on towards the North Atlantic, remaining on the surface for the first few hours. Closer to her diving area, Wreford-Brown ordered the trimming officer to 'catch a trim'. The trimming officer went to the auxiliary machinery area on 3-deck and crouched down in a space with about four feet of headroom, opening a series of valves to fill a big tube with sea water. Using a tried and tested mathematical formula, he calculated the amount of water he needed to flood in or pump out of the compensating tanks to achieve as near-perfect neutral buoyancy as possible. The operation would normally take around half an hour, pumping water either on board or overboard, or from one tank to another. Once the trimming officer was satisfied, the order was given to dive.

The submarine's first dive was to 180 feet, and then immediately the order was given to come back up to periscope depth, which is 68 feet. This is called 'swinging the bubble' and is designed to get rid of any excess air that might be lurking in the main ballast tanks. By making a steep short dive and then coming straight back up at a steep angle, it was possible to force the air out of the tanks.

Once the submarine went deep again, the order was given to crank up the revs: 'Take the plant to the three-quarter power state, revolutions one five zero', which translates into a speed over the ground of slightly more than 20 knots.

Once *Conqueror* was through the North Channel she slowed again while going to periscope depth, heading west off the northern Irish coast and taking pains to listen for any indication of the presence of the 'Malin Head AGI'. (Malin Head is the northernmost point on the Irish coast.) For decades, the Soviets had operated an intelligence-gathering trawler along Northern Ireland's coast, the vessel monitoring and reporting NATO submarines heading to and from the Clyde. On more than one occasion *Conqueror* had steamed off the northern Irish coast and left a few subtle hints to a waiting AGI that she was in the area, and then 'disappeared' as soon as she seemed interested in her. 'Catch me if you can.'

Conqueror then turned north, set her speed to 18 knots and dived to 415 feet, passing well to the west of the Hebrides and then through the great Faeroes–Shetland gap, 200 miles of open sea at the bottom of which lie a series of SOSUS hydrophones which monitor all vessels that pass through – as they do with vessels that pass through the Iceland–Faeroes gap, and the Shetlands–Norway gap. This meant that any vessel en route to, or originating from, a Soviet or Eastern Bloc base could be pinpointed and tracked.

The submarine was now west of Norway and continued in a north-easterly direction, passing Trondheim and then thundering towards the North Cape where the Norwegian Sea meets the Barents Sea.

The major concern for those who knew where they were going was what would happen if they were detected while carrying out an illegal operation in hostile waters. The consequences might be military, dramatic and immediate; there had been several incidents of submarines being depth-charged when they got too close to Eastern Bloc vessels. Or there might be very serious longer-term diplomatic implications if they were caught in the act. Some of those indoctrinated in the secrets of the Barmaid mission believed that the US had asked Britain to carry out this operation precisely in order to avoid the potentially more politically damaging consequences of an American submarine being caught in the act. The two super-powers were well used to deploying satellite states as surrogates when the situation required.

The *Conqueror's* senior officers also knew that this was an operation demanding not only great stealth but also accurate intelligence information, and masterful control of the submarine and the Barmaid equipment itself. *Conqueror* would need the AGI to be cruising at a very slow speed if she was to have the best possible chance of locating and cutting the cable. However, very precise manoeuvring of a near-5000-ton submarine was especially challenging at slow speeds, and the submarine would have to achieve as close-to-perfect buoyancy trim as possible.

Finally, it would of course be impossible to carry out the mission in heavy sea conditions. Huge waves overhead might have relatively little effect on the submarine, but they would mean that the towing cable would be liable to be moving unpredictably, leaving very little chance that the Barmaid cutters could be successfully deployed to do their work.

But of all these complications, the military dangers were perhaps the most pressing of all. The Barents Sea off the far north of Norway and Russia is a difficult, tempestuous ocean that had tested the nerves of British sailors during the convoy runs to

Murmansk during the worst years of the Second World War. Then that ice-free port had been the Soviet Union's lifeline to the world, landing millions of tons of American trucks and planes sent to help the Russians to resist Hitler. Over a hundred ships were sunk and around 3,000 sailors lost their lives in these convoys. In 1982 the dangers for a nuclear-powered submarine came not from U-boats, icy storms or Nazi dive-bombers, but from the might of the Soviet Northern Fleet, which was based at Severomorsk on the coast not far from Murmansk. The *Conqueror* would be edging close to some of the most closely guarded waters in the world. By the 1980s, the Soviet Union regarded the southern waters of the Barents as one of its essential bastions. Severomorsk was the home of a fleet of Victor hunter-killer submarines, of the aircraft carrier *Kiev*, destroyers that embarked anti-submarine helicopters, and of huge Tupolev Tu-142 aircraft, which were equipped with advanced detection systems for use against deep-diving submarines – not to speak of submarines lingering close to the surface. By the late seventies these formidable aircraft had shown they were capable of tracking submarines for hours at a time.

Despite the strict secrecy surrounding the Barmaid operation, the combination of the urgent and unexpected recall and the unusually clandestine behaviour of the senior officers, ensured that some limited information spread throughout the boat. Frequently the captain, the XO and the weapons officer were seen in intensive whispered discussions as they huddled over large diagrams. Nevertheless, false information was posted on the ship's notice board, indicating that the submarine was in a completely different area – but the crew were not easily fooled; even at 400 feet deep, in far northern waters the surrounding sea lowers the inboard temperature. At 400 feet in tropical waters, the crew would have been walking around in shirt sleeves.

'We knew we were heading north rather than south because it was getting colder, not warmer,' said one senior rating. 'Everyone on board was wrapped up with every pullover they possessed.'

'On the other hand,' said another, 'this kind of thing was second nature to us. We knew these waters in a way that we hadn't known the South Atlantic. We knew the enemy and what his capabilities were. This was what we were paid to do.'

As the submarine ploughed through the waters at a depth of 400 feet, sounds of creaking and grinding grew louder. This was always alarming for new submariners because it felt and sounded as though the boat was about to buckle and implode under the pressure. In reality it was just the interior fittings and fixtures adjusting to the changing environment. The pressure at these depths was immense, and it seemed as though every joint and valve was working at the extremes of tolerance and letting the fact be known.

The information from Intelligence was that two Polish AGIs had been seen operating towed-array sonars in the Barents Sea, somewhere close to the border between Norway and the USSR. No one on the *Conqueror* would have known how this information was acquired. Perhaps it was from some double agent in the Polish or Soviet Navy; perhaps it was from observations by an American satellite. In the Cold War, the crew had learned not to be too curious about such matters. Their sole concern was the accuracy of the information received. By the time *Conqueror* arrived in the area, the intelligence would be a few days old, so the precise current position of the spy-ships was unknown. This time they were in luck. After a brief search of the area, the submarine detected the trawlers making a slow patrol in a position not far from the coast.

The sound signatures of AGIs from the Eastern Bloc were well-known to the sonar operators on board *Conqueror*. Though they were supposedly disguised as trawlers, precious little effort was made to conceal the true purpose of these vessels. There could be no mistake that these two were spy-ships.

This was the opportunity they had been waiting for. On the two previous attempts, the vessel involved had been moving at some speed through the water, making it impossible to stage a steady approach with enough precision to be able to cut the cable. This time the selected AGI was proceeding at just 5 or 6 knots. At those speeds, it might be possible to achieve what had proved to be impossible in the earlier attempts.

The target AGI was close to, or inside, the territorial waters of the USSR. Even today, some thirty years after the event took place, the precise location of the action is felt by all those who know it to be too sensitive to talk about. Even those who take great pride in the operation go silent when the subject is raised. However, when given the opportunity to deny that the encounter took place inside USSR territorial waters near the strategic base of Murmansk, none of those involved has taken the opportunity to do so.

'To be honest, most of us would never have known at the time or since,' says one. 'As far as we were concerned we were in hostile waters, and that was all we needed to know.'

Commander Wreford-Brown ordered the submarine to close in and approach from behind the vessel, at a depth of some 500 feet. The TASO was Robin L'Oste-Brown, the navigator was Jonty Powis, and among the others on board were Graham Libby, Steve Archibald, David Perrin, Mike Lewis, Paul Taylor, Grant Louch and Simon O'Keeffe. The operation was a 'baptism by fire' for Sethia's replacement as supply officer, Mike Screech, who, like all new members of the submarine's company, spent most of this first operation getting to know every aspect of every compartment of the boat as part of the familiarisation drill for his new vessel.

The operation took place in the small hours of the morning and this, coupled with the fact that the AGI was apparently drifting along so casually, gave rise to hope that her crew might not be at full alert. On the other hand it also meant that they would be making very little significant noise themselves, so that any bump from the smallest collision would be likely to be heard or felt.

Wreford-Brown ordered the boat back to periscope depth and took another look at his target from a distance of some 1,000 yards;

this was the last and best chance to pinpoint her position before diving. From here on in, the spy ship would have to be approached blind. Having taken his final scan and done the lightning-speed mental calculations he was trained to do, he ordered the boat slowly and quietly to go deep. The plan was to approach the target from behind and below, and then slowly and quietly to come up, to a position more or less directly astern of the trawler.

On board the submarine the silence was almost total. Everyone was under orders that no machinery of any kind was to be used. No one spoke above a whisper. These AGIs were bristling with the latest listening devices, and any accidental noise might be picked up by the target vessel and bring instant disaster. The control room was operating in 'black lighting' in order to give the captain the best chance to see whatever was visible through the periscope. It meant that officers at their stations had to squint through the gloom at monitors which were scarcely readable.

'The control room was in almost total darkness,' says one senior rating, 'and you could hear a pin drop. Everyone present knew the danger and sensitivity of the operation, and the risks of getting it wrong, but everyone was very calm.'

After many minutes of stealthily closing the gap, Wreford-Brown believed that *Conqueror* was coming up to a position directly beneath and behind the trawler. Now the task was to reduce speed and to rise as slowly and gently as possible, in order to come literally within reach of the hull of the target boat, but without actually touching her. It would be the most delicate submarine manoeuvre that it was possible to imagine.

In the forward sonar compartment, the two seamen on duty were 'Reggie' Perrin and Mike Lewis. Lewis bitterly regretted having missed the Falklands War due to illness, and this was his chance to achieve something memorable. The operators of the pincers and the clamp are believed to have been Ron Brooks and 'Bungy' Williams. It was the moment they had trained and trained for. Their position, low and forward in the submarine, was completely blind; it was their job to locate and track the target by sonar, and then to follow instructions from the control room as they operated the cutting gear.

All the time the calculations and readings were checked and re-checked. Detailed charts and tide-timetables had enabled the navigator to calculate the depth of water to the nearest few inches and the echo-sounder enabled *Conqueror* to know the depth of water below her, and therefore above her. Intelligence sources had provided details of the size and draft of the AGI above their heads. The calculations were critical, but the arithmetic could only take you so far. It could not take into account the effect of any surface swell, or buffeting from any wind or surface current.

The depth and darkness of the water meant that the cameras which had been fitted close to the pincers, to monitor their operation, were useless until *Conqueror* got to within inches of her quarry. But the Falklands had enabled the crew of the *Conqueror* to hone their skills in approaching and tracking a target without being detected in critical wartime conditions when their lives depended on it. Inch by inch, the submarine nudged forwards and upwards, gently closing the gap between the two vessels.

Now just feet below the AGI, *Conqueror* edged into its final position. In the control room, Robin L'Oste-Brown peered at the tiny monitor, trying to see through the turbid sea-water the cable attaching the trawler to the towed-array. There she was, the nuclear submarine *Conqueror*, 4,900 tons of machinery, almost literally holding her breath like a giant whale, all but motionless in the water, inching forward in the gloom. A nudge forward. A nudge forward. Through the periscope, Wreford-Brown could now see the hull of the trawler, just yards above his submarine. The ship's propellers were a few feet or so from the periscope mast. And then there it was, visible on the monitors displaying the output of the forward cameras, a three-inch-thick wound-steel cable, within feet of the jaws of the giant pincers which were ready to gnaw their way through it. Through the gloom it was possible to see the powerful cutting edges close around the cable; the order was sent from control room to sonar compartment, and the blades began carefully to cut the cable.

Once it had been cut through, there would still be the danger that the weight of the cable might sink it to the sea-bed. Therefore the Barmaid equipment also included a clamp, which was operated separately by controls within the sonar compartment. The clamp was secured to the cable alongside the pincers, holding it in place once the line had been cut.

Now that the trawler and submarine were physically attached to each other, maintaining a steady course and speed between them was even more critical. Even the smallest tug or tightening of the cable might be felt on the surface ship, and all hell could be let loose. Wreford-Brown and his men knew very well that if the spy-ship were to detect the *Conqueror* and call for assistance from Murmansk or Severomorsk, the 'hell' unleashed might easily take the form of a rocket-propelled depth-charge which could pursue them down to 3,000 feet.

'I was sitting on a step in the corridor at the door of the control room, ready to help if necessary,' says a senior rating. 'It all seemed to take forever, but it was probably only a few minutes. We were all waiting for the signal that the cable had been cut so that we could get out of there as fast as possible.'

In the sonar compartment from where the cutting equipment was also being operated, there was a constant stream of reports back and forth to the control room. Seconds ticked by, and the officers and crew aboard the submarine expected at any moment that their presence would be detected.

'Everyone in the control room was tense,' said another crew member. 'We were just expecting at any time that we would be discovered and were ready to run if necessary.' AGIs were not heavily armed, but they did carry depth-charges, and a depth-charge dropped from the trawler above them could destroy the submarine and kill everyone inside it.

At last the pincers had completed their work, and suddenly the weight of the towed-array was transferred to the submarine. In the event, the captured towed-array had fewer floatation measures than its British and American equivalents to counter its weight in the water, and so was far heavier than had been anticipated. The sudden additional weight caused *Conqueror* to sink quickly, and there was immediate concern that the turbulence beneath the AGI would alert her. The normal response would be to blow out water from the submarine to regain buoyancy, but that carried too great a danger of detection. Only very slowly and gradually did the submarine regain control, and very gently she withdrew into deeper waters, all the while listening carefully for any signs from the AGI that the operation had been detected. It seemed that it had not.

'The submarine turned and ran for a couple of hours,' recalls a crew member, 'dragging the array behind us. Only when we were sure we were in the clear did we send out divers to secure the thing to the submarine.'

When it was felt safe to do so, and at first light, *Conqueror* returned to the surface so that the divers could secure the stolen apparatus to the submarine for the journey home. This was to be another very tricky part of the operation. Though not as long as most of those in use by the UK and the USA, the captured towed-array was heavy and unwieldy. The safest place to stow it was in what was known as the 'trench', a storage area between the outer casing and the water-tight pressure hull of the submarine, which is accessed via the torpedo-loading hatch towards the bow of the boat. *Conqueror* was carefully manoeuvred so that the surface of the water was level with the torpedo-loading hatch, and Graham Libby, Laurie Dymock, Steve 'Archie' Archibald and one other unidentified diver went into the water. With the help of a capstan which is mounted just in front of the torpedo hatch, the divers slowly and carefully fed the captured array into the trench, winding it round and round in a large loop inside as they did so. It was difficult and dangerous work. Once the apparatus was safely stowed, the hatch sealed, and the divers back on board, *Conqueror* turned and headed for home, not stopping or surfacing before she reached the west coast of Scotland.

There were six submarine berths at Faslane and usually *Conqueror* would sail into the red area which was designated for diesel boats or SSNs. On this occasion, for extra security, they were directed into number two berth in the green area which was usually reserved for the Polaris submarines and was guarded by armed Marines. Their return took place in the small hours of the morning, but a crane was on stand-by to lift the precious cargo onto a flat-bed truck. Within hours, the towed-array was on its way to Prestwick airport for a flight across the Atlantic for analysis to try to determine whether its technology was based on stolen secrets or on the Soviets' independent development of sonar. The answer lies somewhere in the Pentagon and perhaps the British Ministry of Defence, but the rest of us may have to wait yet another thirty years before we are allowed to find out. The Barmaid equipment was later transferred to HMS *Valiant*, along with several members of the *Conqueror* crew, in case a further similar opportunity should occur.

The Barmaid mission was complete, the triumph was absolute. On board the submarine, the sense of pride and achievement far outweighed anything that had been experienced during the Falklands War. Commander Wreford-Brown was said to have considered it to be the greatest and toughest operation of his career. Mrs Thatcher was jubilant, and was heard to say 'thank goodness it was one of our submarines which had done it'. Years afterwards, whenever the name of *Conqueror* was mentioned in the Pentagon, senior officials marvelled at the expertise and courage of the men who had achieved success in so delicate an undertaking.

*

The only shadow across what would otherwise be a clear blue sky of satisfaction was the ever-present suspicion that the original improvement in Soviet anti-submarine-warfare capability had been the long-term result of the betrayal of secrets by one or more of the three British spies of the sixties and seventies, Houghton, Vassall and Bingham. For decades the British Intelligence agencies had no choice but to put up with the contempt felt and sometimes displayed by some of their American counterparts, who tended to believe that espionage was a British or European phenomenon, and that home-grown spies were rarely if ever found in the United States.

One can only imagine the joy that was felt in the stony hearts of the UK Intelligence community three years after the success of Operation Barmaid when, one day in 1985, John Anthony Walker Jr was arrested alongside a deserted road in Washington DC after dropping a bag containing 129 classified documents. The arrest was swiftly followed by the revelation that Walker had been spying for the Russians since 1967!

Walker had originally been arrested for burgling a petrol station when he was aged just eighteen. He had been given the choice of jail-time or joining the Navy. Despite these unpromising beginnings, he initially did well in the service and was eventually assigned to the nuclear-powered submarine USS *Andrew Jackson*. However, Walker was a big drinker and womaniser, and was greedy for the good life. Soon after he began his submarine service, he met and married a girl called Barbara Crowley. The two of them opened a bar catering for Navy personnel, but it got into financial difficulties. Things got worse when Walker was transferred to Fleet Headquarters in Norfolk, Virginia, leaving his wife to run the bar. Once at Norfolk, Walker gained access to the top secret codes governing communications with nuclear submarines and other naval vessels around the world. One day in 1967 he travelled to Washington, knocked on the door of the Soviet Embassy, and sold them a top secret document containing the codes needed to decipher secret Navy messages in exchange for several thousand dollars. He then negotiated for himself a salary of $1,000 a week for what he promised would be a steady flow of military secrets.

In the course of the next seventeen years, Walker persuaded his brother, his son and his best friend to join different branches of the military and to pass secrets to him for sale to the Soviets. He also tried unsuccessfully to recruit his daughter. Among the secrets he sold were comprehensive details of how American submarines were able to detect their Soviet counterparts. Using the information provided to them by Walker, the Soviets were first able to address and improve each of the major causes of noise produced by their submarines, and then dramatically to improve their own listening and tracking capabilities.

It is believed that during his time working for the Soviets, John Walker's assistance enabled them to read more than one million encoded messages sent and received between US military installations.

He was sentenced to life in jail. He is still there, gravely ill, and is unlikely ever to be released.

18

The Mystery of the Missing Log-Book

We do not know the reaction in the USSR to the loss of the towed-array. There seem to have been no diplomatic or other protests, and it must be assumed that the disappearance of the array was believed to have been accidental. One can imagine that those on board the AGI would have preferred to report the top secret kit for which they were responsible as having been lost rather than stolen, though probably neither explanation would have been well-received by their Polish and Russian military and political masters. British technicians were confident that the nature of the cut in the cable would be such that it could have been mistaken for a wrench which might have resulted from the towed-array being caught in rocks on the sea-bed.

However, in view of the possibility that the USSR might not be aware of the incident, the need for secrecy was obviously very persuasive, and so when I learned about the story of Operation Barmaid, I kept my counsel and waited.

Nearly thirty years later, in November 2010, I had just finished executive-producing a series of documentaries for BBC2 based on Alastair Campbell's diaries. Alastair had obviously been obliged to have his own diaries cleared for publication, so I asked him to put me in touch with the appropriate person in Whitehall. He introduced me to the civil servant in the Cabinet Office who had read and approved his memoir. I arranged a meeting in her office just opposite the Ministry of Defence, told her the basics of the story, and asked if she could steer me through the process of getting clearance.

My case was that the enemy in question – the USSR – no longer exists, that no one was hurt in the incident, and that the story reflects extremely well on the British in general and the Royal Navy submarine service in particular. The civil servant agreed and offered to broker an arrangement with the MoD. As it was now close to Christmas, she undertook to contact me by the middle of January at the latest.

Nothing happened. I waited, and I waited, and then I started to call. I left messages with a very polite secretary who promised that I would receive a call back, but the call never came. I emailed once, and then twice, and then daily, and never received a reply. From this I assumed that either the system was as inefficient as it is often rumoured to be or, perhaps more likely, that the Ministry of Defence was so horrified that this top secret information was in the hands of civilians, that it was considering who to prosecute.

Eventually I realised that the policy was simply to ignore me in the belief that if I could get no further cooperation I would go away. While I was waiting, more in hope than in optimism, I made a request directly to the Naval Historical Branch for sight of any documents related to Operation Barmaid or any other record of what the *Conqueror* did in the weeks following her return from the war.

There was another long silence and then, just before midday on 29 March 2011, my phone rang. It was Jock Gardner, who is a historian at the Naval Historical Branch based at Portsmouth. He was responding to my enquiry.

I was fully prepared for Mr Gardner to tell me in this telephone call that the information I had requested is still classified, and that I would have to conclude my negotiations with the Ministry before he could release any documents. What he actually told me was that no records exist of the operation I was referring to and, indeed, that the operation had never taken place at all. I was confused.

'So you are not merely saying that you don't have any records of the operation? You are saying that the operation did not actually happen?'

'Yes, I am saying that.'

'But if you have no records, how do you know it didn't happen? Maybe someone moved or destroyed the records?'

'I know that the *Conqueror* did not go on an operation in August 1982 because I know where it was and what it was doing in August 1982.'

'And what was that?'

'In August 1982,' Jock Gardner said patiently, 'HMS *Conqueror* was tied up alongside at the submarine base in Faslane, Scotland. What happened to the *Conqueror* is exactly what you would expect to happen. They had just come back from the war, and the crew was sent off for a well-earned rest.'

At this point I was at a loss. I had no wish to be rude. I could completely accept that the official historian was not allowed to tell me what I wanted to know. Or it might be that the official records available to him did indeed indicate that *Conqueror* was alongside in Faslane. I chose my words carefully.

'It's very good of you to call me,' I said, 'and I completely understand why you are saying what you are saying. It's just that I know as a matter of complete certainty that what you are telling me is not true.'

He appeared not to be offended. I guessed that this may have happened before, perhaps in relation to other secret naval operations.

I explained once again that I have known the bones of the story I wanted to tell for a quarter of a century and that during all that time I had revealed it to no one. I now wanted to tell the story, and would like some help. If we could cooperate, I could at least ensure that I did not carelessly reveal any operational detail which the Navy would prefer to be kept secret. But Mr Gardner was not the right person with whom to be having this conversation, and we terminated the call politely. I was back to square one.

The subsequent negotiation with the Ministry of Defence was laborious and far too extended to describe in detail here. Suffice to say that over the following four months I had a series of discussions with some very understanding and courteous people who work at the Ministry. In these discussions, and in many exchanges of emails, I was repeatedly told that members of the 'Silent Service' are not so-called merely because their submarines slip as quietly as possible through the water; they are so-called because they do not speak about what they do. I was aware of that, I told them, because getting most of what I had already obtained had been like drawing teeth.

I was also told that, even though the best part of three decades have passed since the events I wished to describe, some of the details about operations and capability are the same today as they were then, and that the Navy would not want this to be revealed. I explained that it was perfectly possible to tell the story I want to tell without including sensitive operational detail, and that if we could agree terms of engagement, the Ministry could have a final veto on those aspects of the story.

Finally I was told that, while the Cold War is over, the kind of story I want to tell might (if true) affect our relationship with a foreign power, and that there could be some embarrassment for the Foreign Office. I pointed out that anyone who cares to look through the records in the former USSR would almost certainly already know that the incident took place, and that it is extremely unlikely that anyone would make an issue about it now. We had to agree to differ.

The arguments advanced by the Ministry are all important considerations. However, there are some arguments on the other side of the balance – a number of good reasons why this story should be told. For one thing, it's true. For another, anyone studying the politics of the period, and in particular the significance of the missing control room log-book, would be misled by the existing accounts. The third, and in my mind the most important, is that good men risked their lives carrying out this and other similar operations, and the very least the rest of us can do is to know their stories and remember them.

For weeks and months we went in circles, and I had an increasing feeling that I was being given the run-around. But then one day, to my surprise, there was a development. I was invited to come to the MoD, where I met with Lieutenant Commanders Andy Aspden and Steve Hayton. I had been dealing with Andy for some time, and he was unfailingly courteous and considerate. It seemed, he told me, that there had been a misunderstanding of some sort. Apparently the operation I first enquired about did happen after all. Perhaps, he suggested, I gave the wrong date or the wrong name? Certainly no one had intentionally deceived me. Anyway, in looking through some other papers relating to something else, it had emerged by chance that the incident I was interested in did in fact happen. It took place in August 1982, and it did involve HMS *Conqueror*. She was not, it seems, tied up against the dock in Faslane; she was on an operation – a 'sneaky'. Precisely the 'sneaky' I was enquiring about.

I was surprised and delighted, but the surprises were not at an end. While the Ministry would not authorise any former or current serviceman to talk about Operation Barmaid, and indeed they would remind anyone who asked that it was still subject to the Official Secrets Act, they were sufficiently convinced by my arguments that they would not take active steps to prevent me from writing and publishing my book. So, no help, but no hindrance either. This felt like progress.

The question which now arose was whether it was possible to discover if the control room logs went missing, not because of what they revealed about the Falklands, but because of what they revealed about Operation Barmaid. This was not going to be easy. While all of the officers and men on board *Conqueror* are now authorised to speak openly about anything to do with the Falklands War, none is authorised to speak about Barmaid, or even to acknowledge its existence. When I began making my enquiries and approached a number of senior officers from the submarine, I was told categorically more than once that the incident was a total fantasy. They knew nothing whatever about it, had not heard about it, it could not have taken place. Several of them simply responded by staring into space and would not speak again until I moved the subject back to something else.

When I told the captain of the *Conqueror*, Chris Wreford-Brown, and his second-in-command, Tim McClement, that I thought the control room log had gone missing because it contained information about Barmaid, neither would speak about it. However, they did volunteer that no control room log was likely to go missing because it contained top secret information.

'Why not?' I asked.

Because, they said, since the log was designated at the lowest level of security – 'Confidential' – when the submarine was on a mission with a higher security classification this particular log was not filled in. In the hypothetical case of any operation before or after the war with an even higher security classification, it was unthinkable that the control room log would have been completed. The log was stored when not in use on an open shelf above the chart table in the control room. Anyone could consult it.

This was a significant setback. If the control room log was effectively blank when the submarine was on anything other than a very routine patrol, why would anyone feel the need to 'lose' it at all?

'But what about the Falklands War?' I asked, 'We know that Operation Corporate was top secret at the time, and yet the control room log was filled in routinely throughout the war.'

'No it wasn't,' said Tim McClement. 'That's why none of us could understand what all the fuss was about. Since it was just a confidential log-book, and the operation was top secret at the time, it would have been left blank.'

Now I was even more confused. Firstly because I had heard directly from Narendra Sethia on many occasions that he had filled in the log-book routinely throughout the war, and secondly because I had heard the same from others who had also been on duty. And anyway, if the control room log had been left blank during the Falklands War, why on earth did no one say so at the time? Why did no one say that to the board of inquiry? On the contrary, Jonty Powis told the board that he specifically remembered entering details of the attack on the *Belgrano* into the control room log – which in the view of the board, enhanced its potential value as a souvenir of the war. There was an enormous fuss made about the loss, with Michael Heseltine having to stand up and be humiliated by announcing that a sensitive document had gone missing. If it actually had been left blank, as these men were now saying, would not someone have mentioned this fact? The information would have got everybody off the hook.

I was as sure as I could be that *Conqueror*'s control room log for the period of the Falklands had been completed; but now, even if I thought this was likely, how could I know for sure that the log covering the Barmaid period had also been completed? It had been 'lost' along with the earlier log, but if the submarine captain and his second-in-command were correct, it too would have been left blank, and therefore there could be no reason why it should be 'lost' too.

Then a way to check occurred to me. The control room logs for the period of the Falklands War and the three months following were missing, but the logs for the periods before the war when *Conqueror* made the first two attempts at Operation Barmaid, in the Barents Sea and the Mediterranean, might not be. These two efforts were every bit as secret as the Falklands War and the successful attempt at Barmaid. What is more, as these incidents had taken place in 1980 and 1981, they were more than thirty years old and should be available under the rule that releases official papers after three decades (except, of course, top secret documents). If the captain and XO were right, and I could locate them, they would be blank or contain only minimal information.

The National Archive in Kew is a rare British institution. It works. It was with some trepidation that I sat in front of a computer screen and completed the request form for ADM 173/31840 and ADM 173/32083, which are the catalogue numbers for the *Conqueror*'s control room logs for November 1980 and July 1981. Users are allowed to request up to three documents of this type at a time, so I also asked for the control room log for August 1980, which is the month when I thought the Barmaid equipment had originally been fitted in dry-dock in Faslane. If the captain and XO from the submarine were correct, none of these logs would have been completed, or at the very least there would be blank pages for the times when the submarine was having the Barmaid equipment fitted or was out on its secret operations.

The National Archive system allocates users a locker-number and a desk, and gives an estimate of the time it will take for the requested documents to appear. The minutes passed very slowly. Forty minutes after my request went in, I watched as one of the archivists, wearing white cotton gloves, placed three books with blue covers in my locker, and minutes after that I was sitting at a desk in the reading room and thumbing (carefully) through the pages of the actual control room log-book which was being filled out in August 1980 in Faslane, and another which had been completed in November 1980 in the North Atlantic, and another from July 1981 in the Mediterranean.

I turned the pages. In each one, written in pencil, were the dates, times, courses, rpms, depths, fuel used, and a range of contemporaneous notes made by the officer of the watch. In the log-book for the period in August 1980 when the Barmaid equipment was fitted, you can read a comment on the 9th by the OOD Charlie Hattersley: 'Cleaning the Barmaid structure of barnacles etc is only an overnight job.' Merely to mention the word 'Barmaid' was to step into 'Top Secret' territory, and here it was, written in pencil in a log designated only as 'Confidential'.

Turn the pages of the logs for November 1980 and July 1981 and, if you are familiar with navigation, you can take the point of departure from Faslane, or from Gibraltar, plot the course of the submarine hour by hour, day by day, and work out the approximate location of the submarine. They show that HMS *Conqueror* was in the North Atlantic in November 1980, and in the Mediterranean in July 1981.

The captain and XO were mistaken. The control room logs – designated only as 'Confidential' – continued to be completed during missions which were designated at the highest possible level of security: 'Top Secret [Code-Word]'. If the control room logs for August and November 1980, and July 1981, contain details of top secret installations and operations, it is fair to conclude that the log books for April to June 1982 contained details of the secret operations in the Falklands, and the control room log for August 1982 contained the details of the even more secret Operation Barmaid.

Except that all of these last six, between April and September 1982 are missing.

So we come, as we must, to a hypothetical situation. Just imagine that you are a senior officer on a British nuclear submarine. Just imagine that the submarine is about to go into refit and you have to send all the latest logs and other documents to Navy Records in Hayes or, possibly in this case, to Northwood. Just imagine that you realise that there has been a major breach of security, and that a log-book designated only as 'Confidential' is full of material relating to an operation that is 'Top Secret'. And just imagine that, whereas ninety-nine log-books out of any hundred that you may send off go unremarked and unstudied by anyone outside of the Navy, this batch of six log-books contains details about the sinking of the *Belgrano*. The sinking is the subject of a fierce political battle, which may well end with someone outside of the Navy calling in the control room logs for the period. And if those logs are called for, they will show nothing of significance about the sinking of the *Belgrano*, but what they will show is that HMS *Conqueror* was not tied up alongside at Faslane in August 1982, but was on an operation in the Barents Sea. She was on an operation just exactly at the time and in the place where an Eastern Bloc AGI happened to lose an important piece of equipment.

What do you think a person in that situation would do? What would you do?

If you ask any of the officers or crew who were on board *Conqueror* at the end of the Falklands War and beyond it what they finally think happened to the control room logs, none of them believes that Narendra Sethia stole them. None of them believes that anyone else stole them. To a man, anyone who is willing to venture an opinion says he thinks that the missing logs were shredded or incinerated when the submarine was due to go in for refit around about November 1982.

Accidentally or deliberately? If anyone knows, no one is saying, but the idea that the logs were destroyed accidentally seems implausible. You only have to look at them. Firstly, they are big – A3 size – with a stiff cardboard cover. On the cover is printed 'Confidential (when completed)' – twice – and on the outside of almost every one of the twenty or more originals which I have seen, someone has hand-written 'Do Not Ditch'. Who puts a volume like that in the shredder or incinerator and, more than that, who puts six of them in at one time? Apart from anything else, a bundle of six control room log-books would be nearly 200 pages and would choke the most heavy-duty shredder.

So if the logs were shredded or burned, it is unlikely to have been accidental. I asked the navigator on board *Conqueror*, Jonty Powis, what he thought would happen in the hypothetical case that a log-book designated 'Confidential' was found to contain information about an operation designated 'Top Secret'. He told me:

If the log for which you search is absent it may be that some sensitive information was inserted inadvertently. After any operation the boat would be sanitised, the XO plus one other would examine all records and ensure that everything of the appropriate classification was consigned to the analysts and all innocuous stuff remaining could go to the public record or be destroyed as being of no value.

I asked if this is what he thought had happened in the case of the missing control room logs from HMS *Conqueror*, and he said that he thought the logs had been incinerated accidentally when the submarine had been due to go into refit. Needless to say, I asked Tim McClement whether he knew anything about what had happened to the missing logs, and he repeated what he had told the board of inquiry – which is that he believes that they were accidentally shredded or incinerated when *Conqueror* went into refit.

At the end of it all, I also believe that they were shredded or incinerated – not because of what they revealed about the sinking of the *Belgrano*, as history currently recalls – but because of what they revealed about the top secret mission which took place after the Falklands War. If I am right, I also believe that, given all the circumstances, it was the right thing to do. Only the passage of thirty years and the end of the Cold War makes it reasonable to reveal what those log-books would have revealed in 1982.

The Barmaid operation is one of the high spots in a story of British submarine warfare which is distinguished and of which the nation can be very proud. The Cold War was won, and these men and their machines can take a good deal of credit for maintaining the balance of power and thereby ensuring that it never turned hot. What is a shame, is that the courageous acts of the men on board *Conqueror* in the course of the Falklands War have been blurred by the controversy which followed. These men acted with bravery and distinction, and their story has been ill-served by history. They deserved better.

It is also a shame that, in the effort to keep secrets, one man in particular found himself on the wrong end of the brutal side of the political machine. Extraordinary circumstances, almost none of his own making, put Narendra Sethia at odds with the system, and he paid a heavy price – with his reputation damaged, his personal integrity traduced and his feelings badly hurt. He may have made some money out of it in the end, but neither he nor anyone close to him believes that it was worth it.

Narendra Sethia has never returned to Britain to live. He has spent many years working in the West Indies, and then travelling. He passed some months as a taxi driver in Caracas. At one point, and for just a few months, he was selling imported bits and pieces from a stall in Covent Garden. Today he is happily running another yacht charter business on the beautiful Caribbean island of St Vincent.

Glossary

ADC	Aide-de-camp: personal assistant to a person of high rank, normally a senior military officer
AGI	Auxiliary General Intelligence, the NATO designation for spy-ships operated by the Soviet Union and other Eastern Bloc nations; these were usually disguised as fishing trawlers
ARA	Armada de la Republica Argentina (Navy of the Republic of Argentina): Argentine equivalent of HMS
ASW	Anti-submarine warfare
AUTEC	Atlantic Undersea Test and Evaluation Center
boat	The term used for a Royal Navy submarine by naval personnel
captain	The commanding officer of a ship. The rank of a ship's captain is not necessarily 'captain' but can be any of the more junior officer grades.
CIA	The USA's Central Intelligence Agency
DPP	Director of Public Prosecutions
executive officer	See *first lieutenant*
first lieutenant	The second-in-command of a Royal Navy ship or submarine, answerable directly to the captain; the rank of a first lieutenant is not necessarily 'lieutenant' but can be sub-lieutenant, lieutenant-commander or commander; also known as the executive officer.
GCHQ	Government Communications Headquarters, the British intelligence agency responsible for intercepting and deciphering foreign communications, based near Cheltenham
HMS	Her Majesty's Ship
MoD	Ministry of Defence
MoS	*Mail on Sunday* newspaper
OOD	Officer of the day, the duty officer in charge of routine matters aboard a ship when in harbour
OOW	Officer of the watch, the duty officer in charge of routine matters aboard a ship when at sea
Operation Corporate	Official British military code-name for the military operations of the Falklands War

OSA	Britain's Official Secrets Acts, the first dating from 1911
NATO	North Atlantic Treaty Organisation, also called the North Atlantic Alliance
periscope depth	The depth at which a submerged submarine is close enough to the surface to enable its periscopes and other detection and communication equipment to be raised clear of the water. The depth might be between 50 and 70 feet, according to the type of submarine and weather conditions.
RFA	Royal Fleet Auxiliary, designation given to Royal Navy support vessels
SAS	Special Air Service Regiment, of Britain's Army.
SBS	Special Boat Squadron, a special forces section of the Royal Marines, equivalent to the Army's SAS
SSBN	A nuclear-powered ballistic missile submarine
SSN	A nuclear-powered attack submarine
SNCP	Special Navy Control Programme
TASO	Torpedo Anti-Submarine Officer
TEZ	Total Exclusion Zone
TG	Task Group; the *Belgrano* was part of the group of ships designated TG 79.3 by Britain
Top Secret	Security classification – Top Secret pertains to 'Information and material the unauthorised disclosure of which would cause exceptionally grave damage to the nation'. Other classifications, in descending order of gravity, are Secret, Confidential, Restricted and Unclassified.
VHF	Very High Frequency – VHF radios are used for short-distance communications.
XO	Executive officer

Bibliography

David Aaronovitch, *Voodoo Histories*

Stephen Badsey, Rob Havers, Mark Grove, *The Falklands Conflict Twenty Years On*

Hugh Bicheno, *Razor's Edge: The Unofficial History of the Falklands War*

John Pina Craven, *The Silent War*

Tam Dalyell, *The Importance of Being Awkward*

Lawrence Freedman, *The Official History of the Falklands Campaign*

Arthur Gavshon and Desmond Rice, *The Sinking of the* Belgrano

Robert Green, *A Thorn in their Side*

Hugh McManners, *Forgotten Voices of the Falklands*

Richard Norton-Taylor, *The Ponting Affair*

David Owen, *Anti-Submarine Warfare*

Michael Pitkeathly, *Submarine* Courageous: *Cold War Warrior*

Clive Ponting, *The Right to Know*

Francis Pym, *The Politics of Consent*

W. Craig Reed, *Red November*

Jim Ring, *We Come Unseen*

Mike Rossiter, *Sink the* Belgrano

Peter Sasgen, *Stalking the Red Bear*

Michael Smith, *The Spying Game*

Louis P. Solomon, *Transparent Oceans*

Margaret Thatcher, *The Downing Street Years*

Commander 'Sharkey' Ward, *Sea Harrier over the Falklands*

Index

Index